PUTNAM

BUFFALO GIRL, 2.12¼.

WISE HORSE OWNERS do not propose to save *one cent* in shoeing, and lose the price of the Horse by Cheap Cut Nails.

The PUTNAM is the only SAFE Nail to drive. AVOID BASE IMITATIONS. OVER.

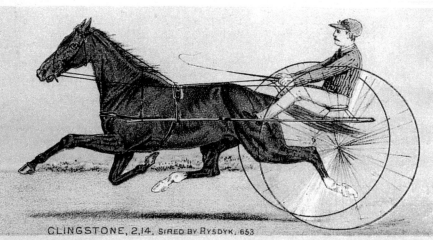

CLINGSTONE, 2,14, SIRED BY RYSDYK, 653.

CHEAP CUT NAILS, with their *sharp, rough edges*, cut the *fiber* and destroy the *life* of the hoof. The SMOOTH EDGED PUTNAM, is the only NATURAL NAIL, as it does not interfere with the HEALTHY growth of the foot. OVER.

# HARNESS

# RACING

# VEHICLES

Susan's Books
455 Coal Mountain Road
Orwigsburg, Pennsylvania 17961


2008

Michael P. D'Amato, Esq.

Susan Green, Librarian

ISBN 978-0-9797013-0-6

I

We would like to thank the following friends, family and organzations who were particularly supportive during the time spent in putting this book together. We would also like to think the individuals at the museums and libraries who were so kind and generous of their time and help, without them this adventure might not have happened.

Penn State Interlibrary Loan Lending
127 Paterno Library, Curtin Road
University Park, Pennsylvania 16802

Waidner-Spahr Library
Dickinson College
Post Office Box 1773
Carlisle, Pennsylvania 17013

Shadek-Fackenthal Library
Franklin and Marshall College
Post Office Box 3003
Lancaster, Pennsylvania 17604

State Library of Pennsylvania
Pennsylvania Department of Education
Forum Building
333 Market Street
Harrisburg, Pennsylvania 17126-1745

Library of Congress
101 Independence Avenue SE
Washington, DC 20540-4574

Smithsonian Institution Libraries
National Museum of American History
12th and Constitution Avenue NW
Washington DC 20560-0630

New York Public Library
Science, Industry, and Business Library
188 Madison Avenue
New York, New York 10016-4314

Hagley Museum and Library
Post Office Box 3630
298 Buck Road East
Wilmington, Delaware 19807-0630

Harness Racing Museum & Hall of Fame
Post Office Box 590
240 Main Street
Goshen, New York

Carriage Museum of America
4089 Iron Works Parkway
Lexington, Kentucky 40511.
*The authors gratefully acknowledge research donated by the Carriage Museum of America in the preparation of this book.*

Jerald Sulky Co. (Tim Gordon)
3050 Wagner Road
Waterloo, Iowa 50703

Marion County Historical Society
164 East Church Street
Marion, Ohio 43301

National Sporting Library
Middleburg, Virginia

Western Reserve Historical Society
Cleveland, Ohio

City Library Association
Springfield, Massachusetts

Springfield Library and Museum
Association, Springfield, Massachusetts

Eastern States Agricultural Fairgrounds
West Springfield, Massachusetts

Historical Society
Utica, New York

Buffalo and Eric County Public Library
Buffalo, New York

Yale University Library
New Haven, Connecticut

Windsor Public Library
Windsor, Connecticut

Connecticut Historical Society
Hartford, Connecticut

State Library, Hartford, Connecticut

Stanton Auctions
Hampden, Massachusetts

Stephen and Lori Roslonek
Wethersfield, Connecticut

Your History Place, Oneida County
Historical Society, Utica, New York

Andrea, Dan, and Ailie Bednarz
Deep River, Connecticut

Michael J. D'Amato, Esq.
Milan, Italy

R. J. Kaprinski, Wallingford, Connecticut

Morphy Auctions, Denver, Pennsylvania

Stephen & Tammy D'Amato

Special Thanks To:
Elizabeth (Betty) D'Amato
&
Mary Jane Green

Courtesy of Connecticut Sate Library.

III

## WEATHERVANES

 Weathervanes have played an important role in the history of art throughout the world. History reveals that the weathervanes in America date back to the Seventeenth Century; "Weathercock" which was made in Holland and brought to America in 1656, was mounted on the Dutch Reformed Church in Albany, New York.

 The earliest known American made weathervane had a date of 1673. The vane was originally mounted atop the second meetinghouse of Concord, Massachusetts.

 This Ethan Allen with Sulky Weathervane is a fine example of the work of renowned weathervane maker A. L. Jewell, Waltham, Massachusetts (A. L. Jewell & Company, 1852-1867). The "Sulky" was added at the factory for a special client that had racing horses. *Courtesy of Morphy Auctions.*

# TABLE OF CONTENTS:

Dedication......page vi-xi

Forward......page xii

Introduction......page1

Two-wheeled Sulky......page 11

Harness Racing Two-wheeled Sulkies......page 123

Four-wheeled Racing Sulky.......page 149

Road Riders and Speed Wagons........page 159

Bibliogrpahy....... page 189

List of Harness Tracks...... page 191

Index.......page 195

### Plates:

Plates 1 & 2 between pages 2-3
Plates 3 & 4 between pages 8-9
Plates 5 & 6 between pages 14-15
Plates 7 & 8 between pages 134-135
Plates 9 & 10 between pages 156-157
Plates 11 & 12 between pages 164-165

Unnumbered Plate of Working Drawing of Sulky
between pages 42-43

# DEDICATION

## THE HORSE,
## IN ENGLAND AND AMERICA-AS HE HAS BEEN, AND AS HE IS.
By William Youatt

Of all the beasts of the field, which, as we are told the Lord formed out of the earth, and brought unto Adam to see what he would call them, none has more engaged the attention of the historian and the philosopher--none has figured more in poetry and romance, than the horse.

Coeval with their domestication, and the knowledge of their admirable capacities to minister to our comforts and pleasures, according to Plutarch, the sentiment has been common to all good men, to treat the horse and the dog with special kindness, and to cherish them carefully, even when the infirmities of age and long service have rendered them useless.

For the volumes which have been written on the *Horse*, whether more or less authentic, as to his original country, his natural history, the time of his subjugation to the use of man, and the various purposes for which he has been employed, whether in the homely gear of field-labour, or in the gorgeous trappings of the tournament or chariot of war on all these points of his history and his uses, we might refer the curious reader to various works, some of them elegant, alike in their embellishments and their literature; but to quote and to collate them here, would be to depart from the line of *practical utility* prescribed for the execution of our task; hence, keeping that object constantly in view, we shall merely glance at what has been written of his early history and services, and so come down rapidly to the period in the history of the *English horse* where, after successive importances of foreign stallions, and the observance of judicious systems of breeding, the stock of the mother country, from which ours is derived, had attained about the days of Flying Childers, in the beginning of the last century, a high degree, if not its maximum of excellence. It was when so improved that the horse was imported into our then British Colonies: and what, after all, it may be asked, is there economical and thrifty in our agricultural and domestic habits--or good in our political and social institutions the elements and general outline of which we have not derived from Old England? ...

None of the writings to which we could point the reader contain more frequent mention, or more glowing descriptions of the power and beauty of the Horse, than. the great *book of books*! The Bible teaches us that from whatever land this animal may have been originally brought into Egypt, that country had already become a great horse market, even before horses were known in Arabia: the country with which we are apt to associate all that is most interesting in the history of thus noble beast. Geological researches, however, have discovered fossil remains of the horse in almost every part of the world, "from the tropical plains of India to the frozen regions of Siberia--from the northern extremities of the new world to the southern point of America." But amongst the Hebrews, horses were rare previous to the days of Solomon, who had horses brought out of Egypt after his marriage with the daughter of Pharoah, and so rapidly did he multiply them by purchase and by breeding, that those kept for his own use required, as it is written, "four thousand stables, and forty thousand stalls." Hence, when honoured by a visit from the beautiful Queen of Sheba, bringing with her "camels bearing spices," and "very much gold and precious stones," it was doubtless in the contemplation of his magnificent stud of horses and chariots, kept for the amusement of his wives and concubines, as well as of his other vast displays of power and magnificence, that her majesty exclaimed, in the fullness of her admiration,--"Howbeit I believed not the words until I came, and mine eyes had seen it, and behold the half was not told me!"

This gallant monarch appears to have enjoyed a large monopoly of the horse trade with Egypt, for which he was probably indebted to his having an Egyptian Princess for one of his wives. His merchants supplied horses in great numbers to the Hittite Kings of Northern Phœnicia. The fixed price was one hundred and fifty shekels for one horse, and six hundred shekels for a set of chariot horses. Thus early was in vogue, as it seems, the gentleman-like fashion to drive four-in-hand, which came down to the good old days when in our Republican country the Tayloes, and the Ridgelys, and the Lloyds, and Hamptons still figured and flourished on the race-courses at Annapolis and Washington.

That there was in the "olden time," something remarkably luxurious in the style of living and equipage at the ancient metropolis of Maryland, may be gathered from the following remarks in " New TRAVELS THROUGH AMERICA," in the year 1781, by the Abbé Robin, chaplain to the French army.--"Their furniture here is constructed of the most costly kind of wood, and the most valuable marble, enriched by the elegant devices of the artist's hand. Their riding machines are light and handsome, and drawn by the *fleetest coursers*, managed by slaves richly dressed. This opulence was particularly observable at *Annapolis*. Female luxury here exceeds what is known in the provinces of France--a French hair-dresser is a man of importance among them; a certain dame here hires one of that craft at a thousand crowns a year salary."

Before the days of Solomon, their honours, the Judges and Princes of Israel, used generally to ride on *Asses* and *Mules*; no less patient and faithful servants of man than the horse; and to whom the editor will endeavour to render justice, in the course of this introduction to the English work.

It is not, be it said, with all our partiality for the Horse, that he possesses any *one* physical or moral trait, in higher excellence than some other animals. In sagacity, he falls short of the ponderous and drowsy Elephant; in muscular development and grace of limb, he surpasses not the Stag; in ardour and constancy of devotion, he can scarcely be said to equal his friendly companion and rival for his master's affections, the faithful Dog; and his courage fails him at sight of a "Lion in the way,"--while in the humbler qualities of patience and availability to the very last, even to the hair and the hoof, that unambitious drudge, the Ox, may well assert his pretensions to comparison, if not to superiority. It is the admirable combination of the several qualities which, taken singly, serve to confer distinction on other quadrupeds, that united in him, fits the horse for employments so various; giving him pre-eminence alike in the wagon or the plough--the coach and the battle-field. While on the one hand, with a flight of speed, compared in Scripture to " the swiftness of the Eagle," he submits his neck, clothed in thunder, to be restrained by a silken rein in the hands of a Di Vernon, his courage in war is thus eloquently described by Job. We give what is esteemed the best translation of a passage often quoted, no less far its appesiteness than for its sublimity.

> "Host thou given mettle to the horse?
> And clothed his neck with ire?
> Dost then command him to spring like a grasshopper?
> The grandeur of his neighing is terror:
> With his feet he beats the ground,
> Rejoicing in his strength;
> And goes forth to meet the embattled foe.
> The fearful sight he scorns, and trembles not,
> Nor from the sword doth he draw back.
> Above him rattle the quiver, the glittering spear, and arrow,
> Under him trembles the earth; yet he hardly touches it.
> He doubts if it be the sound of the trumpet he hears,
> But when it becomes more distinct, then he exults,
> And from afar, pants for the battle,
> The word of command, and the war-cry."

And then as to his gallantry ; where, in all nature, does she exhibit such a magnificent display of that conservative passion, by which alone the Great Jehovah has secured the perpetuity of all his creatures, as in the high-formed, pampered stallion, under the impulse of amatory anticipations!—affording to this resistless necessity of animal organization, proof that should dispel, even in a land of Atheists, all doubt of an overruling design or Providence,

> "Whose work is without labour; whose designs
> No flaw deforms, no difficulty thwarts;
> And whose beneficence no charge exhausts."

It may be the force of early association, but we apprehend it is almost indispensable to have been born and "raised in the country" to estimate fully the attachment which can there alone now up in all its power, between a man and his horse! What conqueror, "from Macedonia's madman to the Swede," so proud as the boy and his horse "Button" or "Bright-Eye," that can beat all competitors in a quarter-race! Alexander was a fool, and Bucephalus a garron, compared to these two great characters, in playtime at a country school.  *"Haud experientia loquor!"*

To the valetudinarian, how delightful to escape from his sick room, and once more throw himself in his saddle, to ride abroad and snuff the fresh air of the morning; or no less to one in the manly vigour of health, to mount his sure-footed, high-mettled steed, and go bounding, at three-quarter speed,

> "Over the hills and far away,"

under reckless excitement of the chase, or sometimes even solitary and alone, ye most agreeably exhilarated by that cheerful turn of thought educed by rapid horseback motion, in the bracing air of the country! He, at least, must have felt these sensations, who described them an happily and with so much enthusiasm, in the old American Turf

VIII

Register and Sporting Magazine; a work since much improved, and now conducted with rare taste and elegance by W. T. PORTER, of New York.

In strong-fear of reproach for departing from the strict line of *utility* laid down for our observance, we cannot forbear to appropriate space enough here to multiply copies this beautiful tribute

"TO MY HORSE."

WITH glancing eye and curving mane,
He neighs and champs on the bridle-rein;
One spring, and his saddled back I press,
And ours is a common happiness
'T is the rapture of motion ! a hurrying cloud
When the loosened winds are breathing loud :--
A shaft from the painted Indian's bow--
A bird--in the pride of speed we go.

Dark thought, that haunt me, where are ye now !
While the cleft air gratefully cools my brow,
And the dizzy earth seems reeling by,
And nought is at rest, but the arching sky:
And the tramp of my steed, so swift and strong,
Is dearer than fame and sweeter than song?

There is life in the breeze as we hasten on,
With each bound some care of earth has gone,
And the languid pulse begins to play,
And the night of my soul is turned to day,
A richer verdure the earth o'erspreads,
Sparkles the streamlet more bright at the meads,

And its voice to the flowers that bend above,
Is sell as the whisper of early love;
With fragrance spring flowers have burdened the air,
And the blue-bird and robin are twittering clear.

Lovely tokens of gladness, I marked ye not,
When last I roamed o'er this self-same spot.
Ah! then the deep shadows of sorrow's mien
Fell, like a blight, on the happy scene ;
And nature, with all her love and grace,
In the depths of the spirit could find no place.

So the vexed breast of the mountain lake,
When wind and rain mad revelry make,
Turbid and gloomy, and wildly tost,
Retains no trace of the beauty lost.
But when through the moist air, bright and warm,
The sun looks down with his golden charm,

IX

And clouds have fled, and the wind is lull,
Oh! then the changed lake, how beautiful!

The glistening trees, in their shady ranks,
And the ewe with its lamb, along the banks,
And the kingfisher perched on the wither 'd bough,
And the pure blue heaven, all pictured below!
Bound proudly my steed, nor hound proudly in vain,
Since thy master is now himself again.
And thine be the praise when the leech's* power
Is idle, to conquer the darkened hour
By the might of the sounding hoof, to win
Beauty without and joy within;
Beauty else to my eye, unseen,
And joy, that then had a stranger been.

We return without further preliminary to trace the progressive improvements which have ended in giving us *the horse of all work* of the present day, and as now employed for ordinary uses. These uses require hardiness and strength for economical and laborious drudgery, and activity and speed for light harness and the saddle; while for every purpose it is essential that he should have *good wind*. The work itself, to which these remarks are but introductory, it will be remembered treats more particularly and fully, and leaves nothing more to be learned about the *anatomy and diseases of the Horse*. How the qualities designated above have been gradually established and preserved from deterioration, it would be impracticable to ascertain and relate without going back as we propose to trace the outline at least of the history of the English Horse, from which ours are descended--and here, before proceed in further, it is deemed proper the better to indicate its importance to every practice husbandman, that we lay it down as a principle, that the horse, in his domesticated condition, where his propagation is conducted arbitrarily and without rule--where the male and female are brought together capriciously, and without care or judgment as to the qualities of each, constant and wide-spread deterioration must be the consequence. On this point, upon which we insist as of the highest consideration, we shall dwell again, to show why it is that animals in a state of nature will preserve a higher standard than when unskillfully and carelessly bred in a state of domestication. In the meantime, in sketching the history of the English horse, it is not deemed essential to go back anterior to the Invasion of England by Julius Cesar. Even at that period it is clear that there existed in that island a good *substratum* for forming a superior race, for that observant and accomplished warrior spoke in the highest terms of the horses he found there. So well was he convinced of their excellence, that he took back with him many to Rome, where English horses soon grew into great demand; and thus early was an inducement offered to the hardy and enterprising Briton, which since then has suffered no abatement, to pay strict attention to this important source of agricultural wealth.

From the book by William Youatt, *The Horse, ...Together With A General History Of the Horse; A Dissertation On The American Trotting Horse, How Trained and Jockeyed, An Account Of His Remarkable Performances; and An Essay On the Ass and the Mule.* published by Leavitt & Allen, New York, [1843]. numerous editions and variations of this title--first published in 1831.

*Leech, in old poetic dialect, means physician.

# THE HORSES IN THE UNITED STATES.

The Boston *Transcript* says:-"The first horses brought into any part of the territory at present embraced in the United States, were landed in Florida, by Cabeca de Veca, in 1527, forty-two in number, all of which perished, or were otherwise killed. The next importation was also brought to Florida, by De Soto, in 1529. In 1608, the French introduced the horse into Canada. In 1609, the English landed at Jamestown, in Virginia. having seven horses, with them. In 1629, Francis Higginson imported horses and other domestic animals in the Colony of Massachusets Bay. In 1625 the Dutch Company imported horses into New York. In 1650, the French of Illinois were in possession of a considerable number of horses.

"According to the census returns for 1850, there were 4,335,358 horses in the Untied States, exclusive of those in cities, which were not returned. The four and a-half millions of those animals in the United States, constitute a proportion of one to five of the inhabitants. New York has one hourse to seven persons; Pennsylvania one to six and six-sixteenths; Ohio, one to four; Kentucky, one to three free inhabitants. In Ohio, and the new States of the Northwest, the increase of horse has kept pace with that of the population.

The number of horses in the Untied States is more than three times as large as that in Great Britain. A recent report in France shows that there are in that country 3,200,000 horses. From the *Journal of the United States Agricultural Society*, published circa 1850, page 76.

[Harness Racing Was Not Just Confined To the Track]. From *Die Gartenlaube*, 1865 page 757.

# FORWARD

What a Marvelous way to spend a day at the harness races and witness a horse race with; a powerful horse, a driver wearing bright colored silks; whip in hand, encouraging his horse with each step to the finish line in a "dead heat," awaiting the results of a photo before a winner could be decided, none better!

There is anxiety felt by the owner of the horse and persons having placed a bet on the horse awaiting the Judges' decision on an inquiry.

Oh, what joy and smiles when the Judges ruled in their favor.

It has been frequently said that the "Horse" should be placed at the head of domestic animals; having in view a treatise on the breeds, properties and uses of each,is a distinction to which he is justly entitled, in reference as well to the beautiful symmetry of his form, and his extraordinary physical powers, as to his admirable docility of temper and high moral qualities fitting him eminently for various purposes of pleasure and business. Yougatt, 1843, page vi.

Ripton & Confidence, Owings/Gimbrede, Engraving, c. 1844, *American Turf Register and Sporting Magazne*, May 1844, (engraving appears opposite p. 259), Courtesty of National Sporting Library, Middleburg, VA.

# INTRODUCTION.

Harness racing--Chariot racing both four horse (tethrippon or quadrigae) and two-horse (synoris or bigae) was a very ancient sport that through artistic evidence is known to have existed in the Mycenaean world. The first literary reference to a chariot race is the one described by Homer in Book 23 of the Iliad, at the funeral games of Patroclus (unknown date between the 8th to 6th century B.C.). It is thought to have been formally organized in the sixth century B.C. by Tarquinius Priscus, the fifth king of Rome (616-579), with the erection of the Circus Maximus as a separate building for horse racing. The sport was as organized as harness racing is today with, pedigrees of horses being kept, betting, loyal spectators, starting gates, rules and regulations and noted drivers with famous charioteers having statues made of them. The ancients were so passionate about

Chariot Race In the Circus Maximus--These Races Were Long the Leading Feature of the Roman Circenses, or Games of the Circus. From a painting by V. Checa.
*Munsey Magazine*, Jan. 1903, page 527.

their sport that rivalry between groups of spectators at chariot races often ignited urban riots. In Constantinople, in 532 A. D., a three-day disturbance left 30,000 dead.[1&2]

## HISTORY OF THE SULKY IN THE UNITED STATES.

In trying to obtain some facts about the history of sulky building we found several discrepancies among the articles on sulkies. We can only conclude that because a new construction feature was introduced the old ideas were still used simultaneously on sulkies; such as sulkies with springs and sulkies without springs. There seems to be a margin of about ten years or more when the use of circular bars and cranked axles were introduced on sulkies. The only thing agreed upon was the first use of the pneumatic tire for sulkies. Since harness racing had become such a popular sport with Americans there were 500 prints published by Currier and Ives alone, on the subject, plus prints by other lithographers. The lithographs of the time yield some insights into a time line of construction details for sulkies, but Peter C. Welsh cautions that printmakers frequently ignored the technical details of harness or carriage appurtenances.[3] From the point of view of the sulky builder they claimed that–history has shown that improvements in sulky

[1 & 2] Chariot racing - *Wikipedia, the Free Encyclopedia.*
[3] Welsh, Peter C. Track and Road: The American Trotting Horses: A Visual Record 1820 to 1900 ... (Washington, DC. : Smithsonian Institution Press, 1967) , p. 16.

# Introduction

building may go hand in hand with winning records of harness horses. A sulky used in 1829 by the celebrated trotting horse Tom Thumb[4] is said to have weighed one hundred and eight pounds and by 1892 sulkies weighed around 50 pounds and had the horse hitched closer to the point of draft.

It is agreed that harness racing in America resulted from the importation of English thoroughbred stallion named Messenger in 1788 or 1790. Messenger's sons and daughters and his following generations of offspring were exceptional trotters. Because America farmers could keep a good horse just as well as a bad horse, a friendly and keen competition soon developed between ordinary people on the country roads for, who had the fastest trotting horse. In 19th century America, harness racing became one of the most popular sports of the people. The first recorded public trot for a stake of $1,000 was in 1818.[5]

## SPRINGS.

One of the earliest lithographs of a trotter to a sulky was published about 1830 by Kennedy & Lucas of Philadelphia a black-and-white drawing on stone by Richard Hillman that shows Whalebone, a great trotter, hitched to a high wheel sulky with a straight axle, with the driver's seat elevated above the shafts and the driver seating in a normal position with his knees bent. This lithograph does not show the use of springs for the sulky between the shafts and axle. Whalebone is shown wearing blinders, a collar and a wide harness saddle. On a muddy Long Island track Whalebone trotted 15 miles in 56 minutes in April 1827.[6]

Whalebone. Harry T. Peters, "America On Stone" Lithography Collection, National Museum of American History, Behring Center, Smithsonian Institution. Cat. no. 60.3564. SI photo 56165. circa 1830.

---

[4]Akers, Dwight. Drivers Up The Story of American Harness Racing, (New York, NY. : G. P. Putnam's Sons, 1947) , p. 61.

[5]American Trotting Horse. *Frank Leslie's Popular Monthly* (Nov. 1885), p. 535.

[6]Welsh, Peter C. Track and Road: The American Trotting Horses: A Visual Record 1820 to 1900 From the Harry T. Peters America On Stone Lithography Collection. (Washington, DC. : Smithsonian Institution Press, 1967), pp. 76-77.

This print "Celebrated American Trotting Horses," Lithograph by W. H. Rease and painted by R. A. Clarke, printed by Wagner & McGuigan, circa 1854, shows some famous trotting horses that were ridden as well as trotters harnessed to two-wheeled sulkies. From the Print Collection of the Library of Congress LC-USZ62-92740 (b&w film copy neg.).

Plate 1

Trotting horse and sulky of 1842: RIPTON: July 19th 1842, beat Confidence, In a Match for $500 a Side, 2 Mile Heats In Harness Over Centreville Course, Long Island, Winning In 2 Straight Heats, Time 5:10 - 5:14½. Lithograph published in 1850 by Currier & Ives. From the Print Collection of the Library of Congress LC-USZ62-92380 (b&w film copy neg.)

Sulky of 1852 showing a wide leather seat valance. "ST. LAWRENCE," published by Currier & Ives in 1852. From thePrint Collection of the Library of Congress LC-USZ62-92076 (b&w film copy neg.)

Plate 2

# Introduction

However the first sulky without springs in the carriage builder's trade journals isn't until May 1872 in the *Coach Makers; International Journal* and the earliest known technical drawing for building a sulky is 1849-1853 showing full elliptic springs.[7]

The next popular trotting horse subject was Sherman Black Hawk who on October 8, 1856 took the first premium at the United States Agricultural Fair held at West

Sherman Black Hawk. Harry T. Peters, "America On Stone" Lithography
Collection, National Museum of American History, Behring Center,
Smithsonian Institution.   Cat. no. 60.3529. SI photo 56196. circa 1856.

Philadelphia. The black-and-white lithograph from a painting by Charles S. Humphreys, by J. H. Bufford, Boston shows the driver's seat slightly lower with the legs of the driver straighter. Again there are no springs shown in the lithograph.[8]

Flora Temple scored a mile in 2:19¾ in 1859 at Kalamazoo, Michigan with a sulky that had bent shafts and weighted eighty-five or ninety pounds, and instead of springs it used stays to support the shafts.[9]

In a colored lithograph by J. H. Bufford and Sons, Boston, Published by Samuel Emerson, Riverside Riding Park, Brighton, 1865 in which the horse Capt. McGowan trotted 20 miles in 58 minutes and 25 seconds. The vehicle is described as a light gig weighing 70 pounds while the driver J. J. Bowen weighed 155 pounds. J. J. Bowen is sitting with his knees slightly bent as opposed to straight and there are no springs shown in the lithograph.[10]

From an interview in 1904 with Uncle Dan Hatfield, wheelwright of Rahway, New Jersey, who made a business of building track sulkies for trotters. He recalls that sulkies prior to 1849: "The sulky old Suffolk pulled must have weighed 125 pounds. It had a straight axle made of hickory, with steel ends driven into the wood about fifteen inches.

---

[7] The Sulky. *Hub* (October 1892), p. 242.

[8] Welsh, Peter C. Track and Road: The American Trotting Horses: A Visual Record 1820 to 1900 From the Harry T. Peters America On Stone Lithography Collection. (Washington, DC. : Smithsonian Institution Press, 1967), pp. 78-79.

[9] The Sulky. *Hub* (October 1892), p. 243. and The Sulky Builder. *Hub* (June 1904), p. 118.

[10] Welsh, Peter C. Track and Road: The American Trotting Horses: A Visual Record 1820 to 1900 From the Harry T. Peters America On Stone Lithography Collection. (Washington, DC. : Smithsonian Institution Press, 1967) , pp. 82-83.

# Introduction

Capt. McGowan. Harry T. Peters, "America On Stone" Lithography Collection,
National Museum of American History, Behring Center, Smithsonian Institution.
Cat. no. 60.3595. SI photo 56513. dated 1865.

[In 1849 a sulky as being built in Western New York with a square iron axle body covered with a casing of hickory, the iron being bedded into the wood and neatly rounded. The wood was a mere shell, but it gave a neater appearance than the square iron.] The seat was set up high from the axle, and rested on heavy springs, a good deal like one of these hackney gigs you see in Central Park nowadays. The fact is, there were no real sulkies in those days. There were only light gigs, and not very light at that. The wheels were five feet high, with spokes over an inch thick; hubs that were four inches through and nearly seven inches long, and the tires were pretty close to an inch wide. The crossbar was set away forward, and perfectly straight, and the shafts were bent only a very little. ... I suppose a trotter had to be hooked anywhere from eighteen inches to two feet further away from the sulky in those times, to avoid hitting, on account of the straight axle and crossbar. That was a big handicap to speed, for the sulky was a whole lot harder to pull, and then it would sway and slip and quiver on the turns so as to throw a horse off his balance and pretty nearly throw the driver off his perch. The system of bracing was nothing at all in those days. This is probably why, they used to raise the seat up two feet or more above the axle with hardly anything to support it, excepting four light iron rods.

"Peter Dubois of New York City, made the first track sulky I ever saw without springs. That was somewhere about 1852, I would say at a guess. It was a big improvement on the old gigs, because it let the driver's seat down and made the vehicle much more rigid. I think that sulky had an iron axle about an inch square, in place of the old hickory axle, but I am not sure. Anyhow, wood or iron, the axle was as straight as a gun-barrel, and the horse had to be hooked just as far away as ever."[11]

From the *Coach-makers' International Journal* of August 1867 plate No. 33[12] we learn that sulkies with full elliptic springs were still considered by sulky builders for their customers. If we believe the artist was accurate in drawing the engraving, "The Trotting Season At Prospect Park Fair Grounds, L. I. –Race Between "Fullerton" and

---

[11]The Sulky Builder. *Hub* (June 1904), p. 117.
[12]See Plate No. 33 on page 14 of this book.

# Introduction

"Goldsmith Maid," Monday, June 8th" published in *Frank Leslie's Illustrated Newspaper*, June 27, 1874, page 253, the sulkies shown have full elliptic springs between the axle and shafts.[13] A sulky built by Crosby, Gilzinger & Company of Rondout, New York in 1876 shows a patented coil spring.[14] We can only conclude that elliptic springs or no springs were a simultaneous occurrence from the earliest use of the sulkies to about 1874.

## CIRCULAR BAR.

From the article "The Sulky" published in the *Hub* October 1892 page 242 the circular bar rather than straight bars seems to have come into use around 1853. "The illustrations, Figs. 1 and 2, are from scale drawings made in the year 1853, at which time the bent cross bar was introduced by which the shafts were shortened, so that the horse could be hitched four inches closer to the axle and the shafts rendered more rigid by the

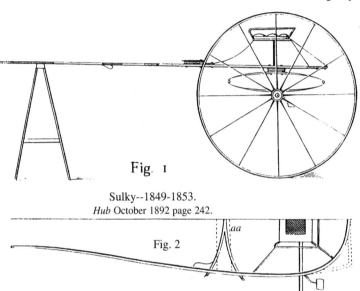

Fig. 1

Sulky--1849-1853.
*Hub* October 1892 page 242.

Fig. 2

braces, than were the straight bars used, as shown by the dotted lines *a a* on Fig. 2. By the use of the bent bar the shafts were reduced in length to 9 feet, 10 inches, forward of the axle. For some horses, this length was insufficient, unless the wheels were made extra high. One of these sulkies weighed 85 pounds, and the builder was congratulated who could, with safety, reduce the weight a pound or two."

When Flora Temple scored a mile in 2:19¾; in 1859 other improvements were beginning to be made–axles were shortened, braces were introduced to give greater rigidity to the frame, closer selection was made in the timber, and the axles and wheels were lightened; but eight years passed before Flora Temple's record was-beaten by Dexter in 1867, who made the mile in 2:17¼. During the next ten years [1867-1877], the record was broken by but three horses Goldsmith Maid 2:14, Smuggler 2:16¼, American Girl 2:16, but during this period many minor improvements in the sulky had been introduced, where greater firmness was secured, together with a decrease in the weight, the latter

---

[13] See page 136 of this book for illustration.
[14] Plate No. 67. Crosby's Sulky. *Hub*. (September 1876). see page 27 of this book.

# Introduction

having been reduced to about fifty pounds,[15] [the wheels were lowered to five feet and the application of a central brace, connecting the shaft on each side with the axle near the collar.],[16] but the long geared load, flying off at a tangent at the turns was there playing havoc with the horse's gait and increasing the draft. It was no uncommon sight to see the inside wheel two or three inches from the ground, while the outside would dig in and slide two to three feet toward the outside, retaining this sliding condition for fifty feet or more.

## CRANKED AXLES.

"The distance of the sulky, back of horse, whereby friction was so greatly increased, caused attention to be directed toward the remedying of this great fault, and in 1877, Joseph Pray of Boston, Massachusetts, built a sulky with the axle bed curved upward, an improvement of greater importance than any other yet introduced. The horse was now brought back to within a few inches of the driver's seat. Many pounds of useless material was removed, greater solidity was obtained, and the load brought closer to horse."[17] In an article published in 1904 about the history of sulkies, the author claims to have made a bow axle for sulky around 1859 first cutting it out of wood and reinforcing it with an iron rod all the way through. It is believed by the time of Dexter's record in 1867 that sulkies with cranked, arched or bow axles were in standard use. "There were great improvements in bracing after Dexter's day, and the axles were bent higher and higher, until you could run the sulky right up on to the horse without having him in it. The improvements in braces was mainly in making them lighter and using more of them."[18]

There maybe various reasons why there are different dates for the cranked axle: 1. The use was isolated to certain areas, therefore it was not know by everyone. 2. They may be talking about degrees of height. 3. Or again the use of cranked axles could have been in use simultaneously with the straight axle from 1859 to 1877 when the cranked axle came into common use.

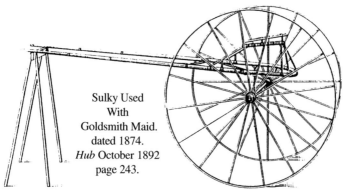

Sulky Used
With
Goldsmith Maid.
dated 1874.
*Hub* October 1892
page 243.

"The impediment to speed, arising from the swinging of the sulky around curves, was materially lessened, and the weight reduced to about forty-five pounds, about one-half what it was in 1859, when Flora Temple made her record, and now commenced the era of increased speed, and from 1877 to 1890 inclusive, two hundred and eighty-one horses made 2:19¾ and better, while eleven stands as the record before that date."[19]

---

[15] see Plate No. 76. Jone's Sulky on page 21of this book. This sulky weighs 46 lbs.
[16] The Sulky Builder. *Hub* (June 1904), p.116.
[17] The Sulky. *Hub* (October 1892), p. 242.
[18] The Sulky Builder. *Hub* (June 1904), p. 118.
[19] The Sulky. *Hub* (October 1892), p. 242.

# Introduction

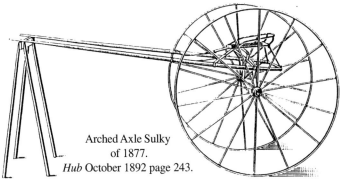

Arched Axle Sulky
of 1877.
*Hub* October 1892 page 243.

"Breeding and training have without doubt, greatly improved the trotter, and increased the number of speedy animals, but it is folly to assert that other causes have not contributed their share. In the year 1874, Goldsmith Maid trotted a mile in 2:14, before an improved sulky of that date. That sulky is shown made from a photograph taken at the time she made her great race. The improved sulky of 1877 has an the arched axle."[20]

## BICYCLE SULKY.

The following history of the pneumatic tired bicycle sulky is from the *Carriage Monthly* published in September 1892. "The accompanying illustration is a reproduction of the pneumatic tire trotting sulky, with which Nancy Hanks and Hal Pointer have recently been making havoc with the world's trotting and pacing records.

"The speed of the pneumatic tire has long been known to bicycle riders, and shortly after its first appearance in England, riders of that style of machine were handicapped 100 yards in the mile. The growth of the popularity of the tire was so rapid, and its adoption by racing wheel men so wide-spread, that it soon had the racing field to itself, as no rider, no matter how speedy, could push the hard tired wheel against a contestant, in his own class, on the new style mount, with any hope of success.

"The rubber tire on sulkies is not an idea of yesterday. Four years ago [1888] Frank Van Ness had a rubber tire fitted to a pair of wheels, and drove Harry Wilke, to them. The result was not a success. It frightened the horse, it is said, without adding to his speed. About a year ago,[1891] when the pneumatic tire on bicycles first bounded into prominence, the idea was advanced that perhaps the small wheel and broad tire could be fitted to a sulky.

"Who first thought of putting pneumatic tires on a trotting sulky is not definitely known. There is no dispute, however, as to priority in practical application of the idea. It is conceded that Sterling Elliott, of the Elliott Hickory Cycle Company, of Newton, Massachusetts, was the first to apply bicycle wheels to sulkies. He used the Pope Manufacturing Company's, Columbia pneumatic tire. C. F. Clark, of Boston, has the credit of using the first of these sulkies for a race, when his pacer, Albert D., won with it easily at Worcester.

[June 8, 1892. It was one of the old-style sulkies, with the 28-inch bike wheels hung at the bottom of rods suspended from the axle arm and braced. This sulky was sent to Worcester with its large wheels on and carried the small wheels in a bag, as I didn't care to hear the remarks which were sure to be made. While I was putting on the little wheels, I was surrounded by an interested circle of stablemen and

---

[20]The Sulky. *Hub* (October 1892), p. 243.

drivers, whose comments you could hardly print in the *Hub*. The man who drove in the new sulky that day was "Jud" Woodbury, who had tried it previously on the private track on Clark's stock farm at Wayland. He had made the private trial with some misgivings, but inasmuch as it was private, he consented to "make a show of himself." The only spectator beside myself was E. D. Emerson, of Waltham, Massachusetts. When Woodbury had made one turn of the track he stopped in front of us and said: "If I was going into a race *for my life* I would take that gig in preference to anything I ever saw." When he got into the sulky at Worcester, he was probably the only man who would have cared to stand the "haw haws" of the crowd in the new rig. After he won the first heat, there was a decided change in the temperature of the audience, and when he had won the race (four heats), I began to have inquiries from horsemen as to where they could "buy one of the d— things."].[21]

That it was not a "fluke," as the Englishmen say, Albert D. proved by winning every other event for which he started.

"The news of this reached Budd Doble, at Terre Haute, Indiana, and he ordered one of the new sulkies. It did not reach him until July 20th, at Detroit. He was so little impressed with its appearance that he would not use it. That day the 2.17 trot was carried over unfinished; and it was suggested to Ed. Geers that he borrow the new sulky, and try his luck with it for Honest George. Harry Hamlin, of Buffalo, the owner of the horse, was willing, and so when the field of six scored up on the following day, Honest George had the bicycle sulky behind him. Hazel Wilkes, the favorite, had one heat, and Honest George two. He had all he could do the day before to make those heats in 2.16½ and 2.16¾, but with the ball bearing, bicycle wheel, pneumatic tire sulky he had an easy time of it, coming home well in front of Almont and Little Albert in 2.16.

"This was the first appearance of the new fangled sulky in society, and the thin edge of the wedge had entered with effect. Budd Doble used it the same afternoon for Jack, in the free for all, and from that day on, the bicycle sulky has, with but two or three exceptions, won every heat in the Grand Circuit. Nancy Hanks pulled it first at Grand Rapids, and made her record of 2.09. It was behind her at Chicago, of course, when she broke the world's record with 2.07¼, and Ed. Geers, who did not receive one until the Cleveland meeting, sat over the bonding tires when Hal Pointer glided like "lightning on a greased track" in 2.05¼. Again, at Independence, Iowa, on August 31st, on a kite track, Nancy Hanks splintered the record made by herself a few days before, trotting a mile in 2.05¼, to a bicycle sulky.

"Every driver and trainer is now satisfied that the high wooden wheeled sulky has been supplanted, and that the easy traveling wheel, with the broad hollow tire, has come to stay. In fact, at Rochester, the bicycle sulky had fairly overtaken the high wooden wheel, and when, in the 2.17 class, with nine starters, J. B. Richardson came out hitched to a Caffrey sulky, old style, it looked as strange as did the small rubber wheel of three weeks before. At the recent race meeting at Springfield, no large wheeled sulky was seen on the track, and one horseman remarked that he would as soon think of hitching his horse to a carry-all.

"The inflated tire on sulkies has, therefore, worked as great wonders as it accomplished on the bicycle racing path. The pneumatic tire is a great benefit to the driver as well as to the horse. The vibration in the old sulky was one of the great drawbacks to increased lightness, and there was a decided draught. The wheel track made by an old style sulky in passing a curve is often several times the width of the tire. Frequently the wheels

---

[21]From a letter by Sterling Elliott to the editor. *The Sulky Builder. Hub* (June 1904), p. 117.

High wheel wooden sulky that was converted to use pneumatic tires. Trotting Mare NANCY HANKS, Record 2:04. Published by Currier & Ives, 1892. From the Print Collection of the Library of Congress LC-USZC2-3101 (color film copy slide).

Grand Trotting Queen NANCY HANKS driven by Budd Doble. Published by Currier & Ives, 1892. From the Print Collection of the Library of Congress LC-DIG-pga-00747

Plate 3

Champion Trotting Queen, ALIX, by Patronage, Record, 2:07 3/4: Winner of the Columbian Exposition Purse $15,000, at Washington Park, Chicago, Sept. 14th, 15th and 16th, 1893, Wining First Heat in 2:07 3/4; Fourheat in 2.1 3/4 Ninth Heat 2:09 3/4. From the Print Collection of the Library of Congress LC-USZC2-2079 (color film copy slide).

## PNEUMATIC TIRED SULKIES OF 1893.

Trotting Stallion NELSON, by Young Rolfe: Record 2:10. Published by Currier & Ives, 1893. From thePrint Collection of the Library of Congress LC-USZC2-3106 (color film copy slide).

Plate 4

# Introduction

slip several inches. All this has an appreciable bearing upon the speed of the horse. The rubber tire does not slip, and the driver has no need to lean over on the side to keep in even keel, but can execute the turn at full speed and sit perfectly square.

"This tire is of rubber, and is pumped up with air, the same as for the bicycle. An 1¼-inch tire, or even larger, is left hollow, and is pumped full of air by means of a small pump. The hole is then made air-tight by a valve, and the tire will remain firm until the air leaks out through a puncture or faulty plugging.

"The striking thing about the new sulky is the low wheels. In the old style sulky the driver sat between them. Now he sits above them. The wheels average from 28 to 30 inches in diameter, about the same as on a safety bicycle. It has ball bearings wherever there is play for an axle. Instead of the wheel turning on a greased axle, as in the old sulky, there is within the hub a row of balls about the size of a buckshot and of the hardest steel. The axle is placed on these balls, which eliminate the cone bearing friction. The rim of the sulky wheel is of wood, and the spokes also, but many horsemen are applying to bicycle dealers for regular bicycle wheels, to be attached directly to the sulky. The common sulky frame is used, the axle of the sulky being placed in a socket, from which two forks run down to the axle of the wheel. The ball bearings are contained in the hub of the wheel, and are regular bicycle bearings. Braces run from the inside of the wheel to the axle of the sulky, and forward from the hub of the wheel to the shaft of the sulky. These are made to attach to any sulky, and it can be easily done by a good sulky maker. This is an awkward and ungainly style of attaching the wheels, and will no doubt be soon done away with. The innovation has become so popular that a cyclone of orders has come to the sulky makers, and they have all they can do to supply the demand, without devoting time to

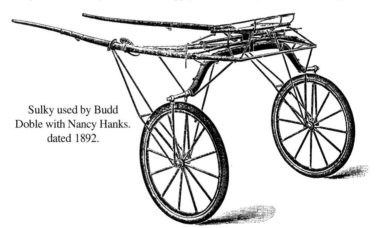

Sulky used by Budd Doble with Nancy Hanks. dated 1892.

improvement. They will doubtless soon make a gearing especially adapted to these wheels, which will not only have advantage in appearance and weight, but will be of much more assistance to the horse.

"The sulky used by Budd Doble with Nancy Hanks is the second ever fitted up by the Elliott Hickory Cycle Company, to whom we are indebted for the accompanying illustration. It is a regular Toomey frame, made by S. Toomey & Company, Canal Dover, Ohio, with the Elliott hickory bicycle wheels, fitted with the finest ball bearings and the celebrated Columbia pneumatic tire a combination hard to beat. Hal Pointer's record was made with a sulky frame made by W. A. Vaughn & Son, Geenville, Pennsylvania, fitted up with pneumatic tire, ball bearing hickory bicycle wheels of the Elliott make, the

# Introduction

machine weighing 49 pounds. They make them as light as 36 pounds. The sulkies that did the best work on the Grand Circuit in the West, recently, had a wheel about 28 inches high.

"The attempts that are being made to use steel bicycle wheels instead of hickory are freely condemned. Steel wheels have been repeatedly tried for road vehicles and sulkies, but have not been found feasible. It is said they are not built to stand the lateral strain, and are more liable to injury from contact with horses' feet than other wheels. Practical persons also consider that the low wheels do not give any advantage; rather that the ball bearings and pneumatic tires enabled the 28-inch sulky to win in spite of the low wheels. They say that the long accepted theories concerning high wheels cannot easily be disproved, and that it will not be long before horsemen will want sulkies having wheels of the usual height, but supplied with the frictionless bearings and inflated tire.

"Among the many new ideas that have been evolved in this movement is a sulky, built in Hartford, Connecticut, certain parts of which are made of steel tubing, the seat of the driver and the body of the sulky being adjustable to different heights, the wheels being fitted with 42-inch Bidwell-Thomas pneumatic tires.[22]

In the very next issue of *Carriage Monthly* published in October 1892 it appears that the criticism for the steel wheel is already old news.

"The first sulky with steel bicycle wheels was fitted by the Buffalo Cycle Works for Chas. S. Green, the well-known driver and part owner of Sprague Golddust, Illinois Egbert, Lucille's Baby, Wilkes Golddust and the Raven. It was given a highly satisfactory trial on August 6th, 1892. "The wheels put on that sulky are still in use, and Mr. Green will testify to their stability and running qualities. Steel wheels have been used with the greatest success on steam fire engines for over twenty years, and have been found feasible and have stood the lateral strain as well as all others. Steel bicycle wheels have been criticized when the fault lay in the improper methods of attaching them to the sulkies. A steel wheel properly designed and constructed, especially for use on the sulky, is stronger than any hickory sulky wheel of the same diameter, and is nearly two pounds lighter.

"Makers of cheap bicycles are putting their wheels onto sulkies, using cheap attachments, without taking into consideration that a wheel made for a bicycle is subjected to entirely different strains on a sulky. Whatever condemnation of steel bicycle wheels for sulkies may have been heard among horsemen, has been directed at this cheap class of wheels, and not at the steel wheel in general. We should be pleased to submit our steel sulky wheels to any test in competition with the hickory wheels. Yours very respectfully, W. S. Bull, of the Buffalo Cycle Works."[23]

In order to accommodate the new style of pneumatic tire within a very short time the truss axle was the new standard for the bicycle sulky as shown by Plate No. 82, Truss Axle Bicycle Sulky, in the *Carriage Monthly* February 1893.[24] The truss axle is simply a double bar, spread apart by means of short braces in the middle and brought together at the ends, where it runs down to the places where the wheels go on. A converted sulky to bicycle wheels weighed up to sixty pounds, were the old style sulky weighed 40 pounds, but the advantages of the new style wheel out weighed the extra weight. With the new truss axle the average weight was reported to be thirty -four to thirty-six pounds in 1904.[25]

---

[22]The Record Breaking Bicycle Sulky. *Carriage Monthly* (September 1892), pp. 183-184.

[23]Steel Bicycle Wheel for Sulkies. *Carriage Monthly* (October 1892), p.211.

[24]See page 60 of this book Plate No. 82 for this illustration.

[25]The Sulky Builder. *Hub* (June 1904), p. 118.

# TWO-WHEELED SULKY

# Two-wheeled Sulkies

**Fig. 42. SULKY WITH SPROUT SPRINGS, AND OLIVER'S IMPROVED WHEEL.**

*Coach-Makers' Magazine*
August 1855.

With this illustration we present something new in the way of a sulky. Messrs. Booth & Bro.'s of Columbus, Ohio have just completed a Sulky with the application of Sprout's spring, [E. T. Sprout patent #s 3729 Sept. 7, 1844 and 5674 July 18, 1848] and which we have had the pleasure of testing to our heart's content, and in justice to the inventor of this valuable improvement we must say that we were never before carried over rough pavements and deep ruts on any two wheeled vehicle with such a soft and steady motion as we were in this Sulky. The easy motion and bracing position of this Spring is peculiarly adapted to vehicles of this denomination. No sensible man will ever be satisfied with an elliptic spring for a sully after he has rode on the one just mentioned. A A are the springs attached to the axle and shafts as seen in our illustration. B is a continuous steel brace running from the vortex of each spring under the cross-bar, and on which brace the singletree rests. C is the centre perch passing from the centre of the axle under the vortex of the brace B and terminating in a scroll takes the cross-bar F.

Some time has elapsed since the main principle of this spring was patented, but within the last three months new principles have been added, and a different form given, which renders it altogether a new thing. It is our opinion, after a practical investigation, that no sulky spring now in use approaches nearer perfection.

To this sulky we have applied the improved carriage wheel of Mr. OLIVES, of Brooklyn, L. I.,[1] for which he obtained a patent on the 30th day of January last. "The improvement," says the *Scientific American*, "consists in the peculiar construction of the wheel, whereby light or small hubs may be used, and a more durable and stronger wheel made than the ones now in common use.

It is customary to use small hubs in the construction of carriage wheels; they are considered ornamental, and add much to the light appearance of the wheel. It will be seen that a small hub with mortises made in it to receive sixteen or eighteen spokes, will be much cut up or weakened, besides there cannot be much of a shoulder allowed for the spokes, as they are close together near the hub. By this improvement the hub has only half the usual number of mortices cut in it, and the long spokes C, may have requisite shoulders at their ends adjoining the hub, so that they may be well supported in the hub, and prevented from working or becoming loose therein. At the same time the felloes composing the rim are well supported, as the usual number of spokes are inserted in them, the ring or band allowing the requisite support to be given the felloes by means of the short spokes, and also diminishing the number of mortises usually made in the hub. Thus a strong and durable wheel is obtained, the spokes are well supported by a ring or band, and prevented from twisting or bending when the tire is shrunk on the rim. Small hubs may be used and the cost of manufacture will not exceed that of the ordinary wheels."

---

1. Patent is registered to John Skelley, Brooklyn #12,330.

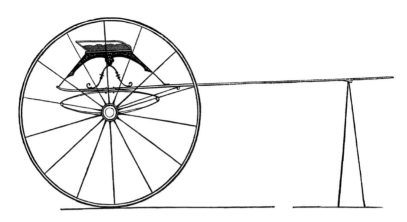

**Plate No. 10. LIGHT ROAD SULKEY\*.**
*Coach-Makers' Magazine* March 1858, page 27.

The design here presented, is one of the most approved style of "road sulkey." The seat is supported upon rods of iron in the usual form, and an ornamental brace put in the centre, on both sides, as represented in the sketch. The vacant appearance so common in the ordinary sulkies about the seat, is in this design very much relieved by the application of the patent leather, fancifully stitched, as shown. It would also add to its appearance to plate the ornamental braces in the centre. This design is by Irving.

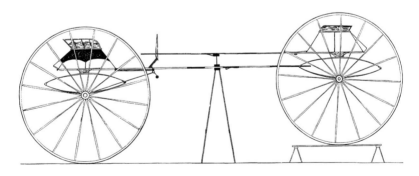

**Plate XXIX. TROTTING AND BUSINESS SULKIES.**
*New York Coach-Maker's Magazine* January 1859, page 150.

We present our readers, this month, with two drafts of the sulky, both on the same plate. We do not offer them as showing any new feature, unless it may be in the formation of the boot of the business sulky. They will, however, answer the purpose for which they are intended that of exhibiting to a customer when such makes a call, and does not exactly know himself what he wants.

\*Sulky with an "e" is an old form of spelling sulky *Pennsylvania Gazette* July 20, 1785; *Pennsylvania Packet* May 6, 1778; and others.

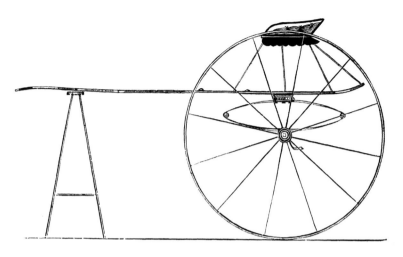

**Plate No. 33. TROTTING SULKY.**
*Coach-Makers' International Journal,* August 1867, page 179.
The circle bars are used back and front.

**TRACK SULKY.**
Made by Chas. Caffrey
*Coach Makers' International Journal*
May 1872 page 143.

The following sulkies were seen on the showroom floor of Chas. Caffrey's light carriage works, ready for shipping. Three of them were ticketed, ready for shipment, and from the cards we made the following memoranda:

"Western Girl," weight 59 lbs., painting, carmine, striped triple lines of black, scroll ends &c., touched up with gold.

"Lucy," 66 lbs. Painted light purple lake, striped, carmine, striped two fine lines of gold.

"Goldsmith Maid," weight, 53 lbs., painting, carmine, striped two fine lines of gold.

One other is painted white, with two fine lines, of gold.

The Queen of the Turf "LADY THORN" driven by Dan Pfifer: Trotting a Mile Heat In Harness In 2:08 3/4, at Narragansett Park, Providence, October 8th, 1869. Published by Currier & Ives, 1871. From the Print Collection of the Library of Congress LC-USZC2-2944 (color film copy slide).

The Celebrated Trotting Mare FLORA TEMPLE, driven by James D. McMann: Best Time In Harness Mile Heat 2:19 3/4, Two Mile Heats 4:50 1/2 to Wagon, Mile Heat 2:25. Published by Currier & Ives, 1872. From the Print Collection of the Library of Congress LC-UsZc2-2143 (color film copy slide).

Plate 5

The Celebrated Trotting Mare LUCY, Passing the Judges Stand: In the Fourth Heat. Winning the $5000 Prize at Buffalo, New York, August 9th 1872. Published by Currier & Ives, 1872. From the Print Collection of the Library of Congress LC-DIG-pga-00637 (digital file from original print).

The Celebrated Trotting Mare HUNTRESS Beating Dutchman's 3 Mile Time: 1872-Sept. 23rd Prospect Fair Grounds Long Island, Purse $1,250 Dash Three Miles, with $1000 Added, to the Horse Beating Dutchmans Time 7:32 1/2 $700 to First, $350 to Second, $200 to Third. Published by Currier & Ives, 1873. From the Print Collection of the Library of Congress LC-USZC2-2139 (color film copy slide).

Plate 6

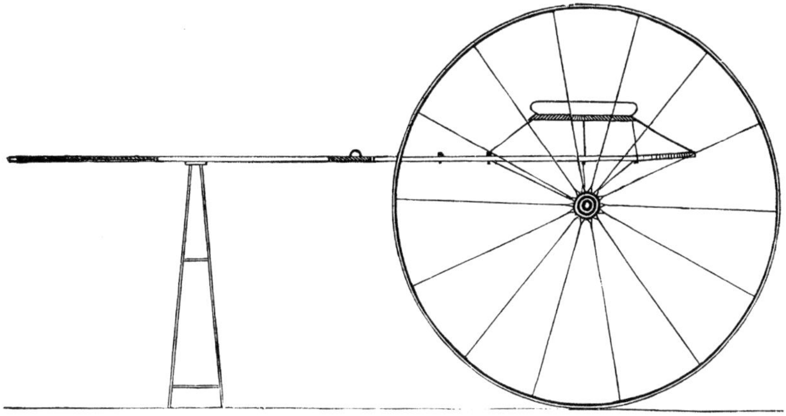

**Plate No. 38. TRACK SULKY.**

*Coach Makers' International Journal,* May 1872, page 132.

This design represents the style of Sulkey that is generally used at the race courses of the present day. We give the dimensions of a sixty pound sulkey, as this is the weight that is mostly used by trainers and drivers of fast horses. There are three bent bars used, two are fastened together in the center with bolts, the ends are boxed into the top of the shafts ⅛ of an inch, 6 feet from the end of the shafts to center of bars, the other is mortised to receive the back end of the shaft which has a tenant on end. The bars are dressed ⅞ of an inch square, with scroll on ends. Back bar: 10 inches sweep. Front bars: 6 inches sweep. From center of axle to shoulder on back of shaft: 7 inches; and from center of axle to center of front bars: 17 inches. Size of shafts: 1⅞ inch wide, and 1½ inch deep from hold back to back of axle, and tapered from these points ⅞ inch. Bottom of shafts from top of axle: 5 inches. Width at points, front end: 24 inches; at whiffletree: 38 inches inside. Seat: 13½ inches by 14½ inches, caned bottom; sets 8½ inches from top of shafts, and ¾ of an inch back of center. Wheels: 4 feet, 8 inches. Hubs: 3 inches by 6 inches. Spokes: ⅞ inch. Rim: ¾ inch ⅞ deep wide. Tire ¾ of an inch by ⅛ inch compound iron. Axles: ⅝ inch, with tapered shank 14 inches long, let in bed. Arms 6 inches long. The axle, should have 1½ inches sweep. The stays that support the seat are made of ⅞ oval iron, with T ends, where fastened to seat. The center stay clips on the shaft. The front stay takes one bolt, fastened to where the bar sets on the shaft. The three back stays have T ends, to form corner stays where the bar is mortice. There is a stay runs from back of shaft to bar in front, as shown in plate; it forms a bar under the axle for clip to fasten through, and there is one stay that forms a bar for clip stay from seat, which clips to the axle 10 inches from shoulder, this stay forms a brace to keep the shafts from rocking. There is a rail on the sides of the seat, but left open on leather back, this rail to be plated. A leather valance of 1½ inches wide, is nailed around the seat, this covers the nuts under the seat. Shafts are trimmed same as common shafts. A band of harness leather is sewed around the axle, (near side,) to step on.

Painting. Blue, with one fine gold stripe.

Philadelphia price: $140 to $160.

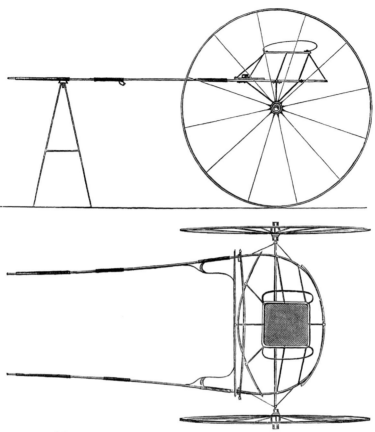

70. SIDE AND TOP VIEWS OF SULKY.—SCALE, ONE-HALF INCH.

## 70. TROTTING SULKY.

*Hub* August 1872, page 121.

The manufacture of carriages for the turf is continually increasing in importance; and in this issue we present our readers with another drawing of a late and tasteful pattern of a sulky, built by Peter Dubois,* of New York City.

Our cut represent the side and top views of which the latter in particular gives a perfect idea of the construction and shape of the stays. The seat is caned with rails on the sides only. The sulkies ranges between fifty and seventy pounds, and the most important dimensions are as follows: Height of wheels, 4 feet, 9 inches. Hubs, 3⅛ x 6 inches, spokes ⅞ inches, axles ⅝ inches, track 4 feet 4 inches.

*Peter Dubois died at his home June 1, 1869, at the age of fifty-four, was for many years engaged in the carriage business, at 202 Green street, New York City. *New York Coach-Maker's Magazine*, Vol. 11 No. 2 (July 1869), p. 29.

# ONE WHEEL SULKY 1870-1910.

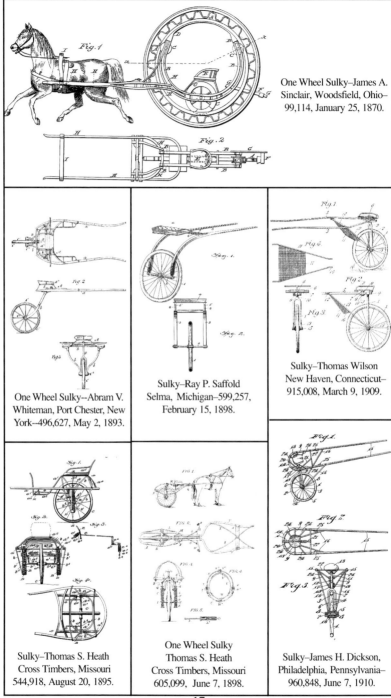

One Wheel Sulky–James A. Sinclair, Woodsfield, Ohio–99,114, January 25, 1870.

One Wheel Sulky--Abram V. Whiteman, Port Chester, New York--496,627, May 2, 1893.

Sulky–Ray P. Saffold Selma, Michigan–599,257, February 15, 1898.

Sulky–Thomas Wilson New Haven, Connecticut–915,008, March 9, 1909.

Sulky–Thomas S. Heath Cross Timbers, Missouri 544,918, August 20, 1895.

One Wheel Sulky Thomas S. Heath Cross Timbers, Missouri 605,099, June 7, 1898.

Sulky–James H. Dickson, Philadelphia, Pennsylvania–960,848, June 7, 1910.

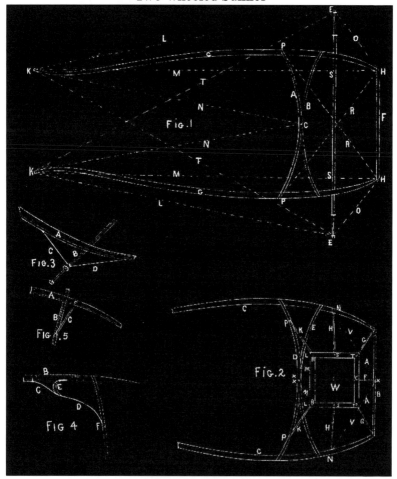

## HINTS TO FINISHERS.

*Carriage Monthly* December 1874 pages 155-156.

HOW TO PUT A SULKY TOGETHER.

While this paper is inscribed to finishers, as its heading sets forth, I doubt not that the smith will also find much to interest hint in the matter of ironing sulkies, as it not unfrequently occurs that the smith engaged upon light work has no other finisher than his helper, and then an inexperienced one.

In the present instance, I favor your patrons with a chapter on sulkies, and to be better understood, furnish you with a number of outline sketches, duly numbered and lettered in such a manner that the most humble smith or finisher will at once be able to clearly understand the whole without any further instructions.

Fig. 1 represents the shafts $G\,G$, the front bar $A$, the front back bar $B$, and back bar $F$; also the axle $D$, as viewed from the top. Our first aim should be to learn whether the shafts are both of the same length, which may be ascertained by measuring from the back corners $H\,H$ to the points $K\,K$, as per dotted lines $M\,M$. To ascertain if the shafts be square, we measure from the center of the two front bars $C$ to the points of the shafts $K\,K$, as per dotted lines $N\,N$. To prove the accuracy of the back section, we measure from the two back corners $H\,H$ to the point where

# Two-wheeled Sulkies

the front bar A connects with the shafts G G at P P, as per dotted diagonal lines R R.

While the putting on of the axle is about the last portion performed, I think it would be better to explain that part before leaving. Fig. 1, as it will avoid future reference and the necessity of a further sketch. Before adjusting the outer stay, as per C D, (in Fig. 3, A, shaft; B, axle,) we prove the position of the axle by first measuring from the back corners H H (Fig. 1), to points on the axle in a direct line as at S S. If we are correct here, we next measure from the ends of the axle E E, to the back corners H H, as per dotted lines O O. Next measure from axle ends E E to ends of shafts K K, as per dotted line L L; and again, diagonally, from axle ends E E to shaft point K K, as per dotted lines T T. This gives or points out any error or discrepancy existing in relation to the axle in its position to the center line between the shafts, as the axle, to be in proper position, must be strictly at right angles with a line drawn from the center between the shaft points K K through C to the center of the back bar F. Next, to prove that our axle does not project more on the one side than it does on the other, we measure from the ends of the axle E E, to points on the shaft immediately above the axle, as at X X.

Presuming that our shafts are true in every particular, the next step is to place the seat in the desired position, that is, in relation to height, pitch, and distance back of front bars. I should have mentioned that before placing the seat in position, we must first find the centers on the seat W, Fig. 2, as per S S and X, also the center of the back bar B, as per X, also the point of attaching the side stays H H on to the shafts C C at N N. We will now consider that we have our seat in nearly the exact position, to prove which, we just measure from the front corners of the seat R R to points on the bars, as per dotted lines L L, and then from the center of the bars at X X, as per dotted lines M M, to the front corners of the seat R R, which at once defines the position of the front of the seat in relation to accuracy. Next, comes the proving of the back portion of the seat, which we do by measuring from the back corners of the seat T T to the center of the back bar D at X, as per dotted lines A A; and, again, from the back corners of the seat T T, to the central points on the shafts at N N, as per dotted lines B B: Again we can measure from the central points N N on the shafts C C, to the side centers of the seat at S S. The side stays H H are then made and adjusted. Next, make and adjust the central back stay F; next, the front corner stays K K, and next, the back corner stays G G. The front stays K K, are adjusted to the front bar D at P P, the points of adjustment being at equal distances from the shafts C C. The front back bar E has no irons affixed to it beyond the whiffletree plates or socket. The seat must be strictly without wind. When looking across the side stays H H, from either side, they must be in range; the front stays K K must also range with each other, as also must the back corner stays G G.

The distance between shaft and axle is not fixed, some makers having 4 inches, and others 5 inches.

Fig. 4 represents one of the stirrups. B, section of shaft; C, front stay of stirrup; back portion, and E, stirrup proper; F, that portion which secures to the under side of the front bar A, Fig. 1. The stirrup must be so, made and adjusted as to afford ample room for the foot, also, what is termed ample leg room. From the front corners of the seat to the stirrup, a distance of not less than 21 inches or greater than 23 inches, ought to intervene, measuring diagonally. To have ample foot room, we require not less than 3½ inches, nor more than 4½ inches. The end F, of stirrup, Fig, 4, is secured to the front bar with the same bolt which secures the front stays K K, Fig. 2.

Fig. 5 represents a section of shaft A, also a section of the axle B; C, being the stay supporting the shaft at the centers N N, Fig. 2, and is held in position or secured by the bolts which secure the side stays H H to the shafts. After the stay C, Fig. 5, is made and adjusted, we make the outer stays as per C D, Fig. 3. The last part executed, less the securing of the whiffletree, is the seat rail, which is secured by the bolts at the corner of the seat R R, T T, Fig. 2, securing the corner stays G G, K K.

# Two-wheeled Sulkies

By way of a genial hint to the smith we would say, that it is unwise to give a sulky axle any gather, as the elevation of the shafts will insure all the gather necessary. Neither should the axle be set under a plumb spoke, and in cases where the sulky is to be used on the track, it would be well to have the spokes, under ones, set outside of a plumb line at least ¼ inch on each wheel, as the continuous moving about a circle has the effect of narrowing the wheels at the bottom.

Any other than an oval-shaped iron fails to give a pleasing effect in the ironwork of a sulky. The sizes of iron used by the different makers vary, ⁹⁄₁₆ by ⁵⁄₁₆ inch being heavy enough for the strongest road sulky, while ⅜ by ³⁄₁₆ inch would be light enough for the lightest track sulky built. LOUIS HOWARD.

---

### IRONING SULKIES.

*Coach-makers' International Journal* December 1871 pages 42-43.

To build a sulky weighing seventy pounds, more or less, and to track about 4 feet 8 inches or 4 feet 10 inches. In this case, we would say, set your shafts about 4½ inches above the axle, and make the shorts stay from the axle to the shafts of ⅝ x ⁵⁄₁₆ inches oval and the long stays of ⁹⁄₁₆ x ⁵⁄₁₆ oval: Set the seat–at the front part: 9½ inches above the shafts; with the back part of the seat ½ or ¾ inches more elevated. Make the two side stays of ⁹⁄₁₆ x ⁵⁄₁₆ inches oval, and all the other seat stays ½ x ⁵⁄₁₆ inches oval. Have the stirrups 22 inches from front corner of seat, and make them of ⁹⁄₁₆ x ⁵⁄₁₆ oval. Make side rails, only, of ⁵⁄₁₆ round, 1½ inches high, and 1 inch flare. Use ¾ x 6 inch axles., well drawn on shank, and let into the bed; and set wheels under a plumb spoke ¼ inch. Use ¾ x ³⁄₃₂ inch tires.

---

### MATERIALS USED TO BUILD A SEVENTY-FIVE POUND SULKY.

*Carriage Monthly* March 1874 page 212.

There are three bars used, made of pieces of bent rims ⅞ inch square, two at the front and one back. The front bars are let in on top of the shafts ⅛ of an inch, and 6 feet from point of shafts to center of bars. The back bar is mortised to receive the tenon on back end of shafts, the bars all finished on the ends with a scroll; front bars sweep 6 inches, back bar sweeps 10 inches. From center of front bars to center of axle on square line, 17 inches; from this point to back bar where framed to shafts, 7 inches. Shafts of best white ash, 1⅞ inches wide by 1½ inches deep from hold-back to part over axle, and from this tapered to ⅞ inch at the back end, also tapered from hold-back to front end to ⅞-inch square. Shafts from top of axle: 5 inches. Width at points, front end: 24 inches. At front bars: 38 inches inside. Seat: 13½ by 14½ inches. Caned bottom sets 8½ inches from top of shafts and center of seat, ¾ inch back of the center of axle; back end of seat elevated ½ to ¾ of an inch. Wheels: 4 feet 8 inches, or 4 feet 10 inches. Spokes: 13-16 inch. Hubs: 3¼ by 6 inches. Rims: ¾ by ⅞ inch. Tire: ¾ by ³⁄₃₂ inch, steel: Axles: ¾ by 6 inches; shank well drawn out to 14 inches in length, and let into the bed. Axle bed: 1½ inches square when got out, arched 1½ inches. After axles are let in, round bed up, leaving squares on the bottom for clip yokes. Short stay from axle to shafts, ⅝-inch oval iron; long stays, ⁹⁄₁₆ inch, oval. The seat stays of ½-inch oval iron. The stirrups 22 inches from the front corner of seat, and made of ⁹⁄₁₆ inch oval iron. Side rails to seat of ⁵⁄₁₆ inch round iron, 1½ inches high, 1¼ inches flare.

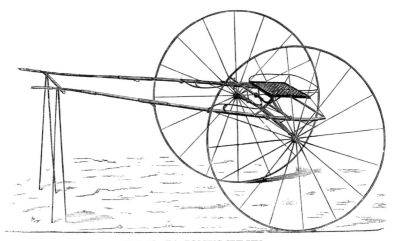

**Plate No. 76. JONE'S SULKY.**
Exhibited by Phineas Jones & Co., Newark, New Jersey.
*Hub* October 1876, page 253 and *Carriage Monthly* August 1876 page 83.

Messrs. Phineas Jones & Co., Newark, New Jersey, in addition to their very creditable display of wheels and wheel timber--which is their specialty--exhibit two track vehicles, a Skeleton Wagon and Sulky, the latter of which we illustrate in the accompanying cut.

The chief novelties in the construction of this sulky consist, first, in the raised cross-bar, upon which the seat rests directly, and, second, in the combination shaft, which is made of two kinds of wood, the upper and larger portion being of light stiff ash, and the lower portion of very tough hickory [about ⁵⁄₁₆ inch thick in the center firmly glued and screwed to the bottom, and tapered each way to the end]. The object of thus combining these two woods in the shaft is to reduce the weight and add to the strength, and, moreover, in case of accident, the ash may break, but the hickory will generally shiver and still hang together. The third novelty consists in the crossbars being crowned or arched, with the seat resting directly upon them, and by connecting, with a brace, the front and back of the seat with the center of the axle, a truss or bridge, as it were, is formed of the whole construction, which possesses the advantages of distributing the weight, and producing a Sulky of unusual stiffness and strength. Weight of the sulky exhibited, 46 lbs. It is unpainted.

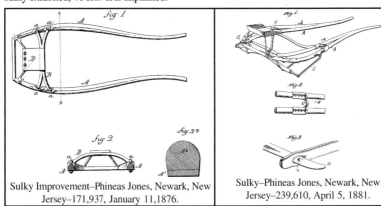

Sulky Improvement–Phineas Jones, Newark, New Jersey–171,937, January 11,1876.

Sulky–Phineas Jones, Newark, New Jersey–239,610, April 5, 1881.

**Plate No. LXVI. JONE'S SPLIT-SHAFT SULKY.**
*Hub* December 1885.

Our Plate in this issue represents a late and improved style of Sulky built by Messrs. Phineas Jones & Co., the well-known wheel manufacturers, of No. 301 Market-street, Newark, New Jersey. Sulkies of this kind are built for the trade, and sold "in the white;" and the utmost care is taken to make them absolutely perfect in every particular, in which aim, judging from the specimen now on exhibition in The Hub office, makers are certainly successful.

The latest improvement, which is patented, consists of a so-called "split-shaft," one made of two pieces, glued together at the ends, while the center or open section is held apart by three bolts, enclosed in wooden spindles, which are heavier in the center than at the ends. A brass ferrule is fastened to the ends, to keep the spindles from splitting The spindles also act as spreaders to prevent the shafts from coming together. The front ends are glued together to about 2½ ft. from the point; and, to prevent any opening of the joint, rivets. are inserted at intervals. The rear cross-bar is lapped to the shafts. As the cross-bar and the shafts are very light at the rear end, they are secured by socket-plates. A corner-plate is fastened to the rear end of the cross-bar and outside of the shaft. Another plate is let in from the top of the bar and shaft, and a similar plate is attached to the bottom, but not let in even with the wood. The rear end of the shaft is further supported by a light iron stay, which extends from the axle. The front cross-bar is secured to the shafts, 2½ in. from the front of the axle, and held securely by a draw-clip. This bar is swept upward as much as the axle in the center. By bringing this front shaft-bar close to the axle, much additional strength is given to the axle; and vibration of the shafts will not disturb the position of the axle or of the wheels.

The whiffletree is secured to the gear, about midway between the front cross-bar and the axle, by an iron stay running from the bar to the axle, and forming a boss in the center for the passage of the bolt used to secure the whiffletree.

The two inside pieces of the shafts are made of the best white ash, while the outside pieces are made of hickory. The combination of these two kinds of timber is claimed to be superior to the use of either one alone, for the reason that ash possesses more stiffness than hickory, and, if bent downward by weight, ash will resume its former position more readily than hickory.

The peculiar merits claimed for this construction of the shafts, as a whole, are greater lightness and more stiffness, and it is also next to impossible for both halves of the shaft to break simultaneously. Even if one half should happen to break, the Sulky will not be disabled, for the other half will be amply strong for continuing the race, without danger. Such an emergency has already occurred in a case where a well-known sporting character held the reins. The inner half of the shaft broke, or rather splintered, but the driver was able to continue the race, much to his gratification, which he afterwards expressed to the makers. This would, of course, have been impossible, had the shaft been made of one piece, in the usual manner.

Another noteworthy improvement in this new Sulky is the application of movable stirrups, also patented by Messrs. Jones & Co. These stirrups consist of two halves, with one half resting on top of the shafts and the other at the bottom, and made of composition metal, which is as pliable as the best iron. The ends form a clamp, which incloses both the outside and inside of the shaft; and the two halves are connected by two bolts. By loosening the nuts, the position of the stirrups can readily be altered to suit the convenience of the driver. The upper half is generally plated in either silver or brass, while the lower half is painted.

The seat-frame is supported in front by a light curved hickory rail, bolted inside the outer half of the shaft by two T-bolts. The heads of these bolts are on the inside, and are bent over the rail to prevent the rail from splitting. Six light iron stays are also introduced, to further support the seat-frames, two being applied on each side, and one each at the front and rear.

The seat-frame, 13½ x 14 in., is made of ash, and covered with canework. The seat-rail, which is very light, is made of steel, and consists of two pieces, welded in the center and at the rear. The uprights at the rear of the seat-rail are not welded, but are drawn from the solid. The axle has a graceful sweep, being curved high enough to effectually prevent the horse's heels from striking.

The weight of such Sulkies, as built by Messrs. Jones & Co., ranges from 45 to 48 lbs. The average height of the wheels is 4 ft. 6½ in. Depths of rims, ⅞ in., well-rounded. Size of spokes, ¹⁵⁄₁₆ in. Number of spokes, 14. Stagger of spokes, the full width of the spokes. Hubs, 3 ⅛ in. diameter. Front bands, 2 in., and back, 2¹⁵⁄₁₆ in., inside diameter. Length of front bands, 1½ in. Length of hubs, 6 in. Tire, ⅝ x ³⁄₃₂ in., steel.

## PHINEAS JONES.
*Carriage Monthly* October 1897 page 217.

Phineas Jones was born in Spencer, Massachusetts; in 1819, and was the youngest of a family of fourteen. He spent his youth between his father's farm and clerking in country stores until he was twenty-one years of age, and until he was thirty-one had entire charge of the

farm. In 1855, he removed to Elizabethport, New Jersey, and went into the wheel business with E. J. and D. S. Whittemore, who had carried on the wheel business before, at East Brookfield, Massachusetts. At the end of the first year Mr. Jones purchased his partners' interests, and for a time conducted the business alone. Afterwards, he took in William H. Baldwin as partner.

In 1858, the business was removed to Newark, New Jersey, and located in a building connected with the carriage factory of the old established house of J. M. Quinby & Co. The growth of the business soon compelled them to make a change, and the firm removed to the old carriage factory of Messrs. Baldwin & Thomas, on Market street, where the firm of Phineas Jones & Co., is now located.

Mr. Jones died at his residence in Newark, on Saturday evening, the 19th of April, 1884.

## HOW TO SET A SULKY SEAT.
*Carriage Monthly* May 1876 page 26.

The best method of setting up a sulky seat for ironing for holding the seat firm.

*Fig. 1* presents what might be termed a seat box. *A*, the box having the proper bevel from back to front, so as to give the seat the proper pitch. The corners of the box are cut out to make allowances for fitting corner stays. The box is secured to the base board *B*, which is furnished with the slot *C* (on each end), to allow of securing the whole to the shafts by means of the hook, as per *Fig. 2*. The short dotted lines *D, D*, represent the seat frame of the sulky as resting on the box. The long dotted lines *F*, represent a plate with hole *E*, through which passes a bolt for securing the seat to the seat box. By screwing pieces on back or front we are enabled to get any desired pitch. The whole may be made in half a day, and will last for years; is steady, and without doubt the best plan which can be adopted.

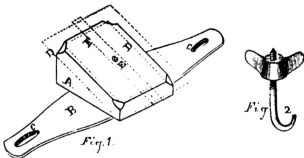

## HOW TO SET A SULKY SEAT, SO AS TO BALANCE.
*Carriage Monthly* December 1877, page 165.

In order to balance a sulky seat it is best to know the height of the horse intended to be used; thus, permitting the shafts to be placed in the position which will be occupied on the track or road, when in use.

We will suppose the sulky is ironed and placed in position, with the wheels on, ready for the ironing of the seat. The seat should be placed in position, as securely as possible, by artificial fastenings. (Perhaps, one which is as good and simple as any, will be found on page 26, May 1876 of the *Carriage Monthly*. The seat frame being in position, thumb screws should be placed upon the shafts, in such manner as to answer in place of the stirrup. Request your helper to take a seat in the sulky....

The helper sits in the position which will be occupied by the driver, if for a road sulky, sitting more erect than for one to be used on the track. Taking the ends of the shafts in the hand, the balancing process may then be commenced, care being taken to keep the shafts in the position to be occupied; should the weight be too much on the hands, move back the seat; or, if too light, move forward, until the position is obtained which will so perfectly balance, as to require you only to steady, and not to hold the end at the shaft.

# Two-wheeled Sulkies

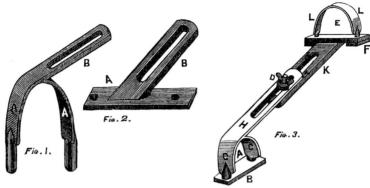

Fig. 1.

Fig. 2.

Fig. 3.

## A HANDY TOOL FOR SULKY IRONING.
*Hub* July 1876.

      The above device is calculated to hold the axle of a sulky in position while fitting the stays. Secure the axle to the shafts.

      *Fig.* 1 shows a clip. *A, A,* with flat projection B, furnished with a slot.

      *Fig.* 2 presents a coupling bar. *A,* furnished with clip holes, and has a flat projection *B,* furnished with a slot.

      *Fig.* 3 presents the tool as a whole or in combination. *A,* the space occupied by the axle formed by the clip *C, C,* and coupling bar *B; E.,* is the space occupied by the shaft formed by clip *L, L,* and bar F; K, is the slotted projection from the bar *F,* and *H* the slotted projection from the axle clip *C, C; D,* is the thumbnut and bolt passing through the slotted projections, which secures the same in position. With this device, we are enabled to place the shafts at any distance above the axle, and fit the axle stays with perfect ease.

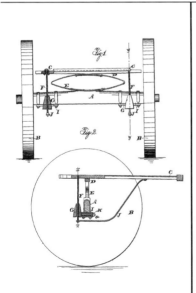

Spring for Sulkies
A. Miller, Angola, Indiana
44,012, August 30, 1864.

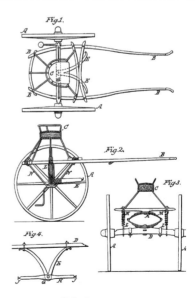

Sulky Improvement
Jacob G. Reiff, Farmersville, Pennsylvania
59,452, November 6, 1866.

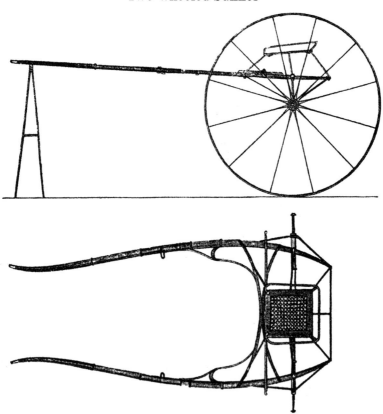

**Plate No. C. HUNT'S TRACK SULKY.** ½-inch Scale.
Exhibited by William Hunt, Camdem, New Jersey.
*Carriage Monthly* December 1876 pages 163-164.

    The exhibition of track sulkies at the Centennial was large, and shows to what an extent this very light work is built in this country. The exhibit comprised those from Boston and Vermont in the East, New York. New Jersey and Pennsylvania in the Middle, and Michigan in the West, showing that the work is not confined to any one section of the country. The designs were very similar, differing mostly in some special points, most all of which were either patented or application for a patent had been filed.

    The accompanying drawing represents a sulky, exhibited by William Hunt, of Camden, New Jersey, which we selected, it being free from patents as far as we know, and it also represents the latest style, together with its beautiful proportions, and, to use the present phrase now in use, "its perfect adaptation to the purpose intended." To fully show the manner of putting together, and give the proper shape of the shafts and stays, we give two views, to wit: side and top view, drawn to ½-inch scale, omitting the wheels in the latter view. The use of a swept bar at the back end of the shafts has been superseded by the straight bar, giving a better stay to the stays, and also is a better support to the shafts sideways. The seat stays at the center are clipped to the shafts, the clip portion forged to the stay end, and the ends of clips passing through the couple formed by the brace connecting with the shaft and axle. The corner stays at the back have T's forged on the ends, which clasp the ends of the shafts and bare on the top and back edge, thus securing the corner in the strongest manner. The front stays are riveted to the bars, which is more secure, than bolts, and they can also be made much lighter, thus leaving more strength at the hole in the bar. The foot braces are secured to the shafts by clips, forged solid to the brace, the top part forming the strap and the lower the coupling, having only one threaded end, which passes through the coupling on the outside of the shaft, thus avoiding all projecting nuts and bar ends for the horse to injure himself by when breaking. The axle brace to the shaft, back and front, is clipped to the axle near the collar, and secured to the shafts by clip at front and rivet at back. These braces, with the inside brace, form a very stiff and strong support, preventing the shafts and wheels getting out of square at the axle. The shafts are of ash, cross bars hickory, seat made with light rail.

Dimensions.—The dimensions of the various parts, with height, and width, are as follows: Wheels: 4 feet 7 inches. Hubs: 3¼ by 6 inches. Spokes: ⅞ inch. Rim: ¹³⁄₁₆ inch deep. Tire: ¹¹⁄₁₆ inch wide. Axles: ¾ inch, the bed forged-flat, and let in the axle bed edgewise. Axle bed in center: 1⅝ inches deep, 1¼ inches wide. Seat: 14 by 15 inches. Shafts: at front point, ¾ by ¾ inch; at the front bar, 1¾ inches wide by 1⅝ inches deep; at back end, ¾ by ¾ in. Cross bars: ¾ by ⅝ in. Height of seat from top of shafts: front, 5¼ in.; back, 7¾ inches. Shafts, from ground: front, 41½ inches; at back end. 36, inches. Width of shafts at front, at the narrowest point, outside: 27½ inches; back, 27 inches; at front bar, 43 inches. The seat is in its proper place over the axle, as shown in the top view. The shafts from center of bars to front point: 6 feet 5 inches. Full length of shafts: 8 feet. 2 inches. Track: 4 feet 4 inches.

Painting.—Black, striped two fine lines light green.

Mountings.—Axle nuts, seat rail and shaft tips: silver plated.

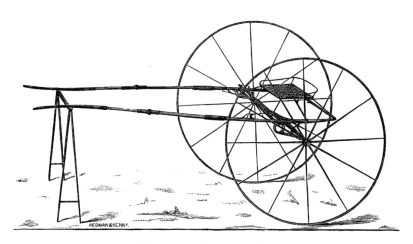

**Plate No. 67. CROSBY'S SULKY.**
*Hub* September 1876, page 213.

Crosby, Gilzinger & Company of Rondout, New York exhibit, by the side of their velocipede, a well made sulky, showing the application of their coil, or "patent Centennial" springs, the form and arrangement of which are plainly indicated in our engraving.

Painting.--Carmine, fine-lined with gold; no striping on rims or sides of spokes.

Mountings.--Silver.

# Two-wheeled Sulkies
## GATHER OF AXLES ON TWO-WHEELED VEHICLES.
### *Carriage Monthly* October 1876 page 125.

It is improper to give the axles of any two-wheeled vehicle the least particle of gather. Make them so that the wheels, from back to front, measuring at the rims and at a point or points equidistant from the ground to the center of the hub, are strictly parallel. The elevation of the shafts in securing them to the horse, owing to the under set of the axle, has the effect of gathering the axle to the front, and with a high horse, sometimes more than is required. To illustrate, after you have secured the axle in position, raise the points of the shafts, at tug bearing, to the same position as when the horse is attached, and measure as above described, and note the results.

Swing is out of date. Sulky axles ought to be set with a view to having a strictly plumb spoke. It is true that the weight of the rider or driver will produce a slight deflection, but the fact of nearly all race courses having their starting and stopping place at the same point, shows that the sulky traverses a regular or irregular circle, which produces a strain upon the wheels and axles sufficient to overcome the deflection, and cause them, the wheels or bottom spokes, to continue nearly vertical.

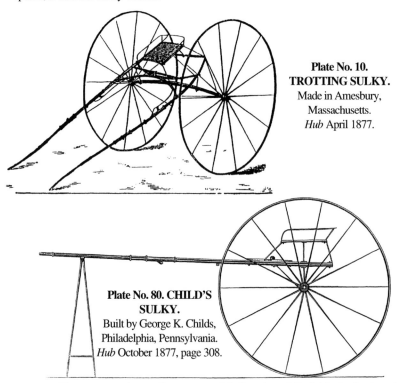

**Plate No. 10.**
**TROTTING SULKY.**
Made in Amesbury,
Massachusetts.
*Hub* April 1877.

**Plate No. 80. CHILD'S SULKY.**
Built by George K. Childs,
Philadelphia, Pennsylvania.
*Hub* October 1877, page 308.

The accompanying cut illustrates a well-built and tastefully finished sulky from the factory of George K. Childs, 307 Union Street, Philadelphia, Pennsylvania. The job was duplicated from the one he exhibited at the Centennial last year, and this is known by him as his "Centennial pattern." We believe that Mr. Childs claimed his sulky at the Centennial, which weighed 47¾ lbs. That it was the lightest in the Exhibition. He now builds the same pattern weighing 47 lbs. Wheels, 4 feet 6 inches, 16 spokes, full staggered. Hubs, 3 by 6 inches. Spokes ¾ inch. Rims ¾ inch. Tires ⅝ by 1⁄16 inch. Axle ⅝ inch, steel.

Painting. Dark carmine fine lined with blue. Mounting. Gold.

# BREWSTER SULKIES, NEW YORK, NEW YORK.

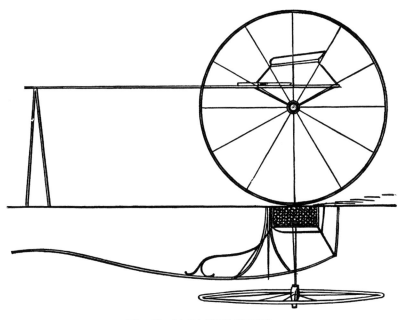

**Plate No. 36. RACING SULKY.**
*Hub* July 1878, page 177.

      Racing Sulky exhibited by Brewster & Company, New York, New York at the Paris exhibit. The shafts and bed of the Racing Sulky (weight 54 lbs.), are of second-growth ash, selected for its lightness and strength. This sulky represents the standard weight used in trotting races, and carries a driver weighing one hundred and sixty pounds. Lighter sulkies (ten pounds less) are made for small horses, and within ten years the standard weight has been reduced by improvements in construction, from sixty-three pounds. The iron used in construction of all our vehicles is of the best quality only. Low moor, Norway, Salisbury, and Burden's Best being used. The latter, an American iron, ranked by the best scientific authorities, after practical tests, as fully equal, and in some respects superior, to Low Moor. The springs are from the best Swedes steel, and the axles from "Burden's Best" iron; homogeneous steel for the lighter axles, and the tires from Hussey, Howe & Company, Pittsburg, Pennsylvania, steel.

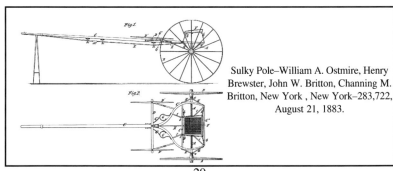

Sulky Pole–William A. Ostmire, Henry Brewster, John W. Britton, Channing M. Britton, New York , New York–283,722, August 21, 1883.

# Two-wheeled Sulkies

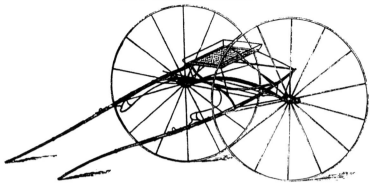

**Plate No. 16. SULKY.**–Half-inch Scale. (not to scale).
*Carriage Monthly* June 1879 page 42.

In reply to several requests for the publication of a sulky, we comply by giving one suitable for a horse about fifteen hands 3 inches high. Mr. W. E. Penrose, of Philadelphia, has the original from which this drawing was taken. Seat 13⅜ inches wide by 14¼ inches deep, caned.

Dimensions.–Wheels: Exterior diameter of wheels, 56 inches. Exterior diameter of hubs 3⅛ inches. Length of hubs 6 inches. Mortise of hubs ¹³⁄₁₆ x ¼ inches. Diameter of bands of hubs 2 x 2⅝ inches. Width of spokes at square end ⅞ inches. Thickness of spokes at square end ⅝ inch. Number of spokes 14. Thickness and depth of rims ⅝ x ⅞ inches. Stagger ¾ inch. Tire, steel ⅝ x ¹⁄₁₆.

Painting.–Carmine, striped with ¼ inch black line.

Mountings.–Gold.

---

## STAYS FOR SULKY.
*Carriage Monthly* March 1879 page 229.

The accompanying illustration is a novelty in sulky ironing, which our sulky ironers would do well to pattern after. *Fig, 1* represents the outer clip complete. *A*, strap, and *B, B*, clip ends; *C, C*, sections of back and front stay from axle, and solid to clip.

To make the same, take Norway iron, proper size, fuller in as at *D, D*, and *E*, draw down *F, F*, and then split from *E*, as per line *G, G*; then as per *Fig. 3*, turn up *H, H*, thus forming *K*, strap of clip, as per *A, Fig. 1*, and stays *C, C, Fig. 1*, by dressing *H, H*, swaging them to an oval and turning them to the proper angle, as per *Fig. 1*. Form the ends *L, L*, as per *B, B, Fig. 1*. This class of stay will lessen weight, will add to appearance, and materially lessen the direct strain on the clip ends *B, B*.

The additional cost for labor will be but trifling, and will more than pay for itself by the enhanced appearance of the stay.

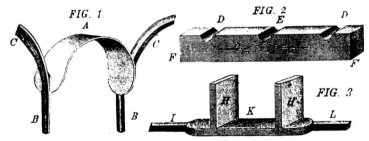

# PRAY, BOSTON, MASSACHUSETTS.

**Plate No. 121. TROTTING SULKY.**
*Hub* March 1880, page 529.

The ingenuity of Sulky builders deserves special credit. When we consider the limited and special use of this class of vehicles, compared with the universal demand for wagons, for example, it is really wonderful to look at the constant improvements made in their construction, insuring at the same time greater durability and a reduction of weight. The double bars under the front of the seat have given place to one full swept cross-bar, and on the cut the rear ends of the shafts are strengthened by two braces, clipped to the center of the axle-bed. This method, we believe, is patented by Messrs. Pray Brothers of Boston, Massachusetts.

Principal dimensions: Wheels, 4 feet. 7 inches. Hubs, 3¼ x 6 inches. Spokes, ⅞ inches. Rims, 1³⁄₁₆ inches. Tire, ¾ inch. Axle, ¾ inch.

In conclusion, the writer begs leave to add that he is prepared to furnish fine colored drawings, either side views or perspective, of any of the above or other fashionable styles for spring, made to any scale up to 1½ inch to the foot, and at prices to suit the times. A good colored drawing is the most satisfactory representation of a carriage which it is possible to show on paper, and it gives a better idea to a customer than even a photograph. ADOLPHUS MULLER

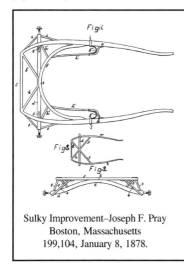

Sulky Improvement–Joseph F. Pray
Boston, Massachusetts
199,104, January 8, 1878.

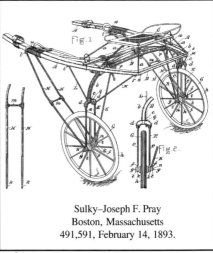

Sulky–Joseph F. Pray
Boston, Massachusetts
491,591, February 14, 1893.

## HOW TO TRACK A SULKY.

*Hub* December 1879, page 396.

Bath, New York, October 5, 1879 To the Editor:

Will you be kind enough to explain how a Sulky should be tracked ? I have just been ironing one, and I tracked it on a plumb spoke, so it was narrower at the bottom than at the top; but the man that owns it had me alter it over, so it was as wide at the bottom as the top. I claim to be right. J. E. Smith.

ANSWER.—Certain conditions in sulky driving demand a departure from established rules. The conditions are these: (1) the track over which the sulky is driven is circular in shape; (2) the wheels of a sulky exceed in height those of ordinary vehicles; (3) the weight to be carried is directly over the axle; and (4) the weight carried is largely in excess of that of the vehicle. These conditions being combined, and the sulky driven at a rapid pace, the vehicle is always liable to inclination beyond the center of gravity. To assist in overcoming this tendency, it has been conceded by turfmen and builders of track work, that sulkies should be so tracked as to bring the under line or bearing of the axle-arm nearly horizontal.

Next, it is a difficult matter to determine the exact distance from the ground to the tug-bearing portion of the shafts. From forty-three inches to forty-seven inches is supposed to be about the correct height. The axle should be set to a plumb spoke, which in ordinary cases would give a spring of from three to four inches, with the draft elevated to forty-three inches, and the axle should be so set as to gather. The distance between the wheels, back and front, at a horizontal line drawn through the center of the axle, should be equal; and we would then find at the increased elevation of four inches, at the point we would have gathered the wheels forward, by reason of the under set, nearly five-sixteenths of an inch, which action would have the effect of increasing friction and retarding speed. The same effect would also be produced were the shafts set at forty-seven inches and then reduced to forty-three inches, the wheels becoming, at the point mentioned, wider at the front than back.

Again, the nearer the bearing portion of the axle-arm approaches a horizontal line, the less the friction incurred. The aim of all sulky builders is to keep the axle as rigid as possible, which is necessary to insure speed; for, with a rigid axle there is but little chance for that deflection which would allow the  wheels to spread at the earth.

The sulky axle, when secured in position and with the shafts at the proper elevation at the front, should be strictly vertical at its front, and back surfaces. To place the shafts horizontal and the axle at right angle with the shafts, would, when the the shafts were at the proper elevation, insure a gathering forward of nearly one inch, which results simply from the under-set of the spindle.

From what has above been set forth, it follows that, in our opinion, presuming the wheels to have the usual dish, then our correspondent is correct in the position he holds; but if the wheels be without dish and the axle spindles be strictly parallel, then the party having the vehicle built is right.

## ABOUT SULKIES.

*Carriage Monthly* January 1880 pages 186-187.

How to iron a speeding sulky to weigh between fifty and fifty-five pounds. With a view to be as nearly correct as possible, we paid a visit to one of our boarding-stables in Philadelphia, where the care of fast trotters is a specialty, and where a number of sulkies by best makers are always to be found, and from them made the selections which we offer.

*Fig. 1* presents one of the corner stays. B, B, the angle which secures to the seat at bottom; A, is the stay proper; Z, the end which secures to the back corner as back stays, or to the front bar as front stays. *Fig. 2* represents the center back stay or center side stays; H, the portion which secures to the seat; K, the stay proper; L, the end which secures to the back bar and shaft. The two stays above mentioned were–*Fig. 1*, ½ x ⁵⁄₁₆ inch; *Fig. 2*, ½ x ¼ inch, both oval. *Fig. 3* is the stirrup; C, the front end, which secures to the shaft; E, is the heel-rest of the stirrup; D, that portion of it which secures to the shaft. These ends

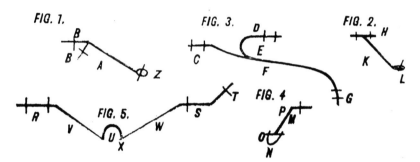

may be secured with screws, bolts or clips, as the builder prefers. Clips entail more labor and add to the weight; screws are quite secure and lessen labor and weight. F is the back part; G, that portion which secures to the front bar; at this point, one bolt–⁵⁄₁₆ inch–is absolutely necessary; or, if preferred, a rivet may be used. This say was ½ x ⁵⁄₁₆ inch oval; the heel portion, E, is half oval, about ¾ x ¼ inch.

*Fig. 4* presents the short stay from the top of the axle to the bottom of the shaft. O, is the coupling bar which rests on the top of the axle, secured by the clips N; M, the stay proper; P, the end which secures to the shaft, under side, with a bolt. This stay we found to be ⁹⁄₁₆ x ⁵⁄₁₆ inch oval. *Fig. 5* is the stay which extends from the outer portion of the axle, near the wheel, to the shafts, front and back; R, the front portion, which secures to the bottom of the shaft; S, the back end, which secures to the shaft; T, a continuation of the same, which extends under and secures to the back bar; V and W are the stay proper; X sets under the axle, and is secured with the clip U.

The axle in nearly every instance, was ⅝ x 6 inches, the tire ⅝ x ¹⁄₁₆ inch; on some the stays were riveted with ⅛-inch rivets; where bolts were used, they were ³⁄₁₆ inch; the clips were ¼ inch; the screws appeared to be about number 9. The seat-rails were some ¼ inch round and others ⁵⁄₁₆ inch round. The track varied from 4 feet 3 inches to 4 feet 6 inches.

# THOMAS H. BROWN, CHICAGO, ILLINOIS

Brown's Novelty Sulky. Thomas H. Brown, of 335 State-street, Chicago, Illinois (the Novelty Carriage Works). The characteristics of this sulky, consist, first, of an axle arched above the plane of the shafts, allowing the horse to be brought closer to the load than in any other sulky, and without any obstruction; second, with a movable seat allowing suitable leg room to be given to the driver, and also allowing the balance to be adjusted for the benefit of the horse;

**BROWN'S PATENTED NOVELTY SULKY.**
*Hub* December 1880.

and lastly and not least, great attention is given to the wheels (made under his own supervision), which are unusually stiff and strong, and prepared to stand the test of making turns around a half-mile track without any fear of springing or "buckling." The price of this sulky (an illustration--of the newest pattern is given herewith), is $150; and in order to meet the competition of Eastern makers, a superior sulky of the more ordinary pattern, with axles less arched, is supplied at $125. To give the absolute dimensions of the sulky illustrated is difficult, for Mr. Brown is accustomed to fit a sulky to the horse for which it is intended, just as the custom tailor is accustomed to fit his suits to individual needs. As sulkies run, the following dimensions are standard: Wheels, 4 feet 8 inches high (they run from 4 feet 6 inches to 4 feet 10 inches). Hubs, from $2\frac{7}{8}$ to $3\frac{1}{8}$ inches, diameter, 6 inches long. Spokes, $\frac{3}{4}$ to $\frac{7}{8}$ inches. Rims, $\frac{3}{4}$ to $\frac{7}{8}$ inches. To the wheels Mr. Brown gives special attention, and herein lies to a great extent his success as a builder of first-class track work. Tire, $\frac{11}{16}$ x $\frac{1}{16}$ inch, steel. Average track, 48 inches. Shafts, rock elm, $1\frac{1}{2}$ inches at centers, tapering toward the end, and turned out a trifle. Length of shafts from 6 feet 3 inches to 6 feet 6 inches. Height of shafts from the axle, 4 to 6 inches. Mr. Brown employs special form of shafts, preventing the liability of the horse being galled by the girth, which is the result of long experience and careful study of the requirements. Axles, $\frac{11}{16}$ inch, steel; arched from 5 to 10 inches. The seat is caned, and provided with a plated rail.

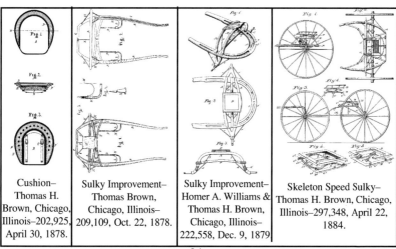

| Cushion– Thomas H. Brown, Chicago, Illinois–202,925, April 30, 1878. | Sulky Improvement– Thomas Brown, Chicago, Illinois– 209,109, Oct. 22, 1878. | Sulky Improvement– Homer A. Williams & Thomas H. Brown, Chicago, Illinois– 222,558, Dec. 9, 1879 | Skeleton Speed Sulky– Thomas H. Brown, Chicago, Illinois–297,348, April 22, 1884. |

# PATENTS for SULKIES 1870-1876.

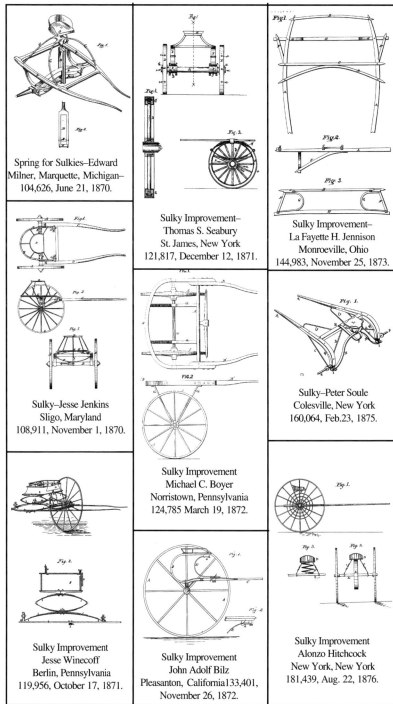

Spring for Sulkies–Edward
Milner, Marquette, Michigan–
104,626, June 21, 1870.

Sulky–Jesse Jenkins
Sligo, Maryland
108,911, November 1, 1870.

Sulky Improvement
Jesse Winecoff
Berlin, Pennsylvania
119,956, October 17, 1871.

Sulky Improvement–
Thomas S. Seabury
St. James, New York
121,817, December 12, 1871.

Sulky Improvement
Michael C. Boyer
Norristown, Pennsylvania
124,785 March 19, 1872.

Sulky Improvement
John Adolf Bilz
Pleasanton, California133,401,
November 26, 1872.

Sulky Improvement–
La Fayette H. Jennison
Monroeville, Ohio
144,983, November 25, 1873.

Sulky–Peter Soule
Colesville, New York
160,064, Feb.23, 1875.

Sulky Improvement
Alonzo Hitchcock
New York, New York
181,439, Aug. 22, 1876.

# PATENTS for SULKIES 1870-1879.

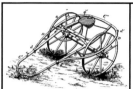

Sulky Improvement–John W. Wood, Owatonna, Minnesota– 187,693, February 20, 1877.

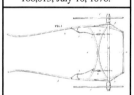

Sulky Improvement–Daniel G. Hetefield, Rahway, New Jersey– 188,013, July 10, 1876.

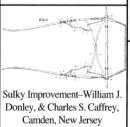

Sulky–William J. Donley, Camden, New Jersey 196,142, October 16, 1877.

Sulky Improvement–William J. Donley, & Charles S. Caffrey, Camden, New Jersey 195,588, September 25, 1877.

Timing Attachment–John L. Boone & Edwin J. Fraser San Francisco, California 197,593, Nov. 27, 1877.

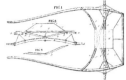

Sulky–Harry B. Paul, Camden, NJ.–206, 606, July 30, 1878.

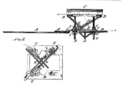

Sulky Improvement–Dennis Bushor, Effingham, Illinois– 207,711, September 3, 1878.

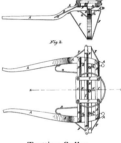

Trotting Sulky-- William J. Hamill St. Catharines, Ontario 210,687, December 10, 878.

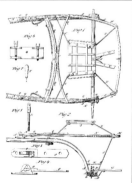

Sulky Attachment–Andrew H. Morse, Norwich, Connecticut216,436, June 10, 1879.

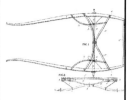

Sulky Braces–Budd Doble, Chicago, Illinois & Harry B. Paul, Camden, New Jersey– 219,924, September 23, 1879.

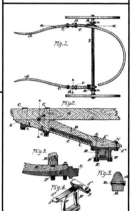

Sulky Improvement John V. Upington, Lexington, Kentucky 221,631, November 11, 1879.

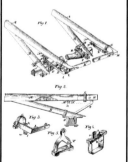

Sulky Improvement–James T. Upington & John V. Upington, Lexington, Kentucky 222,965, December 23, 1879.

# Two-wheeled Sulkies

### HEIGHT OF SULKY WHEELS.
*Hub* January 1881 page 478.

Of course the general principle is, that the larger the circle, the less the shock when an obstacle is encountered. But sulky wheels being made extremely light, they are consequently highly elastic, and after passing a certain point the advantage gained by the large circle is more than counteracted by the vibratory or fluttering movement resulting from velocity and the motion of the horse, this being most perceptible when making short curves. Stiffness, as well as elasticity, is an all-important element in a sulky wheel, and for this reason we consider that it should not be made over 4ft. 6 in. high, and that excessive lightness should be avoided. It should also be remembered that sulkies are ordinarily used on a nearly perfect level, so that the question of passing obstructions hardly enters into the question as a debatable element.

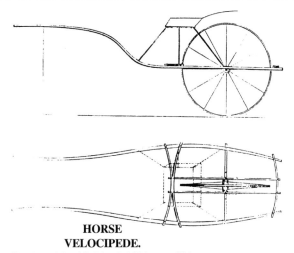

### HORSE VELOCIPEDE.
*Carriage Monthly* March 1881 page 234.

A sketch of this vehicle or cycle was furnished us by Mr. Jos. Haslip, through our Baltimore correspondent. Following are the measurements: Diameter of wheel, four feet; spokes, ⅞ inch ; hub, 4 inches in diameter, 6 inches long. Rims 1⅛ inches deep, ¾ inch tread. Dodge, 2 inches.

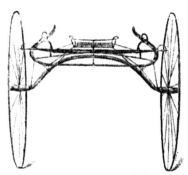

### Plate No. 97. BACK VIEW OF SULKY.
*Carriage Monthly* March 1881 page 238.

This sulkey represents one of Messrs. S. Toomey & Sons' latest improvements. It is finely constructed, and upon the most approved mechanical principles. It has raised cross-bars, making a complete truss brace, giving a very stiff sulkey, enabling the horse to be hitched as close as desired.

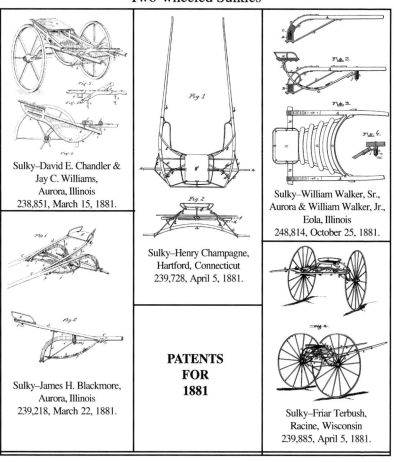

Sulky–David E. Chandler & Jay C. Williams, Aurora, Illinois 238,851, March 15, 1881.

Sulky–Henry Champagne, Hartford, Connecticut 239,728, April 5, 1881.

Sulky–William Walker, Sr., Aurora & William Walker, Jr., Eola, Illinois 248,814, October 25, 1881.

Sulky–James H. Blackmore, Aurora, Illinois 239,218, March 22, 1881.

**PATENTS FOR 1881**

Sulky–Friar Terbush, Racine, Wisconsin 239,885, April 5, 1881.

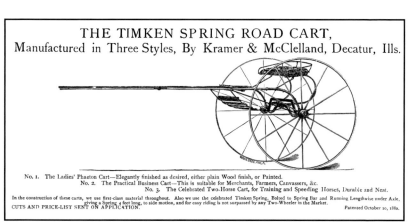

## THE TIMKEN SPRING ROAD CART,
Manufactured in Three Styles, By Kramer & McClelland, Decatur, Ills.

No. 1. The Ladies' Phaeton Cart—Elegantly finished as desired, either plain Wood finish, or Painted.
No. 2. The Practical Business Cart—This is suitable for Merchants, Farmers, Canvassers, &c.
No. 3. The Celebrated Two-Horse Cart, for Training and Speeding Horses, Durable and Neat.

In the construction of these carts, we use first-class material throughout. Also we use the celebrated Timken Spring, Bolted to Spring Bar and Running Lengthwise under Axle, giving a Spring 4 feet long, to side motion, and for easy riding is not surpassed by any Two-Wheeler in the Market.
CUTS AND PRICE-LIST SENT ON APPLICATION.                                    Patented October 10, 1882.

*Carriage Monthly* April 1883.

# Two-wheeled Sulkies

## WHICH WHEEL OF A S UL KY IS SUBJECTED TO THE GREATER STRAIN?

*Hub* October 1883 page 425.

WE have received the following inquiry from Mr. E. F. Bradish, Batavia, N. Y.:

"In making a curve on a level track, which wheel of the Sulky is subjected to the greater strain ? The inner or outer wheel ?

ANSWER.—We have consulted one of the best Sulky-makers in this city [New York City], and after a lengthy discussion, calling into service his long experience and extended observation of this subject, the conclusion was arrived at, that the strain upon the wheels is equal in a properly built Sulky. The near wheel, which is on most occasions the inside wheel of the race track, has a trifle more dish than the outside, or off wheel. Through this arrangement, the strain on the wheel is counteracted, so that in turning a curve it becomes equal, which would not be the case if the dish of the wheels was alike.

## DISH OF SULKY WHEELS.

*Hub* January 1884, page 640.

We had supposed that all fundamental questions relative to the mechanical require-ments of Sulkies had long ago been settled beyond dispute; but it seems not.

In our October number, page 425, appeared the inquiry: "Which Wheel of a Sulky is Subjected to most Strain?" followed by a brief reply furnished by an expert of this city, who has had long experience in track work, and to whom we referred the question as one eminently qualified to do the subject full justice.

We freely confess that his response surprised us: partly because it was just the re-verse of our own theory on the subject; and still more because his two statements (1) "that the strain upon the wheels is equal in a properly built Sulky;" and (2) "the near wheel has a trifle more dish by which arrangement the strain on that wheel is counteracted," seemed obviously contradictory, however, we published his statement, feeling certain that, if incorrect, it would be sure to call out the opinions of other experts ; and this, we are rather glad to add, has proved to be the case. We wish we had room this month to publish all the letters which have since been addressed to us on this subject; but that is impossible, and we must content ourselves with stating that the majority of the writers of these letters, in stating the result of their experience, express the opinion that the greater strain is always on the outer wheel. This is our own opinion, for the reason that the weight of the vehicle and driver must necessarily incline in that direction when the vehicle is moving around a circle. Drivers tell us, moreover, that the inside wheel has often been known to leave the ground while making great speed around a short track, in which case the outer wheel would obviously receive the entire strain. Judging from a theoretical stand-point, the end thrust from the axle, constantly exerted against the outer wheel, would seem necessarily to carry the greater strain to that point. On the other hand, the outer wheel is of course protected by its dish; while the dish of the inner wheel, under the same outward thrust, is calculated to weaken its power of resistance and to render it liable to be turned inside out.

What, now, the experience of Sulky builders as to the result of these conflicting strains? Which wheel, in the experience of the reader, first shows signs of weakness? And what means does the reader take to counteract the unequal strain, if there be any?

The question is still open for discussion in The Hub's columns, and we shall be pleased to receive an expression of opinion from all experts.

## WILLIAM J. WAYNE, DECATUR, ILLINOIS.
continued on next page

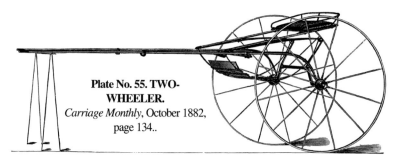

**Plate No. 55. TWO-WHEELER.**
*Carriage Monthly*, October 1882, page 134..

Credit is due Messrs. Wayne Brothers, Decatur, Illinois, for this original plate.

Dimensions. Wheels: Exterior diameter of wheels 48 inches, exterior diameter of hubs 4 inches, length of hubs 6½ inches, diameters of bands of hubs 2¾ x 3¼ inches, width of spokes at square end 1⅛ inches, thickness of spokes at square end ⅝ inches, number of spokes 14, thickness and depth of rims 1 x 1⁵⁄₁₆ inches, stagger ⅜ inches, tire, steel 1 x ³⁄₁₆ inches. Length of arms of axle for 6½ inch hubs, thickness of axle, at square end 1⅛ inches steel.

Painting. Dark green. Mountings. Black.

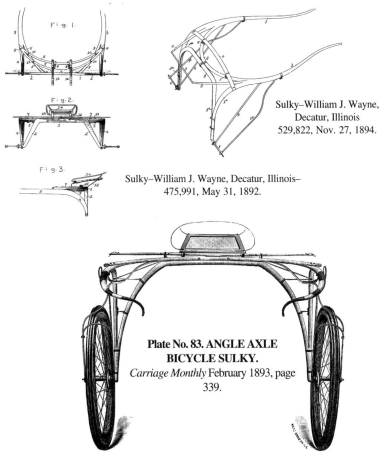

Sulky–William J. Wayne,
Decatur, Illinois
529,822, Nov. 27, 1894.

Sulky–William J. Wayne, Decatur, Illinois–
475,991, May 31, 1892.

**Plate No. 83. ANGLE AXLE
BICYCLE SULKY.**
*Carriage Monthly* February 1893, page
339.

This is one of the remarkable results that has been produced in the evolution of the pneumatic, ball bearing sulky, and is being built for the season of 1893 by the Wayne Sulkyette and Road Cart Company, of Decatur, Illinois. In this pneumatic sulky the ordinary bicycle forks or prongs holding wheels and stay braces are dispensed with. As an improvement over that style of attachment, the wheels are simply slipped on the steel axle arm, and with double nuts produce a perfect ball bearing axle. This makes a quick and convenient manner of removing wheels for repairs or shipment. The distance from the ground to the under side of the axle is 39½ inches by using a 30-inch wheel, and the axle being angle shaped instead of curved, it is the same height for 29 inches in width, thus producing the greatest amount of room for a horse with high action or wide gait. Hock action does not occur in the center of the axle, but at either side of the center. The patented gear is stiff and rigid, and yet when strapped up to the horse has the desired elasticity or spring in the shafts, allowing sufficient room for the easy movements of the horse without chafing. It is claimed that the uncomfortable, back-breaking movement to the driver, so common to many bicycle sulkies is entirely eliminated in this combination. In the construction of this "bike" the best material is used, the painting is done in an artistic manner, and the whole presents to the eye a neat and symmetrical piece of workmanship.

## COMPARATIVE STRAIN ON SULKY WHEELS.

*Hub* February 1884, page 711.

EDITOR OF THE HUB-DEAR SIR; In your October number I noticed a communication from Mr. E, F. Bradish, of Batavia, New York, asking which wheel of a sulky is subject to the most strain, the inner or outer wheel, answered, as you state, by "one of our best sulky builders," to the effect that, "in a properly built sulky the strain is about equal; the inside wheel having a trifle more dish than the outer or off wheel, the strain is counteracted, so that in turning a curve it becomes about equal, which would not be the case if the dish of the wheels was alike."

I would have answered this sooner, but thought I would give him a chance to correct his sad mistake. As he has not, I take this opportunity of doing so, at the same time stating that I have probably had as much experience in the making of first-class sulky wheels as any one in this city.

Your informant has "got the cart before the horse." In making a pair of sulky wheels, I drive the outer or off wheel with a $\frac{3}{16}$ inch dish, and the inner with a scant $\frac{1}{8}$ in. dish. When the wheels are hooped, I want the off wheel to have about $\frac{5}{16}$ inch dish, and the near one $\frac{3}{16}$ inch, with a long rim. It is a very easy matter to spoil a wheel in drafting. If a pair of sulky wheels are made alike and drafted as nearly alike as we can get them, then it is a common occurrence to put the most dished wheel on the off side; but in no case have I ever heard before of putting the wheel with the most dish on the near side of a sulky.

STEPHEN BRIDGE. 725 Eighth Avenue, New-York.

Explanation of Supplement.

## SIDE ELEVATION, HALF OF FRONT AND HALF OF BACK ELEVATION, ALSO HALF OF HORIZONTAL PLAN, TOP AND BOTTOM VIEWS, OF A SULKY–1-INCH SCALE.

*Carriage Monthly* October 1885 page 185.

A working draft of a sulky, showing the different views and drawn to scale correctly, having never been published in an American trade journal, we give one in the illustrations on the supplement accompanying this number, which is correctly represented, and in addition all the measurements are expressed in $\frac{1}{16}$ inches, to enable those desiring to build them to easily determine the weight and height suitable for the horse.

The weight of this sulky is 59 pounds, and it is built for a horse 15 hands high; if it is desired to build it lighter, the measurements must be reduced to suit the weight, and in a future number we will publish one of the lightest sulkies as now made, from which comparisons can be made in the measurements. The diameter of the wheels must be increased or decreased to suit the various heights of horses. The length of shafts from tip to back end is 7 feet 11 inches, and from front tip to center of axle 6 feet $\frac{1}{2}$ inch. The axle, which is let in the axle-bed flush at the bottom, is shown by dotted lines on the front and back view. All the stays are $\frac{1}{4}$-inch round steel, with the exception of the two stays starting from the axle behind the hubs each side and foot rests, which are $\frac{1}{4}$ inch thick by $\frac{3}{8}$ inch deep, and have a sharp oval shape. The rail around the seat is also $\frac{1}{4}$-inch round steel, including the three stays, which are silver plated.

## DESIGN FOR SULKY OR CART CUSHION.

*Hub* March 1884.

To make a sulky cushion, I would begin by fitting a piece of enameled leather or duck to the seat, cutting it the same size and shape as the seat-bottom, which will be the bottom of the cushion.

Paste it out with buckram, and a strip of heavy top leather across the front. When this is dry, stitch two harness-leather straps to the cushion bottom, long enough to go around the seat and buckle, to hold the cushion in place.

The pocket with flap (see A, A, in Fig. 1) is intended to hold weights, as is sometimes necessary in sulky cushions.

We next cut a pattern for the end and back facings, which are cut out of one piece. (See Fig. 2.)

Paste up two-ply of buckram and one of top-leather. When dry, make up the cloth roll. Cut the cloth ½ inch larger all around. Stuff it up with four-ply of cotton wadding, and tuft through the center. (See Fig. 2.)

Make up the cushion top on the bottom, with four-ply of cotton wadding. Blind-stitch the front to the cord across the front. Then sew the facing to the cushion, which can be done with a cord, or it may be bound with a blind binding.

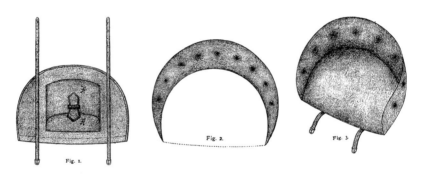

Fig. 1.     Fig. 2.     Fig. 3.

When the end and back facings have been nicely fitted to the seat-rail, with the right flare, this forms a neat-looking cushion, and it is easily made. Fig. 3 shows the cushion complete. C. G. COOK.

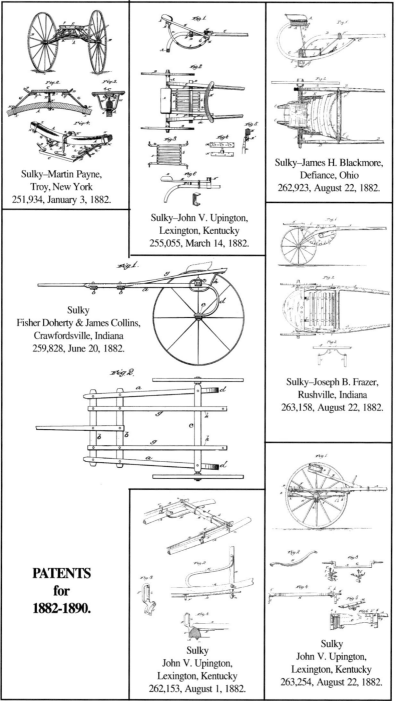

Sulky–Martin Payne,
Troy, New York
251,934, January 3, 1882.

Sulky–John V. Upington,
Lexington, Kentucky
255,055, March 14, 1882.

Sulky–James H. Blackmore,
Defiance, Ohio
262,923, August 22, 1882.

Sulky
Fisher Doherty & James Collins,
Crawfordsville, Indiana
259,828, June 20, 1882.

Sulky–Joseph B. Frazer,
Rushville, Indiana
263,158, August 22, 1882.

**PATENTS
for
1882-1890.**

Sulky
John V. Upington,
Lexington, Kentucky
262,153, August 1, 1882.

Sulky
John V. Upington,
Lexington, Kentucky
263,254, August 22, 1882.

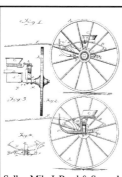

Sulky–Milo J. Reed & Samuel
Shilliam, Waterloo, Iowa–
263,810, September 5, 1882.

Sulky–William M. Boyd,
Rushville, Indiana
267,140, November 7, 1882.

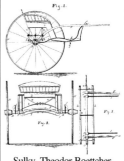

Sulky–Theodor Boettcher,
Mendota, Illinois
274,167, March 20, 1883.

Sulky–Jesse C. Boyd,
Rushville, Indiana
264,615, September 19, 1882.

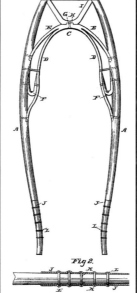

Sulky Shafts–Martin Payne,
Troy, New York
270,838, January 16, 1883.

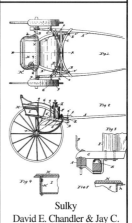

Sulky
David E. Chandler & Jay C.
Williams,
Aurora, Illinois
275,143, April 3, 1883.

Sulky–Fisher Doherty,
Crawfordsville, Indiana
265,035, September 26, 1882.

Sulky–William Yeoman & Edgar
M. Drum, Versailles, Kentucky
272,397, February 13, 1883.

Sulky Spring
Isaac A. Wesson
Wingo, Kentucky
275,445, April 10, 1883.

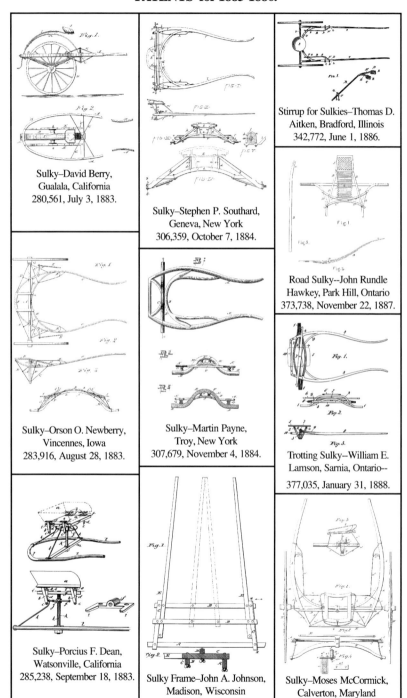

Sulky–David Berry,
Gualala, California
280,561, July 3, 1883.

Sulky–Stephen P. Southard,
Geneva, New York
306,359, October 7, 1884.

Stirrup for Sulkies–Thomas D.
Aitken, Bradford, Illinois
342,772, June 1, 1886.

Road Sulky--John Rundle
Hawkey, Park Hill, Ontario
373,738, November 22, 1887.

Sulky–Orson O. Newberry,
Vincennes, Iowa
283,916, August 28, 1883.

Sulky–Martin Payne,
Troy, New York
307,679, November 4, 1884.

Trotting Sulky--William E.
Lamson, Sarnia, Ontario--

377,035, January 31, 1888.

Sulky–Porcius F. Dean,
Watsonville, California
285,238, September 18, 1883.

Sulky Frame–John A. Johnson,
Madison, Wisconsin
319,264, June 2, 1885.

Sulky–Moses McCormick,
Calverton, Maryland
377,045, January 31, 1888.

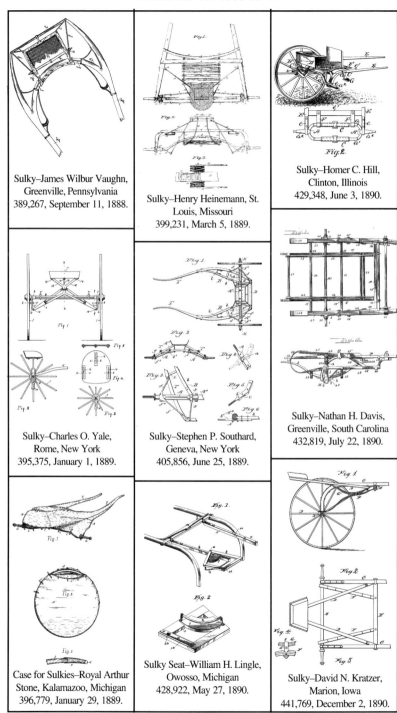

Sulky–James Wilbur Vaughn,
Greenville, Pennsylvania
389,267, September 11, 1888.

Sulky–Henry Heinemann, St.
Louis, Missouri
399,231, March 5, 1889.

Sulky–Homer C. Hill,
Clinton, Illinois
429,348, June 3, 1890.

Sulky–Charles O. Yale,
Rome, New York
395,375, January 1, 1889.

Sulky–Stephen P. Southard,
Geneva, New York
405,856, June 25, 1889.

Sulky–Nathan H. Davis,
Greenville, South Carolina
432,819, July 22, 1890.

Case for Sulkies–Royal Arthur
Stone, Kalamazoo, Michigan
396,779, January 29, 1889.

Sulky Seat–William H. Lingle,
Owosso, Michigan
428,922, May 27, 1890.

Sulky–David N. Kratzer,
Marion, Iowa
441,769, December 2, 1890.

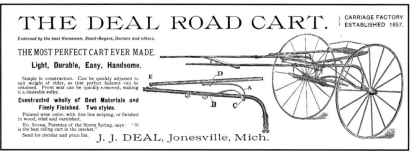

## THE DEAL ROAD CART.

CARRIAGE FACTORY
ESTABLISHED 1857.

*Endorsed by the best Horsemen, Stock-Buyers, Doctors and others.*

### THE MOST PERFECT CART EVER MADE.

**Light, Durable, Easy, Handsome.**

Simple in construction. Can be quickly adjusted to suit weight of rider, so that perfect balance can be obtained. Front seat can be quickly removed, making it a desirable sulky.

**Constructed wholly of Best Materials and Finely Finished. Two styles.**

Painted wine color, with nine line striping, or finished in wood, oiled and varnished.

Ed. Storm, Patentee of the Storm Spring, says: "It is the best riding cart in the market."

Send for circular and price list.

### J. J. DEAL, Jonesville, Mich.

*Carriage Monthly* August 1887.

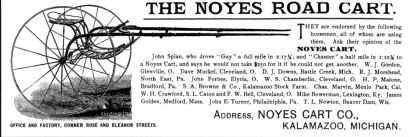

## THE NOYES ROAD CART.

THEY are endorsed by the following horsemen, all of whom are using them. Ask their opinion of the **NOYES CART.**

John Splan, who drove "Guy" a full mile in 2:17¾, and "Chanter" a half mile in 1:10¾ to a Noyes Cart, and says he would not take $250 for it if he could not get another. W. J. Gordon, Glenville, O. Dave Muckel, Cleveland, O. D. J. Downs, Battle Creek, Mich. R. J. Morehead, North East, Pa. John Forbes, Elyria, O. W. S. Chamberlin, Cleveland, O. H. P. Malone, Bradford, Pa. S. A. Browne & Co., Kalamazoo Stock Farm. Chas. Marvin, Menlo Park, Cal. W. H. Crawford, S. L. Caton and F. W. Bell, Cleveland, O. Mike Bowerman, Lexington, Ky. James Golden, Medford, Mass. John E. Turner, Philadelphia, Pa. T. L. Newton, Beaver Dam, Wis.

Address, **NOYES CART CO.,**

OFFICE AND FACTORY, CORNER ROSE AND ELEANOR STREETS. **KALAMAZOO, MICHIGAN.**

*Carriage Monthly* July 1887.

# HUGHSON & SULLIVAN,

## ROCHESTER, N. Y.

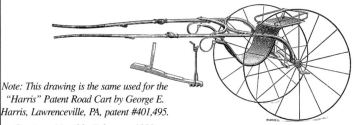

Note: This drawing is the same used for the "Harris" Patent Road Cart by George E. Harris, Lawrenceville, PA, patent #401,495.

*Carriage Monthly February 1889.*

WHILE almost every Carriage Manufacturer in the country has been putting Carts of all kinds and descriptions upon the market for the past few years, we have let the Cart business entirely alone, preferring to wait until such time as we should be able to produce a cart that would answer the purpose, in every respect, for which carts are intended; that time has now arrived. The above cut represents a Cart that has correct principles about it in every way. It is simple in construction, the springs being so arranged that it is the easiest riding cart ever built, and there are no seat bars to climb over when getting in or out. It can be adjusted in a few seconds, without a tool of any kind, from a one-passenger cart to a two-passenger cart and *vice-versa;* or it can be adjusted to carry a heavy person on one side and a light one on the other and ride just as level as though both were the same size. As we intend to make this leading cart of the times, we will build it of only the very best of material, and sell it at a very small margin of profit; a sample job will convince any dealer that it is the best seller, the easiest rider and the most profitable cart he can handle.

*Carriage Monthly* November 1888.

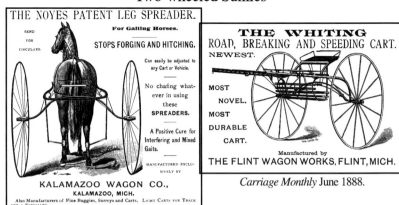

THE NOYES PATENT LEG SPREADER.

For Gaiting Horses.

SEND FOR CIRCULARS.

STOPS FORGING AND HITCHING.

Can easily be adjusted to any Cart or Vehicle.

No chafing whatever in using these SPREADERS.

A Positive Cure for Interfering and Mixed Gaits.

MANUFACTURED EXCLUSIVELY BY

KALAMAZOO WAGON CO.,
KALAMAZOO, MICH.

Also Manufacturers of Fine Buggies, Surreys and Carts. LIGHT CARTS FOR TRACK USE A SPECIALTY.

*Hub* June 1888.

THE WHITING
ROAD, BREAKING AND SPEEDING CART.
NEWEST.

MOST NOVEL.

MOST DURABLE CART.

Manufactured by
THE FLINT WAGON WORKS, FLINT, MICH.

*Carriage Monthly* June 1888.

RUMSEY ROAD CART.
(Patented.)

The best two-wheeled Vehicle on the Globe. Correct in principle of construction. Unsurpassed in quality. Handsome in appearance. Possesses fine riding qualities. Sells rapidly, pleases the public and pays the dealer a good margin.

FOR ILLUSTRATED CIRCULAR AND PRICES APPLY TO

RUMSEY MANUFACTURING CO.,
DETROIT, MICH.

WHOLESALE MANUFACTURERS OF
CARRIAGES, BUGGIES, CARTS, SPRING WAGONS AND SLEIGHS.

*Carriage Monthly* December 1888.

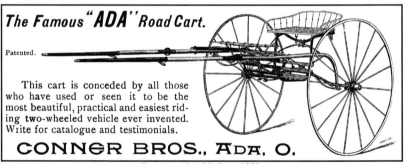

The Famous "ADA" Road Cart.

Patented.

This cart is conceded by all those who have used or seen it to be the most beautiful, practical and easiest riding two-wheeled vehicle ever invented. Write for catalogue and testimonials.

CONNER BROS., ADA, O.

*Carriage Monthly* June 1889.

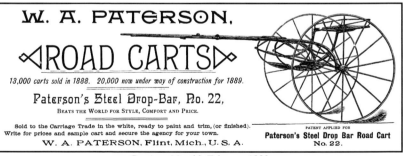

W. A. PATERSON,

ROAD CARTS

*13,000 carts sold in 1888. 20,000 now under way of construction for 1889.*

Paterson's Steel Drop-Bar, No. 22,

BEATS THE WORLD FOR STYLE, COMFORT AND PRICE.

Sold to the Carriage Trade in the white, ready to paint and trim, (or finished). Write for prices and sample cart and secure the agency for your town.

W. A. PATERSON, Flint, Mich., U. S. A.

PATENT APPLIED FOR
Paterson's Steel Drop Bar Road Cart
No. 22.

*Carriage Monthly* February 1889.

*Carriage Monthly* August 1888.

*Carriage Monthly* November 1889.

*Carriage Monthly* April 1890.

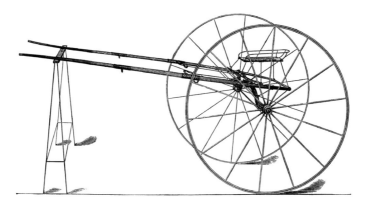

**Plate No. 55. SULKY.**
*Carriage Monthly,*
October 1885, page 180.

Racing sulkies are built much lighter than the one we illustrate in this plate, which was made by one of our best houses, and it is our purpose to publish one of the lightest styles in a future number. This sulky weighs 59 pounds, and is built for a horse 15 hands high. The shafts are bent in the best shape possible, straight on the side elevation, all the bend being from the horizontal view. The circular piece between the shafts is bent, as is also the axle bed and the cross piece above same. The shafts, measured from the side elevation, are 1⅝ inches thick near the foot rest, and 1¾ inches full, measured from the horizontal view; ¾ inch in diameter at the front end, near the tip, and at the back end ¾ inch deep by ¾ inch from the horizontal view. The entire length of the shafts, from the extreme front to the extreme back, is 7 feet 11 inches. For further information, see the supplement accompanying this number, illustrating the side elevation, half front and half back view, and also half of the horizontal top and bottom views.

Painting. Carmine lake, striped two fine lines of red, ¼ inch apart.

Trimming. The trimming consists of the leathers on the shafts, which should be of light hand-buffed patent leather; the straps are all made of the best material, so that they can be made light. The foot-rail is wrapped with harness leather; the leather at this point is creased in diamonds; the seat is caned and the rail plated.

Mountings. Silver.

Dimensions. Wheels: Exterior diameter of wheels 56½ inches, exterior diameter of hubs 3⅜ inches, length of hubs 6 inches, diameter of bands of hubs 2¼ x 2⅝ inches, width of spokes at square end 1 inch, thickness of spokes at square end ⅝ inches, number of spokes 14, thickness and depth of rims ¾ x $^3/_{16}$ inches, stagger 1 inch, tire, steel $^{11}/_{16}$ x $^1/_{16}$ inches.

## CLIP STEP FOR A SULKY.
*Hub* June 1891.

To gain access to the seat, the rider mounts into the sulky from behind using the axle on back end of the hub as a foot rest, by so doing he soon mars the paint and defaces the vehicle. To overcome this and furnish a neat and reliable footrest, the clip step has been introduced. No extra clip is required, all that is necessary is to provide a post and pad in connection with the clip which secures the near or left-hand braces to the axle. In making the clip upset and swage up for the pad and post, making the pad 1¼ inch in diameter, the post ⅜ of an inch at the narrowest point, and ½ inch high, then split the iron and work off the clip straps and bolts. The straps should be ⅝ of an inch wide, and the bolts scant ¼ inch in diameter. The forging of one of these clips is a nice piece of work, but after a little experience the blacksmith should be able to make a neat job. The pad is neatly " jagged " to prevent the foot slipping.

This clip should be made of the best Norway iron, or a low grade of cast steel may be used. A neat manner of finishing is to nickel-plate the neck and pad. If preferred, an octagon head may be used, in place of the round one, but in either case the head should not exceed 1¼ inch in diameter.

## TRUSS FOR A SULKY.
*Hub* December 1891.

A simple but very effective device for supporting sulky axles to prevent their springing or settling down when speeding, is shown by Fig. 1. The several parts are: The tie, Fig. 2, which consists of a link flattened at the ends, and through which the ends of the main arms pass, threads being cut, right and left hand, so that by turning the link the stress increased. Instead of using a right and left hand thread, shown by Fig. 3 may be put upon one of the main arms.

The ends, B B, Fig. 1, are welded on a ⁵⁄₁₆ or ⅜ inch rod; the clip yokes, C C, are loose.     D. H. R.

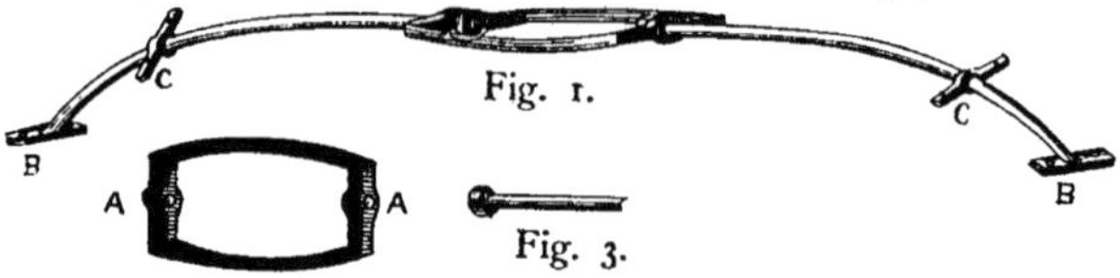

Fig. 1.

Fig. 2.

Fig. 3.

*Carriage Monthly* August 1891.

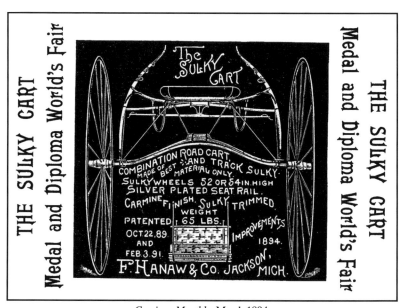

*Carriage Monthly*  March 1894.

# EQUINE BICYCLE

## THE EQUINE BICYCLE
*Hub* March 1891.

The so-called "equine bicycle," exhibited at the recent Horse Show in this city by Mr. T. W. Moore, of No. 40 Elizabeth Street, New-York, apparently called forth more criticisms than compliments from horsemen; but we are inclined to believe that it involves mechanical principle which, in the hands of an artist workman, could be developed into an ideal vehicle for speeding a trotter. The working model shown was certainly not a thing of beauty. Here, for instance, is the greeting I received from the New-York *Evening Sun* -

It is a remarkable-looking affair, and enough to scare any self-respecting horse that meets it on the road. The horse hitched to it is in no position to see what is going on, or he would otherwise protest against having to draw such a combination of the sulky and bicycle. The advantage of the thing lies in the placing of the driver's weight in a place where the horse will least feel it, and in the better control that it gives him over the horse. His weight rests on the axle tree, from which rises a bent band of iron covered with leather and supporting the seat. His feet are braced against the fore part of the sulky, where a railing runs for their support, and the only thing which apparently keeps him from turning over backward is the bit in the horse's mouth and the reins in his hands. The sensation to the driver is almost that of a rider in a saddle, and the man who owns one of these new inventions can enjoy at one and the same time the pleasure of a rider, driver and bicycler.

A first-class mechanic might do much to remove the ungainly appearance of the model exhibited, which seems to us badly proportioned and unnecessarily heavy; but, even in its present clumsy form, we find justice in the claims made for it by its inventor, which are briefly as follows:

The equine bicycle not only relieves the horse of the weight of the rider, but runs so easily as hardly to impede his speed. In no other way yet known can the rider or driver be carried with so little tax upon the horse's strength or power of endurance.

The location of the wheels along the sides and flanks of the horse avoids the friction on the curves of the track. This bicycle does not swing a particle on the shortest curves. The reason is, that the point of contact between the tire of the wheels and the track is opposite the propelling power; and, the greater the distance between the wheels and the sides of the horse, the greater the momentum of the swing and consequent drag on the curves. Sulkies sometimes jump several feet on sharp curves. In this the horse can be turned around in the space he stands on.

The seat is where the rider has perfect control of and can watch his horse better than if nearer the neck, as in a saddle. He is carried over and close to the horse, and his weight is supported by the standards which run up from the axles next to the wheels. The wheels are the same as those of a bicycle, and have rubber tires.

By a careful examination it will be seen that the driver is carried without weighting the horse, with the least possible draught, and that the dragging-back friction of the curves of the course is entirely overcome.

We await with interest the appearance of new and improved editions of the " equine bicycle."

## EQUINE BICYCLE

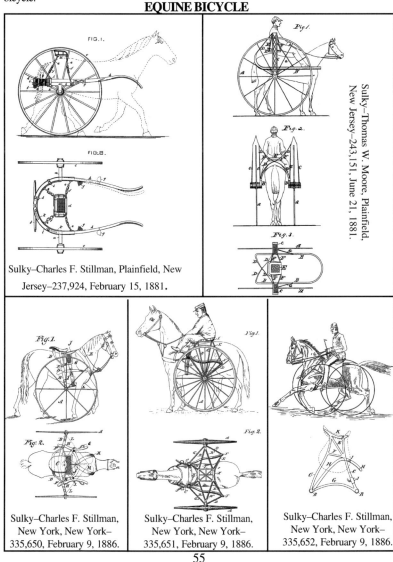

Sulky–Charles F. Stillman, Plainfield, New Jersey–237,924, February 15, 1881.

Sulky–Thomas W. Moore, Plainfield, New Jersey–243,151, June 21, 1881.

Sulky–Charles F. Stillman, New York, New York– 335,650, February 9, 1886.

Sulky–Charles F. Stillman, New York, New York– 335,651, February 9, 1886.

Sulky–Charles F. Stillman, New York, New York– 335,652, February 9, 1886.

# EQUINE BICYCLE

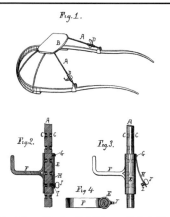

Foot Rest–Charles F. Stillman, Plainfield, New Jersey–244,403, July 19, 1881.

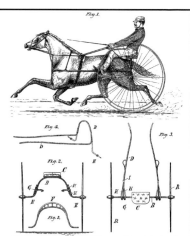

Sulky–Charles F. Stillman, New York, New York–350,169, October 5, 1886.

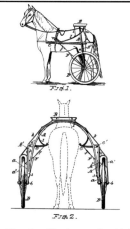

Sulky–Theodore Harrington, Southbridge, Massachusetts–498,790, June 6, 1893.

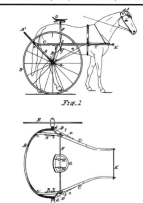

Sulky–Theodore Harrington, Southbridge, Massachusetts–508,707, November 14, 1893.

Sulky–John J. Haywood & Henry Marquedant, Rives Junction, MI.–579,149, March 23, 1897.

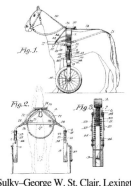

Sulky–George W. St. Clair, Lexington, Kentucky–757,575, April 19, 1904.

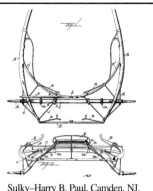

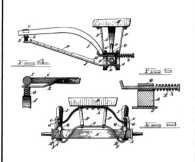

Sulky–Harry B. Paul, Camden, NJ.
444,921, Jan. 20, 1891.

Sulky–Samuel C. Wharton, South Bend,
Indiana–455,781, July 14, 1891.

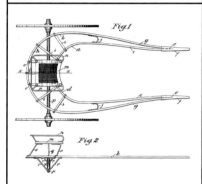

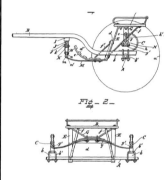

Sulky–George E. Tripp, Stonington,
Connecticut--445,758, February 3, 1891.

Sulky–William D. Harper, Quanah, Texas–
456,565, July 28, 1891.

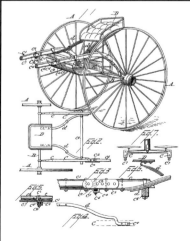

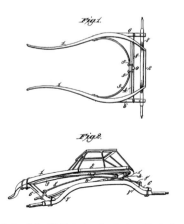

Sulky–John W. Kelley, Columbus, Georgia–
449,542, March 31, 1891.

Sulky–John V. Upington, Lexington, Kentucky–
471,916, March 29, 1892.

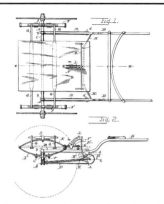

Sulky–Elam A. Oliver, Belleville, Wisconsin, 474,684, May 10, 1892.

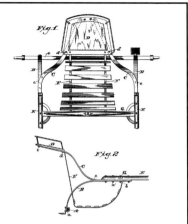

Sulky--John Belmer Armstrong--Guelph, Ontario--482,114, September 6, 1892.

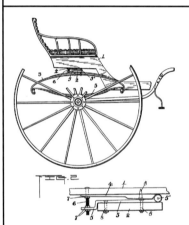

Adjusting Pitch of Sulky–James Hessong, Chillicothe, Ohio–475,218, May 17, 1892.

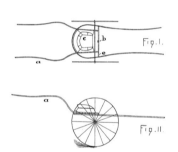

Sulky–Peter H. Bald, Louisville, Kentucky–487,343, December 6, 1892.

Wheel for Sulky–Will A. Fleming, Lewiston, Idaho–476,533, June 7, 1892.

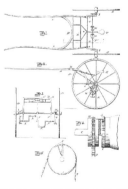

Sulky–Isaac Wood, Minneapolis, MN.– 488,236, Dec. 20, 1892.

## POINTS REGARDING A SULKY.
*Hub* February 1892.

An old sulky builder, in speaking of sulkies, said: " I cannot understand why the inside or near side wheel of a track sulky should be dished more than the outside or off side wheel. In my opinion, if any difference is made it should be with the outside wheel, as the greatest strain is thrown upon it.

"To build a sulky properly the wheels should be alike in dish, and the axle arms and boxes absolutely alike, so that the wheels can be interchangeable and that they should be changed frequently. The wheels should stand as straight on the axle as possible, without gather or underset. In speeding around curves the heaviest strain is thrown upon the off wheel, and were the driver to sit upright the near wheel would leave the ground. The wheel should not be very high to run easy, as the friction from the cramping under of the wheel on the outside is many times greater than the friction from the weight of the driver.

"The weight should be about fifty pounds. To secure this use $1\frac{1}{16}$ in. axles of the best cast steel. The wheels 4 ft. 6 in., or, at the outside, 4 ft. 7 in., high hub 6 x $3\frac{5}{16}$ or $3\frac{3}{8}$ in., twelve or fourteen spokes 1 or $1\frac{1}{16}$ in. at the shoulder, with a true taper to the top. Rim $\frac{5}{8}$ or $\frac{3}{4}$ in. tread, and $\frac{3}{4}$ x $\frac{7}{8}$ in. deep; the spokes staggered full width; the axle head bent wood, arched about 8 in.; the iron head let into the wood the full length. A forty-four pound sulky can be made with a $\frac{5}{8}$ in. axle, 4 ft. 6 in. wheel, twelve spokes; spokes 1 in., rims $\frac{5}{8}$ in. tread. Woodwork of ash. The timber in the wheels of a good, fine grained, tough but not the heaviest wood. The spokes should be tested as to stiffness, and all discarded that do not recoil to the original straight form after being tested. Ash, if the quality is alright, gives better results for shafts than hickory; but it is hard to make the buyer believe that anything can take the place of hickory. The tire and braces should all be of cast steel."

## ONE-WHEEL SULKY.
*Carriage Monthly* February 1894 page 342.

Capt. Alphonse B. Smith. a pioneer of San Diego, California, is the inventor of a one-wheel sulky, which apparently is a success, says the San Francisco *Examiner.* Some years ago he conceived the idea that the time of a horse on a race course could be materially reduced if, instead of the two wheel sulky, a one-wheel cart could be used, and he forthwith set to work to devise a vehicle which would suit the purpose. He feels confident that at last he has succeeded in inventing something which fully realizes his brightest hopes, and something, too, which is destined to come into very general use throughout the world. The axle of the cart is made in two pieces, and is so arranged that the wheel turns very rapidly in any direction the horse can possibly pursue. Attached to the shafts, near where they meet the axle, are stirrups designed to steady the rider in his position on the cart. Made for ordinary, road use one of the vehicles weighs 87 pounds, but when designed for use on a race course the unicycle, as some have called it, may he constructed so as to weigh only 32 pounds. One was recently manufactured at San Diego entirely of aluminum, the weight being a trifle less than 32 pounds, and the vehicle being strong and handsome.

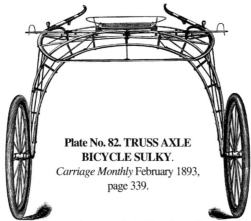

**Plate No. 82. TRUSS AXLE
BICYCLE SULKY.**
*Carriage Monthly* February 1893,
page 339.

This recently improved pneumatic, ball bearing sulky possesses in the truss axle a principle which furnishes the manufacturers, S. Toomey & Company, of Canal Dover, Ohio, unlimited facilities for the perfection of this vehicle. The truss axle gives strength and rigidness with lightness, is self supporting, admits of extension to any height, and enables the production of a sulky, the axle of which is continuous and extends down to the bearing, which is another feature of advantage.

It is claimed in this new sulky, that the bobbing motion which is said to be common with bicycle sulkies has been overcome. Instead of steel tubing, which the manufacturers claim is very unsafe owing to their inability to make a safe structure of it, as well as to its susceptibility to rust on the inside, and the crystallization caused by the continual motion of the horse, all the attachments are solid forged steel and Norway iron, which are properly applied to the best second growth hickory and ash, forming an inseparable structure which is mounted on the highest grade hickory wheels, having the finest ball bearings with the best pneumatic tire. The device for detaching the wheels for shipment or otherwise, is so constructed that by simply loosening the nuts on the spindle bearings, the wheels may be quickly removed and put back to their places again in a secure manner. This sulky is made, in all sizes, adapted to horses of various heights, and with such weights as are consistent with absolute safety to the driver and the highest rate of speed.

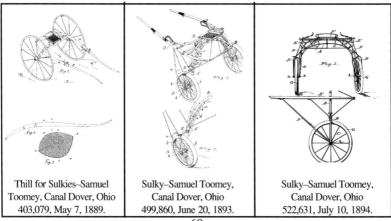

| Thill for Sulkies–Samuel Toomey, Canal Dover, Ohio 403,079, May 7, 1889. | Sulky–Samuel Toomey, Canal Dover, Ohio 499,860, June 20, 1893. | Sulky–Samuel Toomey, Canal Dover, Ohio 522,631, July 10, 1894. |
|---|---|---|

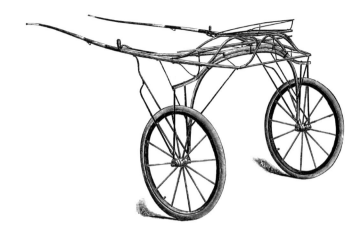

**Plate No. 84. COMBINATION BICYCLE SULKY.**

*Carriage Monthly* February 1893, page 339.

This combination sulky may be used either with the ordinary wood wheels, from 50 to 54 inches high, or with pneumatic bicycle wheels 26 or 30 inches high. The manufacturers, Burch & Hadsell, of Pontiac, Michigan, also supply the large wheels, which are fitted with dust proof, ball bearings of their own design. The spindle of the axle is detachable from the arm or axle bed, and may be securely fixed thereto by a nut and a cone shaped end, which fits into a socket provided on the end and under side of the axle arm. To remove the wheel, it is only necessary to remove the nut on the end of the spindle under side of axle, the spindle and ball bearing mechanism remaining in the wheel intact.

The attachment for the bicycle wheel is constructed of a weldless steel tubing, and consists of a yoke, the lower ends of which are supplied with forked steel forgings, into which are fitted brass bushings with several holes to receive the axle of wheel. These bearings are cut in half, vertically, through the center of holes, and hinged at the bottom, and held firmly in place by the nuts on axle. This device admits of quickly raising and lowering the sulky gear, to fit different height horses. To remove the bicycle attachment, it is only necessary to remove nut on the lug underneath the axle, and unscrew the two set screws. A 28 or 30-inch bicycle wheel may be used, or even a still smaller or larger, and large wheels, from, 50 to 54 inches high, or in cases of necessity, one wheel of each size may be used, and the relative height of the sulky still maintained.

A brake is provided, which is designed to prevent the sulky running under the horse, and throwing him over backward upon the driver in case of rearing, from which cause serious accidents occurred last season. It can be attached to any make of bicycle sulky.

The sulky gear is of novel design, and consists of a combination of bent wood work and irons. It is a model of strength, lightness and beauty, embodying all the essential features of high arch axles, close hitch and width of shafts.

# THOS. D. LINES, SYRACUSE, NEW YORK

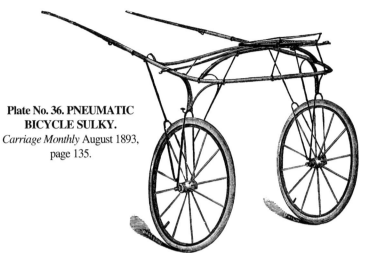

**Plate No. 36. PNEUMATIC
BICYCLE SULKY.**
*Carriage Monthly* August 1893,
page 135.

Built by Thos. D. Lines, Syracuse, New York. Among the many patents which have been issued during the past few years for bicycle sulkies, Thos. D. Lines, the well known inventor and carriage builder, has perfected a bicycle sulky, differing somewhat from others, and which is considered a great improvement. The shafts are bent in a graceful curve, a bent bar across them, to brace the seat, and at the same time a brace to the shafts. The seat is braced with two bent bars and five stays, but the most originality is in the stays or braces, which hold the wheels in position. The object is to give the wheels the same rigidity across, to obviate side motion, And the position of the braces and its size depends entirely on its solidity. The main braces, one on each side, are in a vertical position, with the exception of the bent wood stay, which is bolted to the shafts. The front stays are bolted to the center stays, and clipped to the shafts. This stay is to keep the wheel from shifting backward, and the inside braces to prevent the side motion.

Painting. Carmine or orange yellow, striped two black lines ¼ inch apart.

Mountings. Silver.

*Carriage Monthly* September 1893.

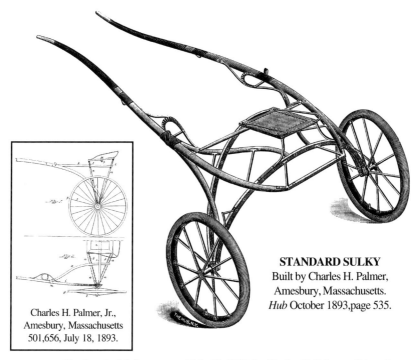

Charles H. Palmer, Jr.,
Amesbury, Massachusetts
501,656, July 18, 1893.

**STANDARD SULKY**
Built by Charles H. Palmer,
Amesbury, Massachusetts.
*Hub* October 1893, page 535.

The Standard Sulky, patented July 18, 1893, by Charles H. Palmer, of Amesbury, Massachusetts, has proved a success in every sense of the word. It is fitted with Æolus ball-bearing, pneumatic-tired wheels, with wood spokes placed in the extreme ends of metal hubs, which makes a very strong and stiff wheel for its weight.

The frame is made of best hickory, with very little metal, it being built in such a way that the wood makes the bracing, and is very stiff both ways. It does not require long metal braces to support the axles, as they are as strong, if not stronger, than those of the high wheel sulky.

By this construction one can use wheels of any height; the frames would have to be made probably for a certain height of wheel, but with a little additional weight can be made to take wheels from 28 to 48 inches high. Wheels 48 inches high can be built on his principle of this height, and be as stiff as one 28 inches. The additional weight of spoke would be small, but the metal rims and tires would add considerable extra weight.

It is a well known fact that wood is the most suitable material for carriage construction; that metal hubs and braces such as are used on nearly all track sulkies will crystallize and break where best hickory and ash will not let go. Mr. Palmer has a sulky that has been in use on the track three months, and in a race has carried a driver that weighed over two hundred pounds. He has not the least hesitancy in saying that it will stand the hardest work that is possible to put on a track sulky, and that it does not have the excessive bobbing motion due to low wheels and insufficient bracing.

The wheels are 32 inches high; he has another 34 inches. The inside bracing is such that it gives more room than the circular brace; this allows a very close hitch. With the front axle sweep smooth with the bottom of the seat, it allows more room than is usual.

Sulkies can be constructed on this principle as light as any other, and stronger for the same weight. Being made almost wholly of wood, they will prove superior to those of other make.

# J. J. DEAL & SON, JONESVILLE, MICHIGAN

No. 1 Speed Cart
made by J. J. Deal & Son.

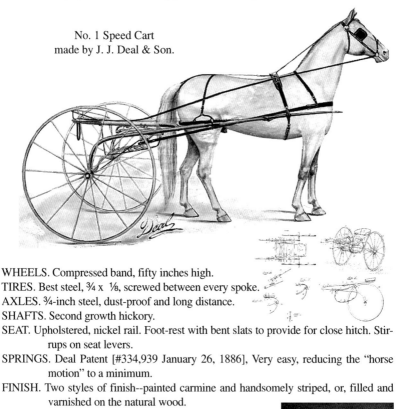

WHEELS. Compressed band, fifty inches high.

TIRES. Best steel, ¾ x ⅛, screwed between every spoke.

AXLES. ¾-inch steel, dust-proof and long distance.

SHAFTS. Second growth hickory.

SEAT. Upholstered, nickel rail. Foot-rest with bent slats to provide for close hitch. Stirrups on seat levers.

SPRINGS. Deal Patent [#334,939 January 26, 1886], Very easy, reducing the "horse motion" to a minimum.

FINISH. Two styles of finish--painted carmine and handsomely striped, or, filled and varnished on the natural wood.

WEIGHT. About 80 pounds.

Jacob J. Deal inventor of the celebrated Deal Road Cart and founder of the carriage factory.

**J. J. DEAL & SON, JONESVILLE, MICHIGAN, Established 1857.**
**from circa 1900 catalog**

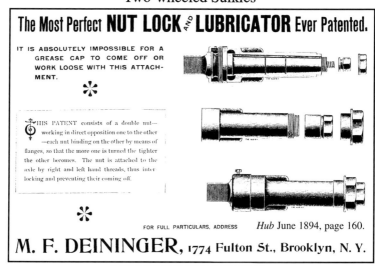

# The Most Perfect NUT LOCK ⅋ LUBRICATOR Ever Patented.

IT IS ABSOLUTELY IMPOSSIBLE FOR A GREASE CAP TO COME OFF OR WORK LOOSE WITH THIS ATTACHMENT.

✳

THIS PATENT consists of a double nut—working in direct opposition one to the other—each nut binding on the other by means of flanges, so that the more one is turned the tighter the other becomes. The nut is attached to the axle by right and left hand threads, thus interlocking and preventing their coming off.

✳

FOR FULL PARTICULARS, ADDRESS *Hub* June 1894, page 160.

## M. F. DEININGER, 1774 Fulton St., Brooklyn, N. Y.

### A GOOD RESULT–DEININGER.

On Tuesday afternoon, November 13th, quite a number of newspaper men and lovers of horseflesh gathered at Koch & Hunter's, on the Ocean Parkway, Brooklyn, to look at a light road cart that had been driven behind fast trotting horses for over eighteen hundred miles without re-oiling. The axle which gave such remarkable results is the invention of M. F. Deininger, the well-known undertaker, 1774 Fulton-st., Brooklyn, who drove the *Hub News* reporter from his place of business in a light road wagon that had been running over nine hundred miles without re-oiling, and from the smoothness with which it ran, when drawn at a clipping gait by a fast trotting mare down the Parkway, one might imagine that it had been oiled just before leaving the stable, and when the hotel had been reached an examination of the axles showed no oil or grease on the outside, such as is usual with the ordinary construction, since close fitting cups prevent the oil's escape and retain it where it is needed, preventing at the same time access of air and too rapid drying of the lubricating material.

The road cart which had been selected for the test had been put in the hands of F. M. Keach, of Parkville, N. Y., who used it constantly to exercise his stable of trotting horses, driving it over a measured course, and keeping an accurate record of the number of miles driven. He started to use it September 29th. During the remainder of the month he drove 95 miles; in October he covered 1,175 miles, and during the first thirteen days of November, 580 miles-a total of 1,850 miles.

Before the wheel was taken off to examine the condition of the axle, the cart was propped up on a jack and the wheel was given a start by hand, running for one minute, twenty-seven and a half seconds. When the wheel was taken off, the axle was seen to be as well lubricated as if it had just been oiled, and after it had stood for a minute a drop of oil fell to the ground, giving every indication that two or three hundred more miles might be rolled off without additional oiling. The axle was in good condition, with no evidence whatever of metallic particles in the oil, showing that, in spite of the high speed at which the cart had been drawn, the lubrication had been perfect.

In starting too use the cart, one hundred and eighty drops of oil had been placed in the cup in each axle, the oil used being known as No. 93 Lubricating.

Mr. Deininger handsomely entertained those who were present, and every one went home pleased with the improvement in axles and the enjoyable afternoon.—*Hub News. Hub* December 1894, page 653. [Patent numbers 380,622 & 482,571 & 537,759].

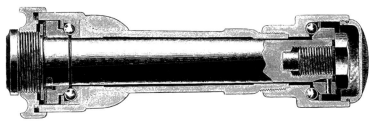
### CRAWFORD BALL-BEARING AXLES.

There is a demand for easy running vehicles. The sulky has demonstrated that ball-bearing axles and pneumatic tires reduce the draft fully sixty per cent., and many claim seventy-two per cent. The adjustment of the bearings in sulkies being exactly like the bicycle adjustment was not to be thought of, owing to its complications in connection with ordinary vehicles when cared for by inexperienced men.

The following advantages are claimed for the Crawford axle. It is adjusted by screwing in the cap screw, the same as any ordinary axle.

It is positively dust and water proof; the latter is very important, as the water must be excluded while the wheel is being washed, or the balls will rust and wear. With the Crawford device, water cannot be forced into the bearing under the heaviest pressure, and it is the only axle on the market which is positively water proof.

All parts are interchangeable, and can be duplicated at small cost.

All wearing parts are thoroughly hardened.

The balls used are the best made.

The axles are carefully adjusted before leaving the factory. All that the user is required to do is to screw in the cap screw until it bottoms in the recess in end of spindle, and the adjustment is perfect, positive and practical. The annoyance of adjusting nuts to a nicety is done away with. The wheels can be taken off like the ordinary wheel; the balls cannot fall out or become misplaced. The manufacturers are the Crawford Wheel and Gear Co., Hagerstown, Maryland. Patent numbers 538,012 and 548,745. *Hub* March 1895, page 914.

# Two-wheeled Sulkies

*Carriage Monthly* October 1892.

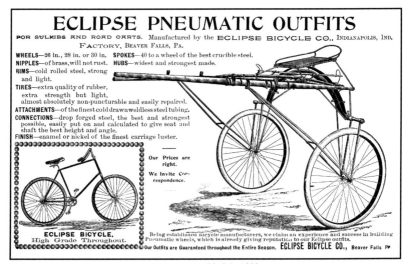

*Carriage Monthly* July 1893.

*Carriage Monthly* October 1892.

# CHARLES S. CAFFREY, AND STERLINGELLIOTT, HICKORY, WHEEL CO., NEWTON, MASSACHUSETTS

## Special
# Caffrey Fittings.

(PATENT PENDING.)

Price, complete, for one sulky, $7.50.

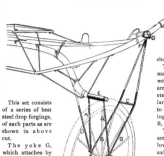

This set consists of a series of best steel drop forgings, of such parts as are shown in above cut.

The yoke G, which attaches by clip to shaft has forged solid taper bolt projecting downward, its shank is accurately "milled" and end threaded to receive standard steel nut.

The two braces B, B, are at their forward ends forged solid to a boss which is reamed to fit the shank of yoke G.

The forging C, is made solid without welds, and its parts are $\frac{7}{8}$ inch in diameter, slightly enlarged at the ends to allow for welding into the braces, B, B.

The forks A, A, are fitted at their lower ends to the axle cone and nut only, and the braces are attached to forks 1⅜ inch up from axle. The object of this construction is that the taking out or adjusting of an axle bearing does not loosen or in any way affect the integrity of the frame as is the case where all parts attach at the axle.

## OUR
# Hickory Wheels

Are 28 inches in diameter.    Hubs, 4½ inches long.
Axles, $\frac{7}{16}$ inch in diameter.
Bearings, NEW and the VERY BEST (fully illustrated in our pamphlet).
Balls, ¼ inch diameter, 24 to each hub.

### Price, $75.00 per pair.

DISCOUNT TO THE TRADE

Hubs, best second growth Rock Elm; Spokes and Felloes, best second growth Hickory; Rims, Cold Rolled Steel, brazed joint.

### THE FAMOUS
# Columbia Pneumatic Tires.

They were the best last year, and they are better this year than ever before.

No trouble to repair, and not very likely to need it. When repairs *are* necessary, an ordinary puncture, such as is made by a nail, can be effectually repaired in less time than in any other tire. In case of a serious accident this tire can be removed and a new one substituted in less than five minutes.

If the horseman doesn't want to bother with it there are nearly two thousand Columbia agents in the United States, any one of whom would be glad to repair a Columbia tire in a few minutes.

.. To the ..
# Carriage Trade.

As you are no doubt already aware, the pneumatic sulky originated with this Company. So far as we know, no one disputes our claim to the credit of having started what has proven a revolution in trotting and pacing records. As we stated in a circular last August, "The embodiment of the idea involved several points of so radical a nature, that our consciousness of what ought to be done, coupled with a commercial reason for doing it, has placed us, we think, in a position where we can reap the reward which is ours by virtue of the constitution."

Any sulky having wheels of less diameter than the distance between the shafts and the ground and provided with any form of elastic tire is an infringement of our patented rights, and we not only owe it to ourselves, but to those sulky builders who are respecting our claims, that all infringements shall be promptly looked after. And we will esteem it a special favor if our agents will notify us of the sale or use of even a single sulky having wheels not made by us.

**ALL OLD STYLE SULKIES** which have had small wheels attached are also infringements of our construction, Patent No. 498,709, issued May 30th, 1893. The use of any such sulky since May 30th (no matter when made) renders the user liable to us for royalty.

# HICKORY WHEEL CO.,

We have a pamphlet on sulkies, wheels, fittings, etc., which we send free to all who ask it.

### Newton, Mass.

*Carriage Monthly* September 1893.

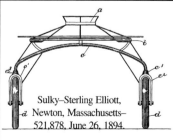

Sulky–Sterling Elliott, Newton, Massachusetts– 521,878, June 26, 1894.

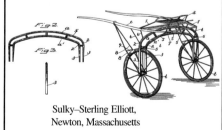

Sulky–Sterling Elliott, Newton, Massachusetts 539,578, May 21, 1895.

# CHARLES S. CAFFREY, AND STERLINGELLIOTT, HICKORY, WHEEL CO., NEWTON, MASSACHUSETTS

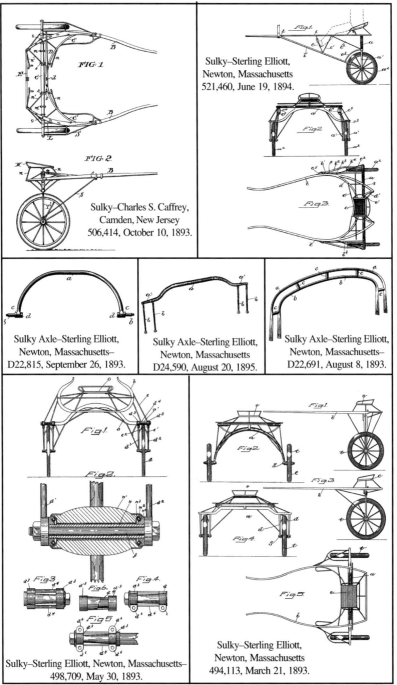

Sulky–Sterling Elliott, Newton, Massachusetts 521,460, June 19, 1894.

Sulky–Charles S. Caffrey, Camden, New Jersey 506,414, October 10, 1893.

Sulky Axle–Sterling Elliott, Newton, Massachusetts– D22,815, September 26, 1893.

Sulky Axle–Sterling Elliott, Newton, Massachusetts D24,590, August 20, 1895.

Sulky Axle–Sterling Elliott, Newton, Massachusetts– D22,691, August 8, 1893.

Sulky–Sterling Elliott, Newton, Massachusetts– 498,709, May 30, 1893.

Sulky–Sterling Elliott, Newton, Massachusetts 494,113, March 21, 1893.

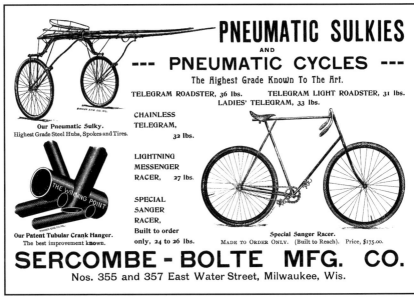

*Carriage Monthly* March 1893.

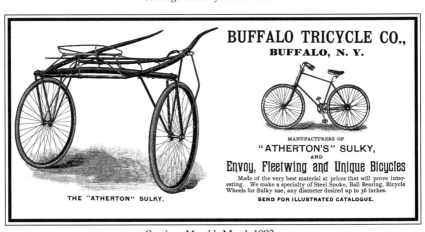

*Carriage Monthly* March 1893.

*Hub* April 1894, page 36. [Patent numbers 492,384 & 511,318]

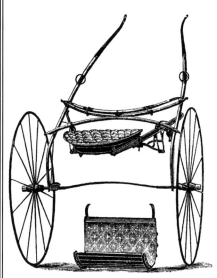
*Carriage Monthly* May 1893

# PATENTS for 1893.

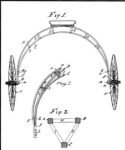

Sulky Axle–James W. Vaughn,
Greenville, Pennsylvania
489,577, January 10, 1893.

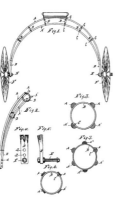

Sulky Axle–James W. Vaughn,
Greenville, Pennsylvania–
489,578, January 10, 1893.

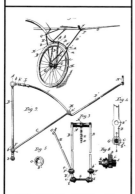

Wheel Frame–William H.
Shortsleeve,
Chicoppe Falls, Massachusetts
490,929, January 31, 1893.

Sulky–John W. Holliday,
Paris, Kentucky
492,725, Feb. 28, 1893.

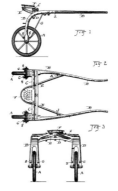

Sulky–Henry H. Garrard,
Cleveland, Ohio
493,582, March 14, 1893.

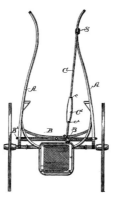

Sulky Attachment–Frank
Lohr, Freeport, Illinois
493,630, March 21, 1893.

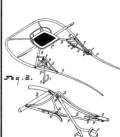

Foot Rest–Charles A. Russell,
Otsego, Michigan
494,648, April 4, 1893.

Sulky–Willie S. Bull,
Buffalo, New York
495,014, April 11, 1893.

Sulky–Willie S. Bull,
Buffalo, New York
495,015, April 11, 1893.

# PATENTS for 1893.

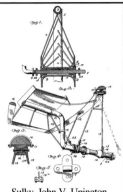

Sulky–John V. Upington,
Lexington, Kentucky
497,224, May 9, 1893.

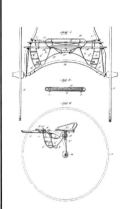

Sulky–Frank E. Brown,
Webster City, Iowa
498,154, May 23, 1893.

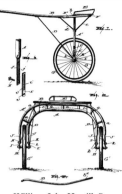

William John Hamill, St.
Catharines, Ontario
503,137, August 15, 1893.

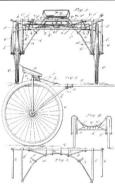

Sulky–William R. Richter,
Benvenue, Pennsylvania
497,501, May 16, 1893.

Sulky--Thomas Freeman,
Dublin, Ireland
502,093, July 25, 1893.

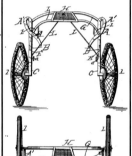

Sulky–Daniel W. Locke,
Bucyrus, Ohio
503,428, August 15, 1893.

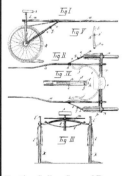

Trotting Sulky--Samuel Rowe,
London, England-
497,894, May 23, 1893.

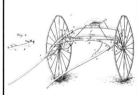

Harry A. McIntosh & Theodore
W. McIntosh,
Brownsville, Indiana
502,984, August 8, 1893.

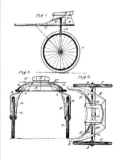

Moses McCormick,
Baltimore, Maryland
504,048, August 29, 1893.

# PATENTS for 1893.

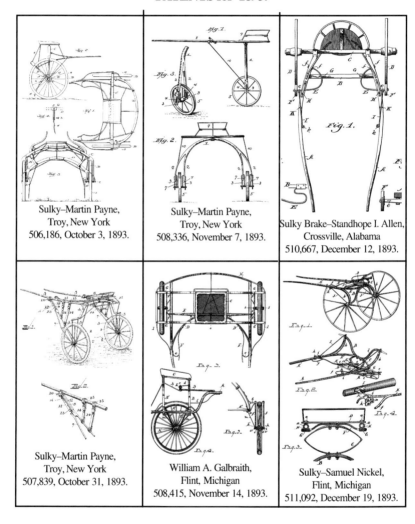

Sulky–Martin Payne,
Troy, New York
506,186, October 3, 1893.

Sulky–Martin Payne,
Troy, New York
508,336, November 7, 1893.

Sulky Brake–Standhope I. Allen,
Crossville, Alabama
510,667, December 12, 1893.

Sulky–Martin Payne,
Troy, New York
507,839, October 31, 1893.

William A. Galbraith,
Flint, Michigan
508,415, November 14, 1893.

Sulky–Samuel Nickel,
Flint, Michigan
511,092, December 19, 1893.

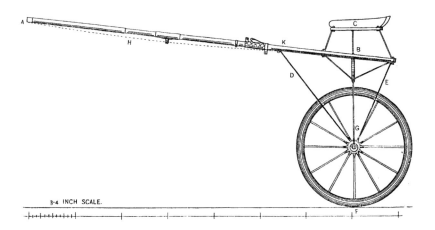

3-4 INCH SCALE.

## PNEUMATIC SULKY WHEELS.
*Carriage Monthly* October 1894.

The results of observing horses tool around the Fleetwood Park, New York, track, is told below and illustrated by means of a sectional outline of a sulky with pneumatic tires, which is explained as follows ; A, point of shaft ; B, section of shaft immediately over axle; C, seat frame; D, front stay from shaft to axle; E, back stay from shaft to axle; F, where wheel rests on the roadway ; G, the hub. The dotted lines H will be duly explained later.

During each of my visits to the park there were from fifteen to twenty or more horses being tooled, the greater number of which were harnessed to pneumatic sulkies. I spent fully an hour at each visit, thoroughly investigating, and invariably with the same results. The fact that there was no bunching of the speeders gave me a good opportunity to notice the action of each horse, sulky and driver. As each horse, sulky and driver sped by the place where I was making my observation, I noticed in unison with the movement of the horse and rider a deflection of the shaft between the point A and the point D, where the front stay connects with the shaft as per the dotted line H. The deflection of the shaft as a matter of course brought down the point K and elevated the point H. The result of such action is readily solved. The wheel at the roadway is momentarily stopped, or suspended from action, perhaps not one-twentieth part of a second, the immediate inflection of the shaft produces a short, jerky motion on the wheel at the roadway, the wheel being dragged forward apparently ½ inch or more.

The same motion was just barely perceptible in the high wheel sulkies, and nowhere near so long in its duration. There was not one-fourth as much lateral motion of the rider with the high wheeled sulkies as with those with the low, pneumatic tired wheel. I also noticed after the vehicles had passed by my position so that I could view them well from the back and side, that as the shaft deflected there was a very perceptible spreading of the wheels at the front, which action was changed to a gathering of the wheels at the front as the shaft receded to and inflected above its normal position.

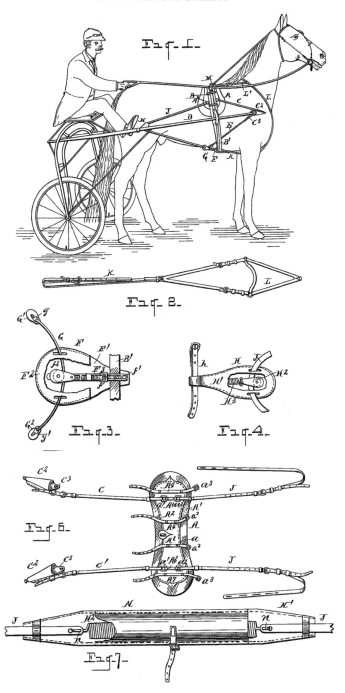

**PATENT SULKY HARNESS** of Mortimer L. Knowles, Detroit, Michigan, #544,310 August 13, 1895.

# PATENTS for 1894.

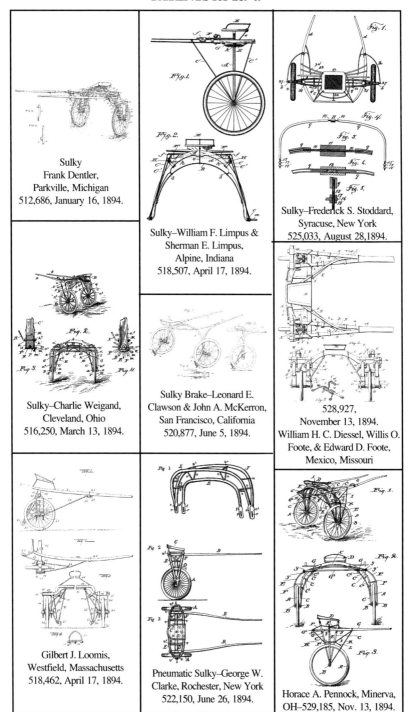

Sulky
Frank Dentler,
Parkville, Michigan
512,686, January 16, 1894.

Sulky–William F. Limpus &
Sherman E. Limpus,
Alpine, Indiana
518,507, April 17, 1894.

Sulky–Frederick S. Stoddard,
Syracuse, New York
525,033, August 28,1894.

Sulky–Charlie Weigand,
Cleveland, Ohio
516,250, March 13, 1894.

Sulky Brake–Leonard E.
Clawson & John A. McKerron,
San Francisco, California
520,877, June 5, 1894.

528,927,
November 13, 1894.
William H. C. Diessel, Willis O.
Foote, & Edward D. Foote,
Mexico, Missouri

Gilbert J. Loomis,
Westfield, Massachusetts
518,462, April 17, 1894.

Pneumatic Sulky–George W.
Clarke, Rochester, New York
522,150, June 26, 1894.

Horace A. Pennock, Minerva,
OH–529,185, Nov. 13, 1894.

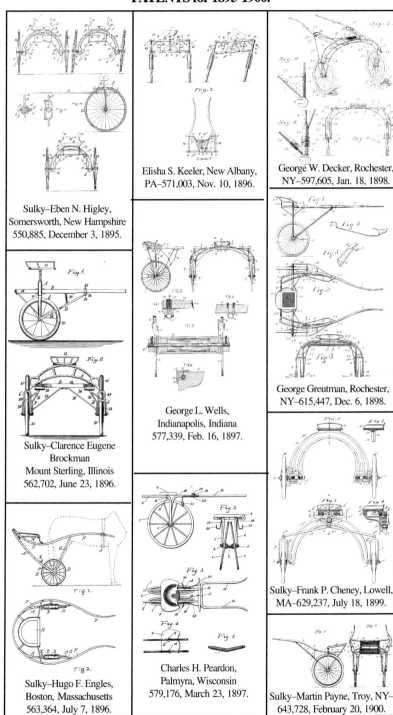

Sulky–Eben N. Higley,
Somersworth, New Hampshire
550,885, December 3, 1895.

Elisha S. Keeler, New Albany,
PA–571,003, Nov. 10, 1896.

George W. Decker, Rochester,
NY–597,605, Jan. 18, 1898.

Sulky–Clarence Eugene
Brockman
Mount Sterling, Illinois
562,702, June 23, 1896.

George L. Wells,
Indianapolis, Indiana
577,339, Feb. 16, 1897.

George Greutman, Rochester,
NY–615,447, Dec. 6, 1898.

Sulky–Hugo F. Engles,
Boston, Massachusetts
563,364, July 7, 1896.

Charles H. Peardon,
Palmyra, Wisconsin
579,176, March 23, 1897.

Sulky–Frank P. Cheney, Lowell,
MA–629,237, July 18, 1899.

Sulky–Martin Payne, Troy, NY–
643,728, February 20, 1900.

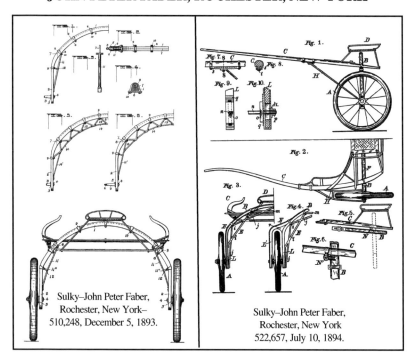

Sulky–John Peter Faber, Rochester, New York– 510,248, December 5, 1893.

Sulky–John Peter Faber, Rochester, New York 522,657, July 10, 1894.

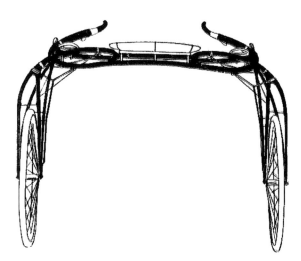

**Plate No. CCI. FABER SULKY.**

*Hub* February 1902 page 484.

Plate CCI shows one of the Faber sulkies, manufactured by the Faber Sulky Co., of Rochester, New York. This sulky is patented and manufactured solely by the company owning the patent. Many of the speediest horses on the track have won before this sulky, and some of the world's records are included in the list.

*Carriage Monthly* June 1895.

### HOW TO STRIPE A SULKY CART.
*Carriage Monthly* June 1896 page 76.

 When gold striping is used on light work, such as buggies and carts, a single stout line or double fine lines, ¼ inch apart, is the prevailing custom. In ordered work, where the wishes of customers are to be considered, there can be at times a radical departure from conventional styles and without glaring contrasts, so long as the same style of striping is used over the entire gear. While the size of the gear often determines the width of the stripe, the customer frequently has his own opinion as to what size and color of stripe will look well. The sulky cart alluded to is probably fitted with wheels having 1-inch spokes. On a jet black ground, we would suggest the use of a gold stripe ³⁄₁₆ inch in width, the striping to be on the flats of the spokes, the more prominent portions of the gear (no stripe is necessary on the face of spoke), and the ends of the stripes should be cut off square with color.

 Runabout wagons of the Palo Alto pattern are frequently striped with a single ⅜-inch stripe of cream, yellow or red on a black ground. This style of striping is very showy, and can be seen at some distance, but for a speeding sulky of sixty pounds we do not advise so broad a stripe, as any suggestion of heaviness would be inappropriate.

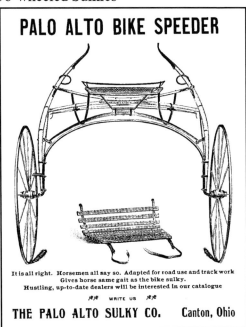

*Carriage Monthly*
March 1898 page 50.

## I. A. Weston Co., Syracuse, New York.

## PATENTS for 1902-1904.

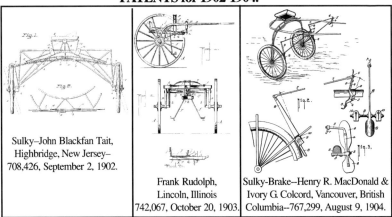

Sulky–John Blackfan Tait,
Highbridge, New Jersey–
708,426, September 2, 1902.

Frank Rudolph,
Lincoln, Illinois
742,067, October 20, 1903.

Sulky-Brake--Henry R. MacDonald &
Ivory G. Colcord, Vancouver, British
Columbia--767,299, August 9, 1904.

## A NEW VEHICLE WHEEL.

*Hub* July 1896 page 285.

The Stamped Steel Vehicle Wheel Co., of Chicago, Illinois, who had their office at 50 Euclid-ave., Cleveland, Ohio, are about to put upon the market a new wheel suitable for nearly all kinds of vehicles.

This wheel is the invention of James White, a mechanical engineer of Cleveland, Ohio, who has had many years of practical experience in various kinds of steel construction.

Expert engineers, who have examined the wheel, pronounce it mechanically perfect in its construction, and being made of sheet metal it will not be affected by changes of weather, and will virtually last until worn out by use.

At the present time steel is conceded to be one of the best metals now in use for strength and durability, and at comparatively low cost, but the company expects to use, as the patent calls for, any kind of sheet metal suitable for the work required.

Some of the first wheels are to be of nickel aluminum sheet, made by the Pittsburg Reduction Co., and will be very strong, light wheels for bicycle or sulky use. For buggies or wagons, steel will be used, as the strength of the wheel is only limited by the thickness of the metal, and any trouble or expense arising from the shrinking or swelling of either hub, spokes or felloe, as is the case with all wheels made of wood in the usual way, is entirely overcome in this wheel. The peculiar construction and shaping of the metal is claimed to make a wheel of 25 per cent. greater strength than one made of wood, both being of the same weight.

The general construction of the wheel admits of the use of any practical tire in the market, either steel, solid rubber, cushion or pneumatic. The hub is also stamped out of sheet metal, and connects the disc plates at the center forming a base or foundation for the arched chords or spokes, which are stamped from the solid plate, the full size of the wheel.

At the center or hub these discs are spread apart enough to give a suitable length of axle with corresponding width of base for the spokes, while at the rim they are securely riveted together with any form of projection suitable to hold the kind of tire used, and make the wheel strong enough to resist almost any side motion or pressure that can be brought to bear upon it, as has been demonstrated by repeated tests. The hubs are constructed to use either balls or roller bearings, and can be easily changed from one to the other.

As timber suitable for carriage and wagon wheels, is becoming scarcer and higher each year, while steel is becoming more plentiful and at less cost as the production increases, the inventor believes that this wheel fills a growing want for bicycles, buggies, sulkies, wagons, motor vehicles of all kinds and wheeled agricultural implements.

The company expects to fill orders for wheels in the near future by special machinery and stamping dies which are now being made by the well-known E. W. Bliss Co., of Brooklyn, N. Y., under the immediate, supervision of Mr. White, who is Vice-President and Superintendent of the wheel company.

## WHEELS AND RUBBER TIRES.

*Hub* April 1896, page 50.

The Michigan Wheel Co., of Lansing, Michigan, are manufactures of sulky wheels, sulky attachments, bike wagons fitted with either cushion or pneumatic tires, and a new tubing sulky fitted with adjustable foot stirrups. They also fit over road wagons with ball-bearing axles and rubber tire used by this firm is what is known as the round cushion tire. It rides easier and will last longer than the strictly solid rubber tire.

# MCMURRAY, MARION, OHIO

### THOMAS J. MCMURRAY.

Portrait Plate No. 170.
Thomas J. McMurray, Marion, Ohio.

Thomas J. McMurray, Marion, Ohio, president of the McMurray Sulky Co., of that place, was born March 2, 1841, at Steubenville, Ohio. At sixteen years of age he started out for himself, and after two years spent at Wooster, entered the paint shop of John Wilhelm, of that place. In three years he was foreman of John Beistle's paint shop, Wooster, where he remained until he enlisted, August, 1862, in the 102nd Ohio Volunteer Infantry, with which he served to the close of the war. After its close, he worked in Florence, Kentucky, and Orrville, Ohio. In the Autumn of 1866, he formed a partnership with R. S. Moore to build carriages. In 1868, fire destroyed the plant, but he resumed and took in his brother J. W. McMurray into the business. The factory was rebuilt as a two-story brick structure 66 by 166 feet on the east side of North Main, Marion, Ohio. In 1870 or 1871, he formed a partnership with W. B. Fisher, (who later moved to New York) and in 1874 J. W. McMurray retired. They made a specialty of track sulkies, in which line they achieved great distinction for volume of output and quality of work. Their sulkies have a national reputation, and are used on almost every track. The company became known as the McMurray Sulky Co. The annual output of the factory amounts to $75,000. The company employs about 30 skilled mechanics. Young blood has been added to the concern, who have given their energy and enterprise to the extension of the business, until it has become one of the largest manufactories of track sulkies in the world. From *Carriage Monthly* October 1897 inside cover.

William Fisher is living in Bolton Landing, Warren Co., New York, as of October 21, 1895, and still joint partner with T. J. McMurray. The McMurray family who is the whole board of directors at this point summons William Fisher back to Marion to offer him a position as president of the company. Mr. Fisher travels back to Marion to meet with the board along with his brother Charles C. Fisher, who is an attorney in Marion, and also on the board of McMurray & Fisher Sulky Co. At the meeting, both Messrs. Charles & William Fisher decide to withdraw their connections with the company, and after 25 years in business, William sells his holdings to the McMurrays and retires from the company and resides in New York as a merchant. His brother Charles also sells his interest, and continues with his law practice in Marion.

Around October of 1896, young William Houghton has been taken under the wing of Thomas McMurray in the same building to be on experimental grounds for Houghtons, promising future of interest. On April 24, 1897, Houghton is allowed to display his whole line of works at the McMurray shop for a grand opening of new carriages made by Houghton in the McMurray name. He displays over 60 vehicles, and the day was a great success in sales.

On August 28, 1897, they anounce a consolidation in the business, where Thomas retires from the business, but sill owns it, making Houghton the new president and manager of the firm as McMurray Sulky Co. (This business is on N. Main Street).

By 1903, Houghton builds his own factory, just across town and next to the same tracks that runs through town on Lincoln Avenue, building carriages under the McMurray name and not his own. By October 1903, Houghton breaks his partnership and moves to his own facilities on Lincoln Avenue, as the Houghton Sulky Co.

Thomas McMurray's son Charles R. McMurray is president of the McMurray Sulky Company, which is still owned by Thomas.

Thomas McMurray dies on September 4, 1908, and the business remains in the management of Charles McMurray, now owned by Thomas' wife Eva McMurray.

In 1926, Eva McMurray dies, and the company is left in the hands of Charles McMurray, her step-son. In the crash of 1929, Charles summons his youngest step brother, Thomas L. McMurray, a real estate salesman in Baltimore, Maryland, to buy him out and become president. Charles retires from the business and Houghton hires him as his sales manager for Houghton Sulky till Charles dies in 1934.

With no interest in the business and having a life of his own in Baltimore, Maryland, Thomas L. puts the business on Main street, up for auction and sells out, putting an end to the McMurray sulky business. There are no heirs to carry on the family tradition of carriage building. *Information sent by Dean Lowe of Marion, Ohio January 08, 2008.*

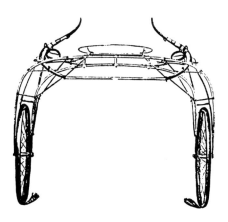

**Plate No. 56. SULKY.**
*Carriage Monthly* February 1898 page 327.
Credit for this style is due to the McMurray Sulky Co., of Marion, Ohio, and covered by patents.

The wheels have pneumatic tires, 1½ or 1⅝ inches diameter, 4¾-inch hubs, wire or wood spokes, and the width of track from center to center is 4 feet, 6 inches. The seat is 42 inches from floor to top of seat, or 38 inches from floor to bottom of lower arch. The width of shafts, front, are 25⅛ inches at points ; 44 inches at center, made of second growth white ash. Wheels are 28 inches and length of hubs 4¾ inches. Front forks are best grade, cold drawn steel tubing, with outside part arranged with an adjustable screw and jam nut to throw wheels out and in of gather, which is patented. All iron braces and clips solid hand forged of ³⁄₁₆, ⁹⁄₃₂ and ⁵⁄₁₆ round U. S. brand iron.

Painting.–Carmine, striped black.

# MCMURRAY, MARION, OHIO

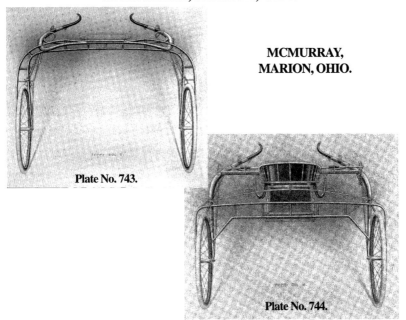

MCMURRAY,
MARION, OHIO.

Plate No. 743.

Plate No. 744.

**Plate No. 743 and 744. PERFECT SULKY AND PNEUMATIC JOG CART.**

*Carriage Monthly* January 1904

The McMurray Sulky Company, Marion, Ohio, have brought out a sulky and pneumatic jog cart which horsemen and trainers will probably find worth their special attention. In these carts strength and speed have been particularly looked after and satisfactory results have been afforded in their use. In the construction a minimum of weight has been reached, which is so highly prized by all horsemen. The science of light construction has been demonstrated in this work and with success.

The peculiar shape of the truss on the sulky prevents it from spreading. The bracing is simple, symmetrical and effective. All wood work is of ideal perfection and the material, it goes without saying, is second-growth timber. The shafts are well bent and heavy in the center where most strength is required, bolted between the two axle braces. A solid truss gives plenty of room for the horse. It will be noticed there is a close hitch, which makes the sulky light in weight and a most desirable running vehicle on two wheels. These features make it one of the fastest sulkys on the track.

The wheels have steel spokes 38 or 40 inches in height, wood rims 54-inch wide track from centers, single tube finest quality; Para rubber tires; weight, from 33 to 35 pounds.

The Buckeye pneumatic jog cart is specially made for jogging, training and matinee driving. It is late and fully up to date and will suit any gaited horse, as long springs ride well for any weight of driver and carry the weight on the heels of the shafts directly over the wheels. The new system of truss and bracing makes it extremely rigid. There is no possible spreading of the wheels, yet they are very light and strong, handsome and practical for both road and track. The wheels are 28 inches in diameter, steel spokes, wood rims, 1¾-inch pneumatic tires, carefully cemented and fastened with lugs through the rims; weight, complete, 65 pounds.

Painting. Rich carmine, striped with black hair lines.

Trimming. Goat skin cushion; plain or blocks.

Finish. Extra heavy pneumatic tires, hand-made weight pockets, dust-proof axle bearings and triple-plated nickel plating.

## *The McMurray Rubber Coated Steel-lined Wood Rim*

To the right is illustrated the best metal lined rims    produced   )u experience with *aluminum* lined rims has been most unsatisfactory   Aluminum being a "greasy" metal the tire cannot be securely cemented and   ver   )u〵 ted with lugs a tire must be well cemented between th  ţ,s else   v:   ,r

rı  cut invalidating the manufacturer's guarantee, besides rolling on the rim materially retards the speed of the wheel.

The McMurray Rubber Coated Steel Lined Wood Rim removes all these objections, further it is light, strong and durable; three essential features in a true, light running wheel.

## *McMurray "Bolt-on" Palmer Tires*

It is an absolute fact that practically all world's records have been made on Palmer tires yet the plain Palmer meets with some objection from drivers on half-mile tracks.   The The new McMurray "Bolt-on" Palmer retains all the speed and resiliency of the regular Palmer with the security of the lugs for bolting to rim.   Four plys of thread fabric embedded in pure rubber doubles the life of the tire, making it the most satisfactory ever offered.

No. 1 "Champion" plain Palmer tires, special make. 24, 26 or 28x1¼ or 1⅛ inches without lugs.   This is an exceptionally fast tire.

No. 1 "Champion" Racer is a lug tire, as illustrated above, 24, 26 or 28x1¼ or 1⅜ iı ᐧhes with lugs to bolt on.   These tires have a double tread and reinforced ᐧ ı seat.

No 15 "Perfected" Sulky tires, double tread and reinforced rim seat, are furnished in 24, 26 or 28x1⅜ inches, with lugs to bolt on.

No. 80 "Flyer" Speed Cart tires with raised tread, reinforced rim seat. 26x1½ or 1⅜ inches with lugs to bolt on.

No. 90 "New Idea" Speed Cart tires, double tread, reinforced rim seat, 26x1½ inch, with lugs to bolt on.

No. 30 "Buckeye" Cart tires, double tread, reinforced rim seat, 28x1⅝ or 1¾ inches, with lugs to bolt on.

**McMurray tires are made in one grade, positively the best and are absolutely guaranteed for one year, and in the majority of cases they last for two or more seasons.**

From the 1916 catalog of McMurray Sulky Co.

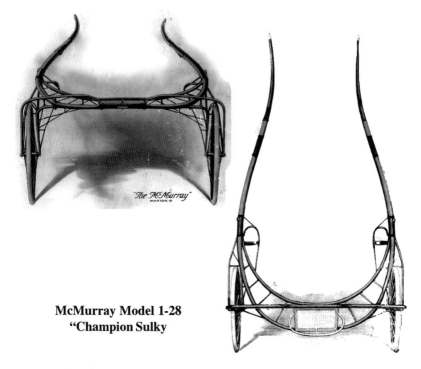

**McMurray Model 1-28**
**"Champion Sulky**

The stirrups hang well below the shafts and at an angle to fit the foot, precluding the possibility of chafing or cramping the foot or ankle of driver.

The construction of the circle bar, top axle arch and front of seat into a solid unit, with the diagonal steel truss braces between it and the lower axle rib leaving wood truss smooth on the bottom, gives the greatest amount of clearance under the arch with a given height of seat, and furnishes the neatest yet strongest complete axle arch known to the art of Sulky building.

**Standard Sizes**--From 26 to 30 inches under axle. 48, 50 or 56 inch track center, which is 43, 45 and 51 inches between inside axle nuts.

Sulkies carried in stock with shafts as long as 85 inches; on special order we furnish any desired length. The special shape of the shaft in the McMurray Sulky has always been preferred by all drivers.

**Wheels**--McMurray special wheels.

**Tires**--McMurray tires 28 x 1¼ Palmer racer being regular. McMurray bolt-on Palmer furnished when ordered.

**Painting**--French Carmine neatly striped is regular; any special color combination painted to order, and many carried in stock.

**Trimming**--Hand buffed black patent enamel or Russet leather of finest quality, stirrup spot is reinforced, and the leathers on the points of the shafts are sewn on, so that there are no tacks to cut the harness.

**Equipment**--Standard equipment furnishes a fine, hand-sewed, hair filled imported Corduroy cushion, large serviceable tire pump, and wrenches. From the 1916 McMurray Sulky Co., catalog.

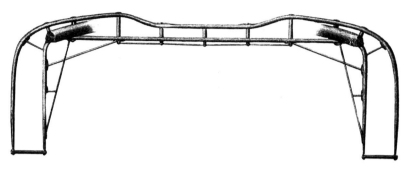

## *The McMurray "Double Truss" Sulky Axle*

The axle truss is the most vital part of any Sulky. A careful study of the illustration above is convincing of the extreme strength of the McMurray "double truss" Sulky axle, the most rigid ever designed.

The extra strong, yet simple wood truss, composed of continuous, (there are no spliced axle ribs in the McMurray Sulky axle), second-growth hickory ribs, is doubly strengthened by the steel truss rod immediately below the lower axle rib, forming a continuous inside bracing from wheel to wheel, producing a truss as strong as any other possible form, with the extra strength of the steel truss added. The McMurray "double truss" Sulky axle will carry a driver of any weight over the roughest track with perfect safety.

The axle and fork tips or ends are hand forged from solid imported Norway iron, and absolutely will not crystallize.

**You are "safe" when riding a McMurray.**

## *The McMurray Low, Leather-Covered Drop Stirrup*

prevents chafing, cramping, or pinching, and affords the driver the most comfortable position. Each stirrup is attached to the shaft and circle-bar at three different points in such a manner as to make them doubly secure,—*a tremendous factor in safety.*

From the McMurray Sulky Co., catalog of 1915.

# McMurray "Speed Attaining" Wheel

McMurray wheels really aid in attaining speed. All horsemen will verify the statement that to the wheel construction more is due than to any other factor in the development of speed.

This is plainly exemplified by reference to the more modern records of horses, for example: "Major Delmar" was able to draw a Sulky with wood rims and pneumatic tires in less than two minutes, while his best record to the metal bound wood rim wheel was somewhere around 2:08.

McMurray wheels are conceded by the majority of successful trainers and drivers to be built on the principle which alone can furnish a wheel of greatest speed. On page 12 is shown a sectional view of the McMurray lock-joint wood rim, a rim that is preferred for obvious reasons. It is light, strong, resilient, therefore fast, and without any metal lining, so that the tires will stay "put." A tire that is not securely cemented to the rim over all the rim surface, regardless of whether it is fastened with lugs, will not give satisfactory wear, but will rim cut and invalidate the manufacturer's guarantee, besides it is slow and retards the speed. As stated above, a metal bound wood rim cannot possibly be as fast as a plain substantial wood rim mounted with lively, fast, resilient pneumatic tires. *This fact has been proven* beyond all arguments. The lock-joint wood rim is light. A heavy wheel will tear the frame of a Sulky to pieces. It runs hard, stiff, and is positively a bar to that required attainment—speed.

The McMurray wheel is composed of well tried parts, which are hereinafter described. (See pages 11 and 12.)

From the 1915 catalog of the McMurray Sulky Co.

# McMurray Frictionless, Dust and Waterproof Hubs

The superiority of McMurray Sulky and Cart hubs is conceded by every McMurray user. The hub illustrated above is not only frictionless and extremely light running, but water- and dust-proof.

By keeping these elements away from the bearings the special graphite semi-fluid lubricant with which the hub is packed is retained and automatically oils the bearings. The hub is very simple, hence easily understood and requires practically no attention. The two cones, one stationary and the other adjusting, attached to a hollow sleeve, permit a knock-out axle bolt, a very essential feature and improvement over the old style hubs with the stationary axles. In connection with this hub is used the direct spoke, eliminating all possibility of spokes shearing off at the hubs, as is common with the old flange style.

The balls are very large in size, and made of finest Chrome nickel steel, are all carefully tested for accuracy and hardness, eliminating friction, rendering the hub one of absolutely easy service. The balls are held in place by a retaining washer when the cones are removed. Next to the ball retainer is a large felt washer, outside of this a dust cap holding the felt washer in place. This dust cap is made with a flange which, when in place covers the spoke hole, the hub, preventing any oil from running down the spoke of the wheel. All McMurray Sulky and Cart hubs are absolutely guaranteed, and any defective part will be replaced free of charge.

The axle bolt is large in size, a very important factor in safety. The McMurray special hub, in connection with the Diamond "E" spokes of finest grade, together with the lock-joint or the McMurray rubber coated, steel lined wood rim, form the most complete and perfect wheel possible to produce.

From 1916 catalog of the McMurray Sulky Co.

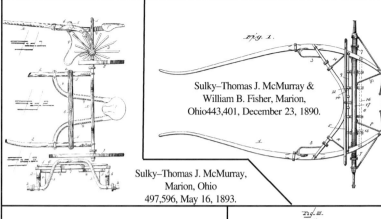

Sulky–Thomas J. McMurray &
William B. Fisher, Marion,
Ohio443,401, December 23, 1890.

Sulky–Thomas J. McMurray,
Marion, Ohio
497,596, May 16, 1893.

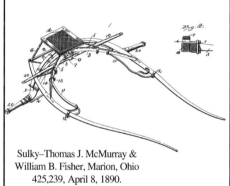

Sulky–Thomas J. McMurray &
William B. Fisher, Marion, Ohio
425,239, April 8, 1890.

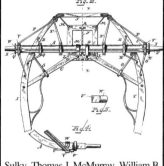

Sulky–Thomas J. McMurray, William B.
Fisher, Marion, Ohio
324,140, August 11, 1885.

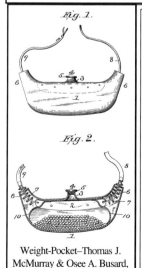

Weight-Pocket–Thomas J.
McMurray & Osee A. Busard,
Marion, Ohio
462,575, November 3, 1891.

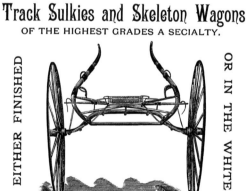

# W. S. FRAZIER & CO., AURORA, ILLINOIS

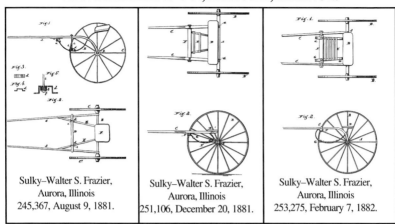

| Sulky–Walter S. Frazier, Aurora, Illinois 245,367, August 9, 1881. | Sulky–Walter S. Frazier, Aurora, Illinois 251,106, December 20, 1881. | Sulky–Walter S. Frazier, Aurora, Illinois 253,275, February 7, 1882. |

## W. S. FRAZIER & CO., AURORA, ILLINOIS.
*Carriage Monthly* June 1900 page 123.

W. S. Frazier & Co., Aurora, Illinois, claim to be the pioneers and leaders in the manufacture of vehicles embodying ball-bearings and wire or steel spoke wheels. They have been turning out such work since 1893. Naturally they think this extensive experience enables them to furnish a superior article. They make their own wheels and ball-bearing axles and a fifth wheel which embodies many durable features not known elsewhere. Their wheels contain an unusual number of spokes, and are believed to be proportionately stronger for that reason.

The Frazier patent ball-bearing [#482,896 Sept. 20, 1892] is so constructed that the bearing parts are all independent of the axle arm. The great advantage of this is that the bearings can be adjusted before shipment, thereby saving the dealer any annoyance or expense in that direction. Their wheels are built with either double tube pneumatic, or solid rubber tires, and have given great satisfaction. The Frazier fifth-wheel [#658,361 Sept. 25, 1900] itself is a novel and simple arrangement which does away with the necessity for rub irons, as the wheels cannot touch the body, no matter how short the vehicle is turned. Consequently there is no danger of overturning, and that a vehicle with this wheel is safer for ladies' use seems to be clearly demonstrated. This fifth wheel is also particularly well arranged to resist the leverage of high arched axles.

The firm have a salesroom at No. 371 Wabash avenue, Chicago, but the main office and factory are at Aurora.

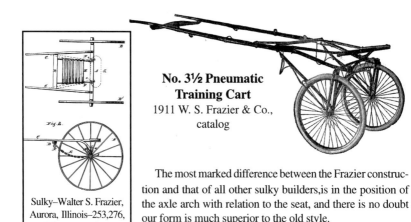

### No. 3½ Pneumatic Training Cart
1911 W. S. Frazier & Co., catalog

Sulky–Walter S. Frazier, Aurora, Illinois–253,276, February 7, 1882.

The most marked difference between the Frazier construction and that of all other sulky builders, is in the position of the axle arch with relation to the seat, and there is no doubt our form is much superior to the old style.

...We refer to the relation of the seat to the axle arch. On all other sulkies the seat overhangs the axle arch and the weight is carried on the rear part of the shafts, back of the axle. This part of the shaft is not stiff and cannot be made so. Therefore the seat is constantly springing under the driver's weight, laming his back, and tending to throw the horse off his stride and chop his gait. In the case of the Frazier sulky the rigid axle arch supports the rear of the seat, thus eliminating the springing so objectionable in other sulkies, and ensuring a better riding hitch, a better drawing one for the horse, and a faster one than it is possible for anyone to produce using the old style construction.

Another great advantage found in the Frazier relates to the design of the arch. In placing the arch at the rear of the seat we are able to retain its full depth, as it is so far back that a horse cannot possibly strike it with its hocks. The strength of any truss is in direct proportion to its depth, as is well known by mechanics, engineers and architects, and we are able to and do turn out sulkies which, at even weights, are much stiffer in the arch than any others, the axles of which are made shallow in the center under the seat where the arch is naturally the weakest. ...The Braces of the Frazier are shorter and consequently stronger than the corresponding ones of any other sulky made.

All other sulky builders depend entirely upon a single nut to keep the wheel in position. Our spindles are screwed through the fork so that we have a postive safeguard against the loosening of a wheel from its position, therefore, the Frazier is much safer to ride. From the 1911 catalog of W. S. Frazier & Co.

### Frazier Track Sulky
1911 W. S. Frazier & Co., catalog

**Peerless Carts**

**Nos. 1 and 2 Carts**

**No. 21 Cart**

**No. 6 Chicago Breaking Cart**

Circa 1911 catalog

# W. S. FRAZIER & CO., AURORA, ILLINOIS

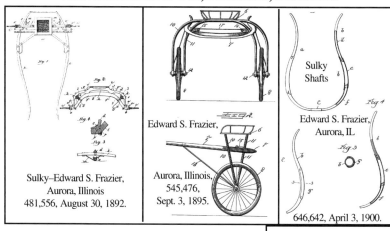

Sulky–Edward S. Frazier,
Aurora, Illinois
481,556, August 30, 1892.

Edward S. Frazier,
Aurora, Illinois,
545,476,
Sept. 3, 1895.

Sulky
Shafts

Edward S. Frazier,
Aurora, IL

646,642, April 3, 1900.

Sulky--Edward S. Frazier
Aurora, Illinois
762,038, June 7, 1904.

## WIND-SHIELD and DIRT-SHIELD

Pace-Maker with Wind-
shield.

Wind-shield
and
Dirt-shield.

In 1903 the Wind-shield and dirt-shield was tried in order reduced the atmospheric pressure created by a horse's own thirty mile wind. It was not accepted by the racing officials as safe and they rule against horses setting a record by such artificial means. From *Trotting and the Pacing Horse In America* by Hamilton Busbey, 1904 pages 13 & 23.

# PARSONS-HOUGHTON CO. / HOUGHTON SULKY CO.

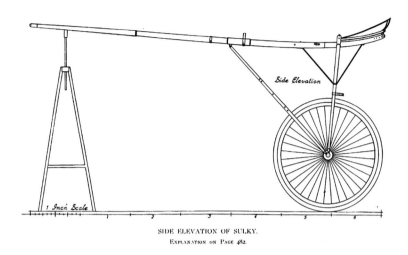

SIDE ELEVATION OF SULKY.
EXPLANATION ON PAGE 482.

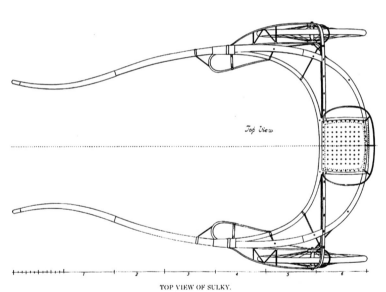

TOP VIEW OF SULKY.

## SULKY BUILT BY THE PARSONS-HOUGHTON CO., MARION, OHIO.

*Carriage Monthly* January 1905 page 482.

We give elsewhere four views of this light sulky, one of the lightest built, showing a side, top, bottom and back view.

The shafts are well bent, as shown on top and bottom view, and are jointed about 6 inches front of axle, and from there is a circular steel drawn tube, 1⅜ x 1½ inches at the joint, and ¾ inch at the center. The front tips of shaft are ¾ inch diameter and 1 ¼ inches long. The greater part of the shafts are finished oval on top surface.

# PARSONS-HOUGHTON CO. / HOUGHTON SULKY CO.

The circular piece in front of seat is connected with the upper axle truss and seat, the three being on a level. The size of the circular bent piece is rounded top and bottom, and is only 1¹⁄₁₆ inches in diameter. The upper axle truss has a drop in the center, in order to be in the same line with the seat and circular bent piece. The rear of seat rests on three spools, which rest on the steel-drawn tube of the shafts. The front of seat rests on the lower axle truss, with spools between. Most braces are ¼-inch round steel, but some are oval, ³⁄₁₆ x ½ and ¼ x ⁹⁄₁₆ inch. The bracing of this sulky is ingenuous, and the weight, being 175 pounds, settles the wheels in a vertical direction. The width of track is 4 feet 3 inches, center to center.

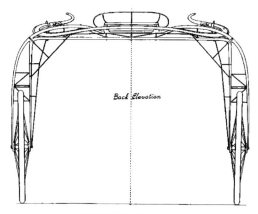

BACK ELEVATION OF SULKY.
EXPLANATION ON PAGE 482.

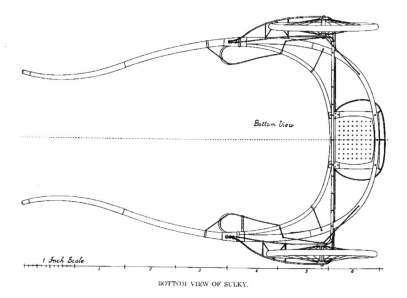

BOTTOM VIEW OF SULKY.

97

# PARSONS-HOUGHTON CO. / HOUGHTON SULKY CO.

William H. Houghton.                    Charles J. Parsons.

### CARRIAGE FACTORY OF PARSONS-HOUGHTON COMPANY.
*Hub* June 1904, page 142.

Marion, Ohio, is to have a new carriage factory, construction of which is now under way. The promoters of the new company are William H. Houghton, formerly of the Houghton-Merkel Co., and Charles J. Parsons, formerly of the Parsons Vehicle Company. The Parsons Houghton Company has been incorporated with $50,000 capital stock.

The first factory illustration of which appears herewith, will be three-story brick with basement, and occupy a space 60 x 180 feet. It will be equipped with the most improved machinery, and the company will manufacture novel pleasure vehicles largely. The past experience of Mr. Parsons is a guarantee that the styles will be new and original, as he ranks as one of the foremost designers in the business.

A great complement has been paid the new concern by dealers writing for agencies even before a brick was laid in the plant.

Mr. Houghton is president and Mr. Parsons secretary and general superintendent of the concern.

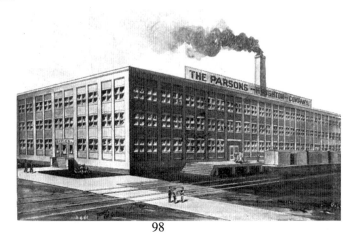

# PARSONS-HOUGHTON CO. / HOUGHTON SULKY CO.

## WILLIAM HENRY HOUGHTON.

Excerpts from the History of Marion County (1907) by J. Wilbur Jacoby

William H. Houghton is officially identified with a number of the leading manufacturing concerns of Marion County. He was born in Wayne County, Ohio, November 17, 1864, and after completing a common-school education, Mr. Houghton learned the carpenter's trade at which he worked until 1884. His chance for promotion came when he was appointed superintendent of the buildings for the new State Fair Grounds, at Columbus, Ohio. After he served two years as such, he went into the lumber business, purchasing a half interest in a mill at Dalton, Ohio. The business prospered under his management until 1890, when he went to Harriman, Tennessee, where he engaged in the same business. Two years later he established himself, with his father-in-law, Martin Schultz, at Dalton, Ohio, in the manufacturing of wagons and carriages, one of their specialties being the manufacturing of circus wagons. They continued to push this wagon business until the spring of 1895, when the plant burned down and Mr. Houghton lost everything he had.

In October 1895 he removed to Marion, Ohio and became superintendent of The National Wagon Company of this city. After one year's management of this concern, he had so matured his plans that he was able to organize his own company, under the name of The Houghton Buggy Company. At the end of the first year, he and T. J. McMurray formed a partnership and re-established The McMurray Sulky Company, and continued both the buggy and sulky business under one management until 1901.

October 1, 1903, Mr. Houghton sold his interest in The McMurray Sulky Company and the year following established The Houghton Sulky Company, of which he had been president from its organization.

The Houghton Sulky Company was organized under the laws of Ohio in 1904, with a capitalization of $50,000.00. The company manufactures high-grade racing and pleasure vehicles. About 70 men, nearly all skilled mechanics, are employed. The factory, a three-story, brick building with basement, was erected in 1904, on Lincoln Avenue, just north of the "Big Four" and Erie Railroads, at a cost of $30,000.00. The plant is a modern one, employing many skilled workers. The value of the annual output of the company is $120,000.00.

The officers of the company are: W. H. Houghton, President and Treasure; Hoke W. Donithen, Vice President; and Vernon Gordon Stair, Secretary.

The Houghton-Merkel Company was organized under the laws of the State of Ohio, December 1, 1901 to take over the buggy business of the McMurray Sulky Company. The capital stock of the company paid-in is $26,000.00 (as of December 1906). The company wholesales and retails all kinds of vehicles and farm implements.

Its specialty is building high-grade buggies and delivery wagons of all kinds to order, besides running a general buggy repair shop. The officers of the company are W. H. Houghton, President; L. W. Ireland, Vice-President and Charles E. Merkel. secretary and treasurer. Investors include J. B. Gunder. William Henry Houghton died on March 20th, 1941 at age 76.

The remains of the Houghton Sulky Co., were bought by Jerald Sulky Co., in 2007.

# PARSONS-HOUGHTON CO. / HOUGHTON SULKY CO.

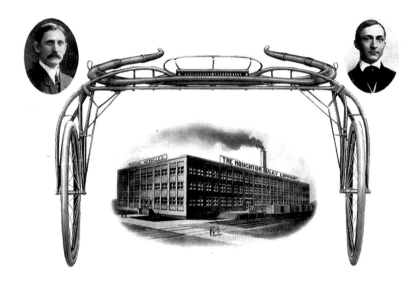

**From a circa 1908 catalog of Houghton Sulky Co.**

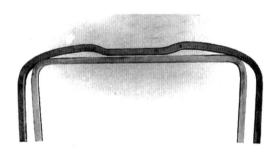

The Houghton Sulky axle truss is conceded to be the most rigid on the market. The accompanying illustration shows plainly its splendid formation. Two pieces of select second-growth hickory (the best material for this purpose) form the foundation. These pieces after being properly shaped are glued, screwed, and clipped at each corner. This positively prevents rolling or spreading. The central part of the truss is divided by means of perpendicular spools into rectangles. These being tied with diagonal braces remain perfectly true, insuring unequaled strength and rigidity, leaving the axle on the bottom perfectly smooth and free from any additional and unnecessary trusses. All hand-forging of high-carbon steel; all vital points are clipped, leaving the wood full strength, a construction which is much more expensive but very important. The shafts have ample width, and very rigid at the points. The stirrups are dropped below the level of the shafts making a more comfortable position on the low-seat sulky.

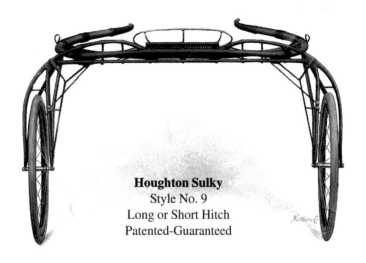

**Houghton Sulky**
Style No. 9
Long or Short Hitch
Patented-Guaranteed

Any height from 28 to 40 inches under axle, any width between axle nuts--long or short-hitch shafts. Standard in long-hitch half-mile, 31 inches high, 48 inches wide. Standard in long-hitch mile tracks, 29 inches high, 46 inches wide.

From 29 to 34 pounds. Crated for express shipment 70 pounds.

**Houghton "Highball"**
Style No. 99
A Favorite Hitch at the Matinee

In this sulky is used the patented axle truss in connection with the well tried double wood truss bar, a formation that is extremely rigid, carrying the heaviest drivers on roughest and short-turn tracks with perfect safety and alignment.

**From a circa 1908 catalog of Houghton Sulky Co.**

## Wheels and Bearings

Much depends upon the bearings of a light-running cart or sulky. The Houghton hub is mechanically perfect. It is exclusive in the following features; Tubular knock-out axle with cones adjusted and locked with lock nut, by which means wheels may be removed from frame without disturbing the adjustment.

Direct spokes, "Diamond E" grade, with special locking device at hub; ball retainers; finest quality tool-steel cones and extra large balls; heavy felt washers saturated with lubricant, automatically oiling bearings; outer dust-caps making it dust and water proof. The name, "The Houghton Sulky Co.," stamped on each hub--a criterion of quality. All parts are interchangeable; duplicates furnished promptly. Wood wheels--Exclusive pattern 28 inches high with 1⅛-inch cushion tires (see cut). Furnished

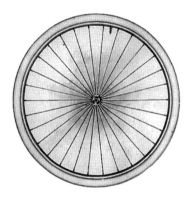

on styles Nos. 3, 4, or 55 carts only. Made of finest second-growth hickory, equipped with Houghton bearings, interchangeable with wire wheels.

The accompanying illstration shows a sectional view of the Houghton original "aluminum-lined" rims, also the manner of lug fastening of tires to rims so especially desirable

for foreign or half-mile track use--in case of puncture the race may be finished without fear of tire rolling off. A special wood rim, after being white-leaded, is lined the entire circumference with a sheet of aluminum, which, though very light (weighing no more than wood removed), greatly strengthens and stiffens the wheel. Don't take chances on your life with a non-supported glue joint--use a Houghton and let the other fellow worry.

**From a circa 1908 catalog of Houghton Sulky Co.**

# PARSONS-HOUGHTON CO. / HOUGHTON SULKY CO.

## Houghton Light Speeding Cart

Style No. 77

Weight 40 pounds.

Equipment includes hand-made cushion, oxidized dirt-shield, detachable dust protector (Keeping all dirt and dust out of the lap and face of the driver), whipholder, foot-pump, wrenches, repair outfit. Crated ready for shipment at 70 pounds. From circa 1908 catalog of Houghton Sulky Co.

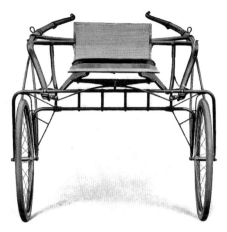

EMPLOYEES OF THE HOUGHTON SULKY CO., circa 1937.

Honor Roll of Craftsmen who have been connected with the Houghton Sulky Company for twenty years or more: Standing, 1. To r., Frank Foster, Vice-President, 22 years of service; George Lehner, Wood Department Foreman, 23 years of service; Bert Radebaugh, Smith Department Foreman, 27 years of service; Sam Hollenbaugh, Tool and Die Worker, 38 years service; H. B. Smith, Wood Department Expert, 35 yeas of service; Philip Kimberling, Wood Worker, 25 yeas of service; Ernest Kipp, Smith Forging, 23 years of service; Ed. Walker, Painter, 28 years of service; Ed. Paulus, Striper, 38 years of service; Bert McWherter, Paint Department Foreman, 35 years of service; Walter McLain, Painter, 20 years of service, Sitting, 1. to r., Harry A. Hoffman, Smith Finisher, 35 years of service; V. R. Harrell, Trim Department Foreman, 20 years of service; Fred Schneider, Wheel Department Foreman, 27 years of service. Courtesy of the archives of the Jerald Sulky Co.

# PARSONS-HOUGHTON CO. / HOUGHTON SULKY CO.

One wheel sulky developed by Houghton Sulky Co.
Courtesy the archives of Jerald Sulky Co.

View of the Houghton Sulky Co., with some of the workmen looking out the window.
Courtesy the archives of the Jerald Sulky Co.

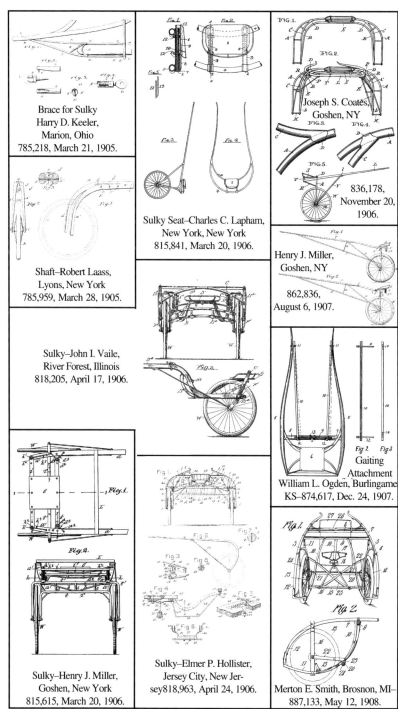

Brace for Sulky
Harry D. Keeler,
Marion, Ohio
785,218, March 21, 1905.

Shaft–Robert Laass,
Lyons, New York
785,959, March 28, 1905.

Sulky–John I. Vaile,
River Forest, Illinois
818,205, April 17, 1906.

Sulky–Henry J. Miller,
Goshen, New York
815,615, March 20, 1906.

Sulky Seat–Charles C. Lapham,
New York, New York
815,841, March 20, 1906.

Sulky–Elmer P. Hollister,
Jersey City, New Jer-
sey818,963, April 24, 1906.

Joseph S. Coates,
Goshen, NY

836,178,
November 20,
1906.

Henry J. Miller,
Goshen, NY

862,836,
August 6, 1907.

Gaiting
Attachment
William L. Ogden, Burlingame,
KS–874,617, Dec. 24, 1907.

Merton E. Smith, Brosnon, MI–
887,133, May 12, 1908.

# JERALD SULKY COMPANY, WATERLOO, IOWA

## HISTORY OF JERALD SULKY COMPANY

Samuel Jerald

Samuel E. Jerald, Sr. while working as a cabinet-maker in the early 1890's, made himself a fine carriage and soon others were asking him to make them one. It was not long before he had a reputation of being one of the finest craftsmen in the carriage and wagon business and completed his first successful sulky in 1895 in the little town of Osage, Iowa where he lived. Business grew rapidly, and in 1898 the Jerald factory was moved to Waterloo to obtain better shipping facilities and raw materials. Building racing sulkies and carts for the harness horse people, Jerald soon gained the reputation of being the most progressive in utilizing the very latest design, materials, and methods along with pioneering many of the new improvements in the sulky/cart race industry.

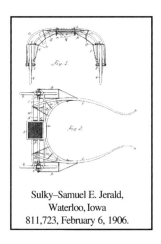

Sulky–Samuel E. Jerald,
Waterloo, Iowa
811,723, February 6, 1906.

Stanley Jerald

Samuel's son Stanley E. Jerald quit college to take over running the business when his father took ill. Stanley ran the business until his death in 1957 and Stanley's son-in-law, Bill Card ran the company from 1957 until the spring of 2005. Jerald was a family owned business for 107 years with some great history. New ownership, effective April 15, 2005, moves forward to continue the legacy of Jerald Sulky Company. Todd Gordon and Kevin Ireland experienced businessmen come to Jerald with extensive pony hackney background and the desire to carry the company forward.

During the early days at the height of the racing business, there were over a dozen sulky manufacturers. The introduction of the automobile and the crash of 1929 left only two sulky manufactures. During the war when there were no materials and no sulky business, Jerald manufac-

# JERALD SULKY COMPANY, WATERLOO, IOWA

tured thousands of field ambulance carriers for the army. After the war a number of new sulky manufacturers appeared but of those, only Jerald remains today.

Toward the last of World War II, Jerald got busy and turned out hundreds of training carts for horsemen who had not been able to get any new equipment since before the war. Material shortages made it necessary to use substitutes at that time. Research during the war brought out many new materials which were very superior to anything prewar. Because of this, Jerald vehicles improved in quality and have continued to do so as new materials and technology developed.

In the forties there was an increased interest in harness racing contributed to the development of the starting gate, pari-mutual betting, and night racing. The big races still exist today ... the Hambletonian and the Little Brown Jug, just to name a couple of the annual events. In more recent years the show horse industry has grown and Jerald is very active in producing carts and buggies for the horse, pony, and miniature horse, show and pleasure customers.

In business since 1898, Jerald is the oldest established concern in the business, maintaining a standard of excellence that has produced finely crafted carts, buggies, and sulkies for various breeds for the show, pleasure, and race industries. Every Jerald vehicle is designed to provide outstanding comfort, strength and safety. The sulky's superior aerodynamic design reduces drag and provides for faster performance for the horse racing industry. Each vehicle is uniquely painted and hand striped to the customer's specification with accessories to match. Known for outstanding quality, excellent finish and appointments, Jerald's attention to detail is obvious. Jerald is known as the "blue ribbon addition to your stable".

The company has its main office and manufacturing facility in Waterloo, Iowa. Located at 3050 Wagner Road, Jerald built its own facility in 1962 and still resides there today. A satellite branch in eastern Pennsylvania assembles and finishes new rigs, repairs and refinishes used rigs, and services the east coast horse race customers [Now closed]. While employing approximately 15 people, the company enjoys an amazingly low turnover with the majority of employees being with Jerald ten years or more. One employee has worked for Jerald for over 40 years. Many are craftsmen and artisans skilled at manufacturing these carts ... machine shop, wood shop, paint shop, leather working and upholstery shop, wheel shop, repair shop.

The company utilizes dealerships to sell its products covering both national and international markets. Products may also be bought directly from Jerald. For further information or assistance, their phone number is (319) 234-6195 and their web address is www jeraldsulky.com. Information courtesy of the Jerald Sulky Company.

New factory of the Jerald Sulky Co., in 1939, replacing an old place destroyed by fire.
Courtesy of the Jerald Sulky Co., archives.

From the
## S. E. JERALD SULKY COMPANY, WATERLOO, IOWA
Catolog of 1915. Courtesy of the Jerald Sulky Co.

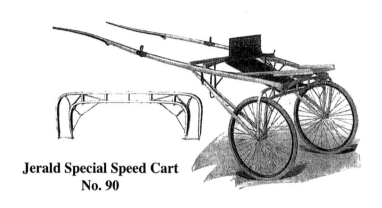

**Jerald Special Speed Cart
No. 90**

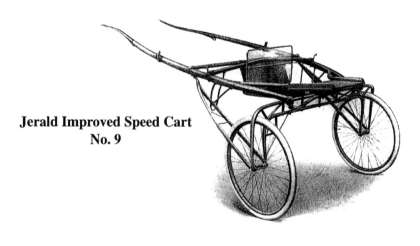

**Jerald Improved Speed Cart
No. 9**

**Jerald Breaking Cart
No. 15**

S  E  JERALD  SULKY  COMPANY  WATERLOO  IOWA  U  S  A

# How We Make the Jerald

IN a racing sulky, especially if it is to be used on half mile tracks, the one great point of **dependability** and **excellence** should be the arch, as a sulky is often given severe use and strain in scoring and around the turns. This is especially true in a large field of horses.

For the past nine years Jerald Sulkies have been used principally on half mile tracks and their great popularity has been largely due to our success in building them to meet the most severe requirements to which they may be subjected.

Jerald Sulkies are constructed by skilled workmen from the best materials that money can buy. Specially selected second growth wood is used for all wood parts. A special high grade steel, much stiffer than the steel used on the average sulky, is used for bracing and assures every Jerald Sulky being a durable, safe vehicle.

The style of bracing shown in the illustration on this page has been adopted for our improved sulkies No. 1 and No. 10. It is the result of long and careful study and experimenting to find a method of bracing that would be **superior** to anything now on the market. During these experiments we ironed arches with different styles of bracing on each side of the frame, drawing the arch slowly together at the axle bolts to learn which style of bracing would stand the greatest strain, continuing the strain until the weaker style would break.

In addition to these tests the different bracings were subjected to tests made by forcing the arches apart to learn which styles were of a standard that might be adopted for Jerald Sulkies. In our experiments we did not confine our tests to our own styles, but tested the wheels and arches of other well known sulkies. The result of all our experiments and tests gives us confidence in saying that the Jerald Improved Bracing will withstand **more strain** than any other now on the market.

S  E  JERALD  SULKY  COMPANY  WATERLOO  IOWA  U  S  A

As demonstrating the great strength of Jerald Improved Sulkies, we are showing here two illustrations taken from actual photographs in our factory. The first illustration shows a test that few sulkies would withstand. Here are five men, 700 pounds live weight, applied to the Jerald arch. Not much danger of a Jerald arch straightening out as do those used in some sulkies selling for even more money than the Jerald. The lower illustration demonstrates that there is little chance of a Jerald "buckling" in scoring or on the turns. These two men weigh 300 pounds, yet we found after these tests were made that the frame was not sprung and that the wheels lined up perfectly.

All details of manufacture are performed by skilled workmen under direct supervision of an expert. Every point of a Jerald must be up to the Jerald standard of superior construction. There are other sulkies that sell for more money than the Jerald, but there are none that are **superior** to it in style, weight or construction.

The painting of the Jerald receives just as careful attention as does every other feature of construction. Our paints give an elegant appearance and **wear well**.

Trimmings are of the best quality stock. We do not believe in the practice of using cheap trimmings. Poor trimmings soon make a sulky look shabby. Jerald Sulkies have the best trimmings we can buy.

We have told you here something of our methods of manufacture and any Jerald user will substantiate what we claim. "Jerald" to Harness Horsemen Stands for Honest Goods at Honest Prices.

Bourbon Stock Farm,
Phoenix, Arizona.
S. E. Jerald Sulky Co.,
Waterloo, Iowa.
Gentlemen: I think I will be in the market for a sulky soon. I think you will appreciate my telling you that the first of the three sulkies that I purchased of you is still as good as new and has had very hard use.     Yours respectfully,
J. T. CLARK.

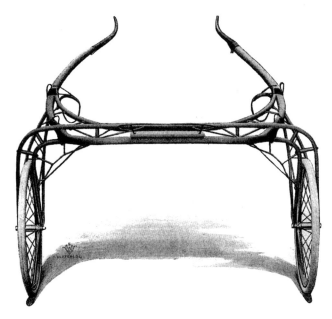

# Jerald Improved Racing Sulky No. 1

THE strongest and best half mile track sulky built.  See preceding pages. Stock size—28 and 29 inches under arch, 52-inch track center; 29 and 30 by 54 inches and 30 and 31 by 56 inches; stirrups set to best fit driver with 31 or 32-inch pants measure.  Can build 50 and 58-inch track centers and from 26 to 34 inches high.  Heights are given with 26-inch wheels.  If 28-inch wheels are ordered, sulkies are one inch higher.  Track centers are 6 inches greater than distance between axle nuts.  Stock color—bright red.

We will also carry sulkies in sizes above in the lead, ready to finish in dark color, which we can put out, nicely finished, in 10 days.  We can fit stirrups any length.

**Trimming**—Pebble Grain Morroco, dull finish on shafts, the most durable light leather we have ever seen.  Fine corduroy hair stuffed weight pocket cushion, foot pump, wrench and oil can.

**Wheels**—26-inch regular.  Option, 24 or 28-inch.  Best that money can buy.  See page 10.

|  | PRICES | C. O. D. | Cash With Order |
|---|---|---|---|
| With wheels fitted with Diamond Bolted Tires—no cover | | $58.50 | $55.58 |
| With wheels fitted with Diamond Bolted Tires and cover | | 64.00 | 60.80 |
| With wheels fitted with Hartford Bolted Tires—no cover | | 60.50 | 57.48 |
| With wheels fitted with Hartford Bolted Tires and cover | | 66.00 | 62.70 |

Palmer Single Tube Unbolted, same price as Hartford.

Crated for express shipment, 70 pounds; with shipping cover, 80 pounds.

## DESIGN CHANGE

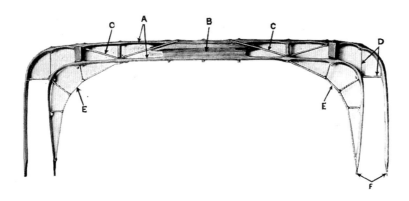

## JERALD GRAND CIRCUIT SULKY NO. 10.

.... The one great point of efficiency in our sulkies is this arch, which is perfect in design, superb in workmanship and very light but has exceedingly great strength and durability. So perfect is the design of our Number 10 Arch that a careful study of its bracing and the class of material used will convince any one that our sulkies have no superiors in *Looks, Durability and Speed.*

The arch here shown if fitted with 26" wheels would be 29" from floor to lower arch and 54" track centers.

(a) Arches of second growth hickory, bent to our special pattern, hand worked and finished, leaving arches full size at point of greatest strain, and working wood away where the strain is less.

(b) Solid Arch Center. The point of greatest strain on a bridge is the center. Most high priced sulkies spring at this point.

(c) Bridge Arch Bracing, making arch very rigid the entire length of top.

(d) Solid forged brace connecting arches together above the wheels.

(e) Inside arch braces make from special high grade steel which makes it possible for us to use lighter iron and yet have a very rigid and durable brace. From this combination of bracing, we are able on our No. 10 sulky, to produce the lightest and yet the most durable arch made.

(f) Arch End Irons. Many sulkies of all makes including some of ours which were built before February 1914, give out at this point. This is caused by crystalization of the iron. We now use arch end irons, while of the same design as formerly, yet are a little heavier at the weak points and these now receive a special heat treatement which greatly toughens the steel so that the vibration takes no effect on the iron. This style of irons was used on nearly all of our sulkies built in 1914 and on a large number in 1913 and we find that not one single iron has given out.

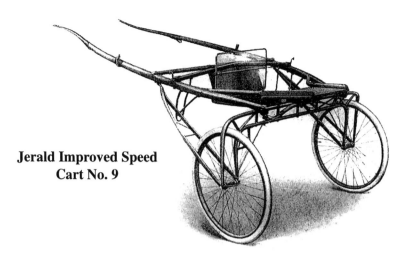

**Jerald Improved Speed Cart No. 9**

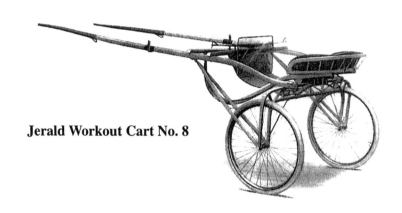

**Jerald Workout Cart No. 8**

**Jerald Road Cart No. 4**

Jerald New No. 4
"Solid Comfort" Road
Cart

Jerald New No. 5 "
Competition" Road Cart

Jerald New No. 6
"Competition" Road Cart

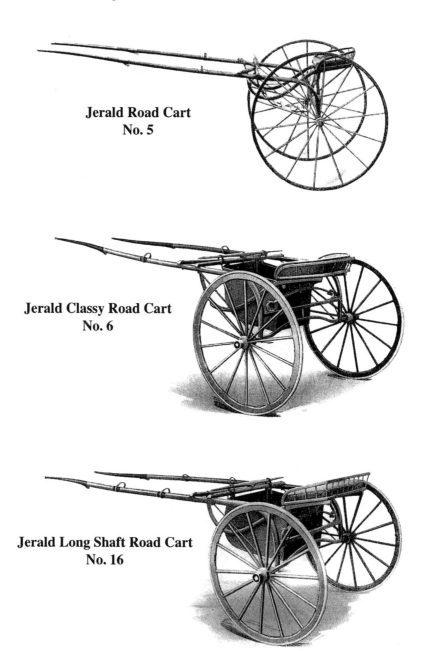

Jerald Road Cart
No. 5

Jerald Classy Road Cart
No. 6

Jerald Long Shaft Road Cart
No. 16

End of
S. E. JERALD SULKY COMPANY, WATERLOO, IOWA
Catolog of 1915.

**Parts of Hub**

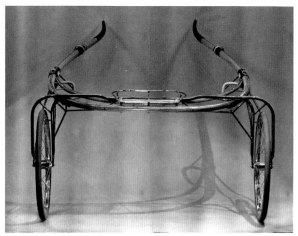

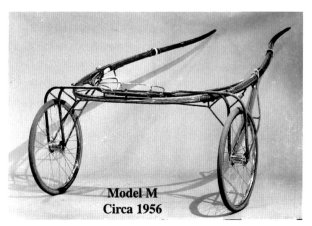

**Model M
Circa 1956**

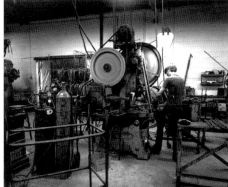

Jerry Barman Working On Press
April 27, 1971

Louis Sanska, Sander
April 27, 1972.

Trimming--Putting Leather on Shafts.

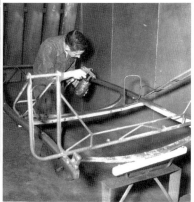

Dick Siglin, Painting a Vehicle (cart) in
Booth, 80 Webster Street.

Donnell Kelling, Assembler
April, 27, 1972.

Hand Striping, Donald Kraming, 80
Webster Street.

16 Rigs Ready for Shipping, Summer 1955.

# JERALD SULKY COMPANY, WATERLOO, IOWA

Jerald Sulky Co., employees, and Stanley Jerald, (back left corner).
Courtesy of the Jerald Sulky Co., archives.

The Jerald Sulky Company Plant, in 2007.

**Plate No. 816. SPEEDING CART.**
Built by W. A. Paterson Co., Flint, Michigan.
*Hub* July 1907, page 119.

Plate No. 816 illustrates a cart which may be arranged for sppeding purposes or for jogging along the road. When desired for speeding the foot rest is raised to the height indicated by dotted lines, while for jogging it is used as shown. Wheels are 48 inches high. The average weight of this cart is 100 pounds.

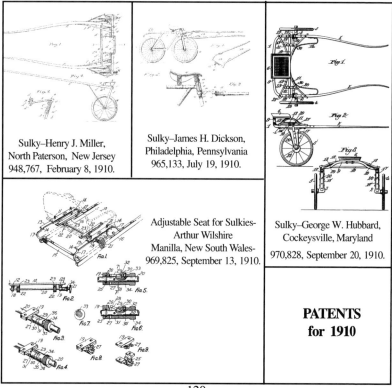

Sulky–Henry J. Miller, North Paterson, New Jersey 948,767, February 8, 1910.

Sulky–James H. Dickson, Philadelphia, Pennsylvania 965,133, July 19, 1910.

Adjustable Seat for Sulkies– Arthur Wilshire Manilla, New South Wales– 969,825, September 13, 1910.

Sulky–George W. Hubbard, Cockeysville, Maryland 970,828, September 20, 1910.

**PATENTS for 1910**

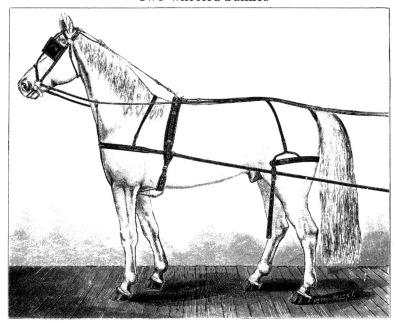

1721 First Quality, Single Strap Light Driving or Speeding Harness, Traces Sewed on.

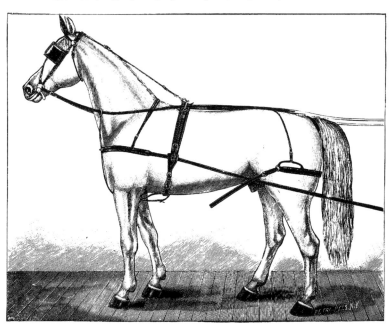

1722—First Quality, Light Driving or Speeding Harness, Enameled Leather Folds, Traces Sewed on.

LIGHT DRIVING or SPEEDING HARNESS--
C. M. Moseman & Brother, New York, New York. 1892.

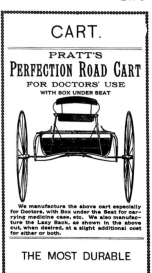
ADVERTISEMENTS
FOR
BUILDERS

# Harness Racing

# Two-Wheeled

# Sulkies

SMUGGLER, Who Beat Goldsmith Maid at Cleveland, July, 1876.
*Frank Leslie's Popular Monthly* November 1885, page 540.

## HARNESS RACING IN AMERICA–FOR TWO-WHEELED SULKIES.

Harness racing in America just seemed like a natural fit for one of the most popular American past times, once roads began to be established there were the friendly road races with ones neighbor. Just like automobiles are such a part of everyday life for many Americans today, so was the horse before the automobile, therefore it only seemed natural to organize the everyday buggy horses into organized competitions with lots of land being available for race tracks. In the early 1800's, trotting competition was given a great impetus because of the outlawing of thoroughbred horses racing in New York, New England and most other Northern states. The tracks were closed because of the "rowdies, racketeers, and scalawags" the sport was said to attract. But trotting was allowed to flourish, for this version of the sport was not felt to be truly competitive in a horse vs. horse manner....By the 1820's, when the thoroughbred ban was lifted, trotting competition had gained an important foothold on the American sporting scene."[1] As it is human nature with most good things someone is always looking for the way to make more doing less, so that by the 1850 harness racing had fallen into extreme disfavor: some churches in New York and New England branded harness racing as "evil."[2]  Most agricultural fairs that had started out to demonstrate and exhibit improvements in agricultural techniques and animal husbandry–were being corrupted "by the exciting scenes upon the circular track." [3] Because of media communications and print makers  such as Haskell and Allen of Boston, and Currier and Ives of New York harness racing had become such a popular past time with most all of the different classes, that what was needed was ways to make it better and the National Trotting Association was formed in 1870. The adoption of a system of track law almost at once, said *Wallace's Monthly*, "dissipated the pestilential fogs. The change from infamy to respectability was magical."[4] Although serious scandals came to light from time to time the image of harness racing continued to gain respectability.

Other advantages to having a national association were that before the Civil War every track association arranged its own meetings oblivious to the schedule of other tracks, this could lead to conflicting engagements, with half-filled racing cards in one city and over-crowed cards in others. A systematic organization was brought about through a federation of local clubs into racing circuits. A racing circuit was first conceived in Cleveland, Ohio in 1871 and later put in effect in 1873 with Cleveland, Buffalo, Utica and Springfield as the "Quadrilateral Trotting Combination." By 1875 Rochester and Poughkeepsie were added to the circuit changing its' name to "The Central Trotting Circuit." In 1876 the Charter Oak track, of Hartford, Connecticut was added to the circuit. This sequences of meetings nicely adjusted to each other, with big audiences guaranteed and liberal purses provided became known as "The Grand Circuit."[5] With the image of harness racing being cleaned up and an organized circuit the sport continued to grow even more making it a major spectator sport for Americans. Mass marketing continued to promote it from  weather vanes to collectors cards with a portrait of the harness horse such as published by Putnam Nail Co., and Lawrence, Williams & Co., promoting their caustic balsam for veterinary use.

At present harness racing is still a growing industry and a major recreational sport in America.

1. Sullivan, George. Harness Racing. Fleet Press Corporation : New York, 1974 page 18.
2.Sullivan, George. Harness Racing. Fleet Press Corporation : New York, 1974 page 18
3. Welsh, Peter C. Track and Road: The American Trotting Horse A Visual Record 1820 To 1900 From the Harry T. Peters America On Stone Lithography Collection. Smithsonian Institution Press, Washington, D. C., 1967, page 47.
4. Busbey, Hamilton. The Trotting and the Pacing Horse In America. Macmillan Co. : NY, 1904 page 163.
5. Akers, Dwight. Drivers Up : The Story of American Harness Racing. New York : G. P. Putnam's Sons, 1947, page 141

**EXTRAORDINARY TROTTING MATCH AGAINST TIME.**

45 Miles in Two hours and 55½ minutes. [Pair of brown horses driven by Mr. Burke of Hereford in 1839]. From the Horse by Youatt, 1843.

1796 " Mr. Stevens made a bet which was decided 5th October, 1796, that he would produce a pair of horses, his own property, that should trot in tandem from Windsor to Hampton Court, a distance of sixteen miles, within the hour; notwithstanding the cross country road, and great number of turnings, they performed it with ease in fifty-seven minutes and thirteen seconds. Horse by Youatt, 1843, page 52.

## HORSE. TROTTING

1814, "Boston Blue," Lynn turnpike, one mile, sulky, in 2 min. 54 sec.

1829, "Tom Thumb," Sunbury Common, England 16.5 miles, harness, 248 lbs., in 56 min. 45 sec.; and 100 miles, in 10 hours 7 min., including 37 min. in rests.

1830, "Top gallant," Philadelphia, PA, 12 miles, harness, in 38 min.

1834, "Master Burke" and "Robin," Long Island, NY 100 miles, wagon, in 10 hours, 17 min. 22 sec., including 28 min. 34 sec. in rests.

1837, "Mischief," Jersey City, NJ, to Philadelphia, PA 84.25 miles, harness, very hot day and sandy road, 8 hours 30min.

1867, "John Stewart," Boston, MA, half mile track, 20 miles, harness, in 58 min. 5.75 sec., and 20.5 miles in 59 min. 31 sec.

1869. "Morning Star," Doncaster, England, 18 miles, harness (sulky 100 lbs.), in 57 min. 27 sec.

1835, "Black Joke," Providence, RI, 50 miles, saddle, 175 lbs, in 3 hours 57 min.

1855, "Spangle," Long Island, NY, 50 miles, wagon and driver 400 lbs., in 3 hours 59 min. 4 sec.

1853, "Conqueror," Long Island, NY, 100 miles, harness, in 8 hours 55 min. 53 sec., including 15 short rests.

1873, M. Delancy's mare, St. Paul's Minn., 200 miles, race track, harness, in 44 hours 20 min. including 15 hours 49 min. in rests.

1875, "Steel Grey," Yorkshire, England, 10 miles, saddle in 27 min. 56.5 sec. *Mechanics' and Engineers' Pocket-book...* New York, NY : Harper Brothers, 1920, pages 439-440.

**GRAND TROTTING MATCH.**

*Illustrated London News* August 12, 1843, page 104.

On Tuesday the trotting match for 10,000 francs, in which the celebrated American horse, Confidence, was to trot in harness six miles in 16 min. 30 sec., in three starts, came off at the East Surrey race-course, Peckham. He was to do it within four hours from the time of the first start to the completion of the match. The course was prepared for the occasion, and during the afternoon there was a large attendance of company. The following is the result:—1st 2 miles 5 minutes 26 seconds–2nd 2 miles 5 minutes 35 seconds–3rd 2 miles 5 minutes 45 seconds.

The match was, consequently, lost by 16 seconds. Confidence is a fine bay, and stands 15 ½ hands.

The proprietor, Mr. Gill, was the driver. The course presented a very animated appearance. Among the company were Mr. Batty, in his car, with a band of music, driving his fourteen horses, and followed by the dramatis person of "Astley's" on horseback.

# Harness Racing --Two-wheeled Sulkies

Race Course On Long Island--Union Course, Long Island on the 22nd, the horses run on the occasion were Black Harry, Ralph, and Dutch Charley, 1 mile heats, best three in five, in harness; sweepstakes $100.00 won by Black Harry.
*Gleason's Pictorial Drawing-Room Companion* May 17, 1851 page 36.

Ten Mile Race for $10,000 at Centreville, Long Island, Between "Prince" and "Hero."
*Gleason's Pictorial Drawing-Room Companion* November 26, 1853 page 340.

## TEN MILE RACE IN CENTREVILLE, L. I.

Above we give a correct representation of a ten mile race that lately came off on the Centreville course between ch. g. Prince (trotter), and g. g. Hero (pacer), witnessed by from six to eight thousand spectators, in and outside of the track. The day was fine, the atmosphere clear, cool, and bracing; the track in most excellent order; and, in fact, everything was in favor of the horses for speed. They both appeared in superb condition, and capable of going the ten miles with

127

ease. Hero was the favorite, and one hundred to eighty and a hundred to seventy-five were staked on him in very large sums, probably in the amount of forty or fifty thousand dollars. The horses went in harness, carrying 165 lbs., the trotter being driven by Hiram Woodruff, and the pacer was handled by George Spicer. At the time appointed to start (2:1 2 P. M.), the horses made their appearance on the track, and were soon after called up by the judges for the race. They were started at six minutes before three o'clock, the pacer having the pole, and leading round the first turn. On the backstretch he waited for the trotter, and let him take sides with him, it being apparent at this early stage that Spicer did not intend to go any faster than the trotter would make him, at the same time keeping the trotter on the outside all the way round, thereby making him go a greater distance in the race. They lay side by side until they reached the lower turn, when the trotter fell in behind Hero, and waited until he reached straight work on the homestretch, where he drew out, and the horses came to the score with the hubs of their wheels as close together as it was possible to get them without touching. The first mile was done in 2:44. Leaving the stand on the second mile, the trotter struck his quarter and broke up, losing a length or so, but trotted the faster after he recovered, and was yoked again with the pacer at the quarter pole. The pace of both horses now became accelerated, and it was evident that Hiram intended to force his adversary to a breakdown, believing that his horse would prove the longest liver. Spicer kept the pacer in hand, and would not go any faster than he was absolutely compelled to. The trotter again fell in behind on the lower turn, and again made a brush up the homestretch, coming to the score head to head. The time of this mile was 2:36. On the third mile, Woodruff put on more steam round the turn, which compelled the pacer to add a little more pressure, and away they dashed round the upper turn and down the backstretch at a killing pace. Hiram, instead of dropping back on the lower turn, as he had previously done, kept his horse up at the top of his speed, and used every effort to take the lead. The pacer still had a little left, whenever he was called on, and they came up to the stand yoked, Hiram exclaiming as he passed there, "I've got him, sure!" The time was 2:33 1-2. The gray was opened as he left the score on the fourth mile, and he drew away from the trotter a few lengths on the upper turn ; but there was no let up for him. The trotter was even with him again at the quarter pole, and without falling off in the slightest, forced him onward. On the lower turn the pacer again dashed away from the other; but he was collared again before he reached the homestretch, and an excited struggle ensued to the score, the two passing there side and side, making the mile in 2:39. Both nags now began to show the effects of the speed at which they had been going; but as it was a "do or die " affair with the trotter, he kept up his speed. This was the fifth mile, and, instead of falling off, the horses went the faster. They hung together, side and side, all the way round, and crossed the score in 2:37, with as much apparent vigor as previously. On the sixth mile the trotter became the favorite. Any amount was offered on him, without takers. He took the pole on the upper turn, in spite of Spicer's efforts to force the pacer onward, and the latter began to show symptoms of distress.

He struggled on; but the trotter opened the gap at every stride. It was now evident the affair was near a close. At the half mile pole the trotter was fifty yards in front, without the slightest abatement to his speed , but on the lower turn Hiram let him up, and took it more moderately up the homestretch, crossing the score in 2:46, having performed the six miles in 15:55 1-2-an average of less than 2:40 during the six miles. When the pacer reached the score, it was evident that he had given it up, and he was stopped at the upper draw gate. A more exciting race, as long as it lasted, was never seen. The trotter was then stopped to a very slow gait, as it was unnecessary to drive him up to his speed any longer, and he was walked and jogged for the next three miles, keeping as fresh as possible for the last mile, his owner having a wager of five hundred dollars that he would perform the tenth mile in less than three minutes. The time of the seventh mile was 5:08 1-2, the eighth, 6:18, and the ninth 6:19 ; but he was let out on coming to the score, and started to decide the wager, dashing off at an astonishing rate of speed, which he kept up throughout the mile, performing the distance in 2:39-the greatest feat ever known.

Celebrated Trotting Horses, FLORA and MAC.
*Gleason's Pictorial Drawing-Room Companion* September 9, 1854 page 153.
At the New York Union Course.

Great Boston Horse Exhibition, At the Agricultural Fair Boston, October 1856.
*Ballou's Pictorial Drawing-Room Companion* November 19, 1856 pages 344-345.
Race between Flora Temple and Lancet.

General View of the United States Fair Grounds, Powelton, Near Philadelphia, PA., Showing the Grand Stand, Great Banquet Tent, Show Grounds. *Frank Leslie's Illustrated Newspaper* October 18, 1856 pages 296-297. Fourth annual exhibition of United States Agricultural Society. Competing against horses from all parts of the United States, Sherman Black Hawk took the first premium at the United States Agricultural Fair. Welsh, Peter C. Track and Road: The American Trotting Horse A Visual Record 1820 To 1900 From the Harry T. Peters America On Stone Lithography Collection. Smithsonian Institution Press, Washington, D. C., 1967, page 47.

American Trotting Horse, In Harness. Noted trotting horse "Mac" raised in Kennebec, Maine. *Ballou's Pictorial Drawing-Room Companion*, February 20, 1858 page 117.

Great National Horse Fair, Eclipse County, Long Island, New York. *Frank Leslie's Illustrated Newspaper*, November 6, 1858 cover.

Great Two Mile Trot Between Flora Temple and George M. Patchen.–Patchen Victor in Two Straight Heats.–June 12th, 1860. *New York Illustrated News*, June 23,1860 pages 104-105.

EIGHTH ANNUAL EXHIBITION OF THE UNITED STATES AGRICULTURAL SOCIETY, NEAR CINCINNATI, OHIO, COMMENCING SEPT. 12TH, CLOSING SEPT. 20TH, 1860.--FROM A SKETCH BY MR. HENRI LOVIE.--SEE PAGE 281.

Eighth Annual Exhibition of the United States Agricultural Society, Near Cincinnati, Ohio, Commencing Sept. 20th 1860–From a sketch by Henri Lovie.

*Frank Leslie's Illustrated Newspaper*, September 22, 1860 pages 274-275.

JACKEY, the Winner of the Late Aintree Trotting Stakes at Liverpool.
*Illustrated London News* December 14, 1861, page 602.

Hartford Horsefair.–View In Front of the Judge's Stand.–The Decision.
*Frank Leslie's Illustrated Newspaper*, November 8, 1862 pages cover & 104.
Included a large variety of races: trotting horse races for tandem teams, pairs,
singles, and running matches for ridden horses.

# Harness Racing --Two-wheeled Sulkies

National Horse Fair at Riverside Park, Cambridge, Massachusetts.–Exciting Contest
Between the celebrated Horses Empress, Frank Verrian, Dan Mace, and Capt. McGown,
Saturday, September 22.–From a sketch by Robert D. Wilkir.
*Frank Leslie's Illustrated Newspaper*, October 14, 1865 page 52.

Fast Trotter "Ethan Allen."–From an instantaneous photograph by Rockwood.
*Harper's Weekly* August 3, 1867 pages 484-485.

A Good Send Off,-Go!: GOLDSMITH MAID, AMERICAN GIRL, LUCY and HENRY, Trotting At Fleetwood Park, Morrisania, New York, July 9th 1872. Published by Currier & Ives, 1872. From the Print Collectionof the Library of Congress LC-USZC-3392 (color film copy slide).

The Champion Trotting Stallion SMUGGLER owned by H. S. Russell, Milton, Mass.: By Blanco, dam by Herod's Tuckahoe. On the Back Stretch In the Third Heat "Coming Away" and Winning the Great Stallion Race for the Championship of the United States In the Presence of (Estimated) Forty Thousand Spectators, at Mystic Park Medford, Mass. Sept. 15th 1874. Published by Currier & Ives, 1875. From the Print Collection of the Library of Congress LC-DIG-pga-00655 (digital file from original print)

Plate 7

SWEETSER, SLEEPY GEORGE and LUCY, Pacing for a Purse of $1000 at Hartford, Conn., Aug. 22, 1878. Artist John Cameron, published by Currier & Ives, 1878. From the Print Collection of the Library of Congress LC-USZC2-3059 (color film copy slide).

Trotting For a Great Stake. Artist Louis Maurer, published by Currier & Ives, 1890. From the Print Collection of the Library of Congress LC-USZC2-3477 (color film copy slide).

Plate 8

Great Trot at the Buffalo Driving Park, August 12, 1869.–sketched by J. P. Hoffman.
*Harper's Weekly* September 4, 1869.

Race Between the Celebrated Trotters, Lady Thorn and Mountain Boy, at the Prospect Park
Fair Grounds, Brooklyn, Long Island, September 3rd–The Start.
*Frank Leslie's Illustrated Newspaper*, September 18, 1869 cover.
There were three heats with Lady Thorn winning all.

The Promising Colt.–drawn by J. W. Ehninger.
*Harper's Weekly* May 21, 1870 page 329.

New York.–The Trotting Park at Buffalo–The Race for the $10,000 Purse, August 6th, 1872,
Won by Sleepy John.,–From a sketch by George W. Gibson.
Seventh annual trotting meeting of the Buffalo Park Association, there were eleven different
sections and the $10,000 purse was for all horses.
*Frank Leslie's Illustrated Newspaper*, August 24, 1872 pages 379-380.

Trotting Season at Prospect Park Fair Grounds, Long Island.–Race Between "Fullerton" and "Goldsmith Maid," Monday, June 8th.
*Frank Leslie's Illustrated Newspaper* June 27, 1874 pages 251 & 253.

Goldsmith Maid, the Celebrated Mare That Trotted A Mile In 2:14¾, at Rochester Driving Park, August 12th.
*Frank Leslie's Illustrated Newspaper* August 29, 1874.

# Harness Racing --Two-wheeled Sulkies

## How the Old Horse Won the Bet.

### by Oliver Wendell Holmes

'T was on the famous trotting-ground,
The betting men were gathered round
From far and near; the "cracks" were there
Whose deeds the sporting prints declare:
The swift g. m., Old Hiram's nag,
The fleet s. h., Dan Pfeiffer's brag,
With these a third--and who is he
That stands beside his fast b. g.?
Budd Doble, whose catarrhal name
So fills the nasal trump of fame.
There too stood many a noted steed
Of Messenger and Morgan breed;
Green horses also, not a few,--
Unknown as yet what they could do;
And all the hacks that know so well
The scourgings of the Sunday swell.

Blue are the skies of opening day;
The bordering turf is green with May;
The sunshine's golden gleam is thrown
On sorrel, chestnut, bay, and roan;
The horses paw and prance and neigh,
Fillies and colts like kittens play
And dance and toss their rippled manes
Shining and soft as silken skeins;
Wagons and gigs are ranged about,
And fashion flaunts her fray turn-out;
Here stands —each youthful Jehu's dream–
The jointed tandem, ticklish team !
And there in ampler breadth expand
The splendors of the four-in-hand ;
On faultless ties and glossy tiles,
The lovely bonnets beam their smiles
(The style's the man, so books avow:
The style's the woman, anyhow)
From flounces frothed with creamy lace
Peeps out the pug-dog's smutty face,
Or spaniel rolls his liquid eye,
Or stares the wiry pet of Skye–
O woman! In your hours of ease
So shy with us, so free with these !

"Come on ! I'll bet you two to one
I'll make him do it !" "Will you? Done !"
What was it who was bound to do?
I did not hear and can't tell you,--
Pray listen till my story's through.

Scarce noticed, back behind the rest,
By cart and wagon rudely prest,
The parson's lean and bony bay
Stood harnessed in his one horse shay--
Lent to his sexton for the day.
(A funeral-so the sexton said;
His mother's uncle's wife was dead.)

Like Lazarus bid to Dives' feast,
So looked the poor forlorn old beast;
His coat was rough, his tail was bare,
The gray was sprinkled in his hair;
Sportsmen and jockeys knew him not,
And yet they say he once could trot
Among the fleetest of the town,
Till something cracked and broke him down,
The steed's, the statesman's, common lot!
"And are we then so soon forgot? "
Ah me' I doubt if one of you
Has ever heard the name " Old Blue,"
Whose fame through all this region rung
In those old days when I was young !
"Bring forth the horse! " Alas! he showed
 Not like the one Mazeppa rode:
Scant-maned, sharp-backed, and shaky-kneed,
The wreck of what was once a steed,
Lips thin, eyes hollow, stiff in joints;
Yet not without his knowing points.
The sexton, laughing in his sleeve
As if 't were all a make-believe,
Led forth the horse, and as he laughed
Unhitched the breeching from a shaft,
Unclasped the rusty belt beneath,
Drew forth the snaffle from his teeth,
Slipped off his headstall, set him free
From strap and rein–a sight to see!

So worn, so lean in every limb,
It can't be they are saddling him!
It is ! His back the pig-skin strides
And flaps his lank, rheumatic sides ;
With horsey wink and saucy toss
A youngster throws his leg across,
And so, his rider on his back,
They lead him, limping, to the track,
Far up behind the starting-point,
To limber out each stiffened joint.

# Harness Racing --Two-wheeled Sulkies

As through the jeering crowd he past,
One pitying look old Hiram cast;
"Go it, ye cripple, while ye can! "
Cried out unsentimental Dan;
"A Fast-Day dinner for the crows! "
Budd Doble's scoffing shout arose.

Slowly, as when the walking-beam
First feels the gathering head of steam,
With warning cough and threatening wheeze
The stiff old charger crooks his knees,
At first with cautious step sedate,
As if he dragged a coach of state;
He's not a colt; he knows full well
That time is weight and sure to tell;
No horse so sturdy but he fears
The handicap of twenty years.

As through the throng on either hand
The old horse nears the judges' stand,
Beneath his jockey's feather-weight
He warms a little to his gait,
And now and then a step is tried
That hints of something; like a stride.

Go !" —Through his ear the summons stung
As if a battle trump had rung ;
The slumbering instincts lone unstirred
Start at the old familiar word ;
It thrills like flame through every limb--
What mean his twenty years to him?
The savage blow his rider dealt
Fell on his hollow flanks unfelt ;
The spur that pricked his staring hide
Unheeded tore his bleeding side ;
Alike to him are spur and rein,--
He steps a five-year-old again !

Before the quarter pole was past,
Old Hiram said, "He's going fast."
Long ere the quarter was a half,
The chuckling crowd had ceased to laugh ;
Tighter his frightened jockey clung
As in a mighty stride he swung,
Te gravel flying in his track,
His neck stretched out, his ears laid back,
His tail extended all the while
Behind him like a rat-tail file !
Off went a shoe,–away it spun,
Shot like a bullet from a gun.

The quaking jockey shapes a prayer
From scraps of oaths he used to swear ;
He drops his whip, he drops his rein,
He clutches fiercely for a mane ;
He 'll lose his hold--he sways and reels —
He'll slide beneath those trampling heels!
The knees of many a horseman quake,
The flowers on many a bonnet shake,
And shouts arise from left and right,
Stick on! Stick on! "Hould tight! Hould tight!"
"Cling round his neck and don't let go
That pace can't hold--there! steady! whoa!"
But like the sable steed that bore
The spectral lover of Lenore,
His nostrils snorting foam and fire,
No stretch his bony limbs can tire ;
And, now the stand he rushes by,
And "Stop him! —stop him! " is the cry.
Stand back! he's only just begun--
He's having out three heats in one!

"Don't rush in front! he'll smash your brains ;
But follow up and grab the reins!"
Old Hiram spoke. Dan Pfeiffer heard,
And sprang impatient at the word ;
Budd Doble started on his bay,
Old Hiram followed on his gray,
And off they spring, and round they go,
The fast ones doing " all they know."
Look! twice they follow at his heels,
As round the circling course he wheels,
And whirls with him that clinging boy
Like Hector round the walls of Troy ;
Still on, and on, the third time round!
They're tailing off! they're losing ground!
Budd Doble's nag begins to fail!
Dan Pfeiffer's sorrel whisks his tail!
And see ! In spite of whip and shout,
Old Hiram's mare is giving out !
Now for the finish ! At the turn,
The old horse–all the rest astern–
Comes swinging in, with easy trot ;
By Jove ! he's distanced all the lot !

That trot no mortal could explain ;
Some said, "Old Dutchman come again !"
Some took his time,–at least they tried,
But what it was could none decide ;
One said he couldn't understand
What happened to the his second hand ;

# Harness Racing --Two-wheeled Sulkies

One said 2.10 ; *that* couldn't be–
More like two twenty two or three ;
Old Hiram settled it at last ;
" The time was two — too dee-vel-ish fast!"

The parson's horse had won the bet ;
It cost him something of a sweat ;
Back in the one horse shay he went ;
The parson wondered what it meant,
And murmured, with a mild surprise
And pleasant twinkle of the eyes,
"That funeral must have been a trick,

Or corpses drive at double-quick ;
I shouldn't wonder, I declare,
If brother Murray made the prayer! "

And this is all I have to say
About the parson's poor old bay,
The same that, drew the one horse shay.

Moral for which this tale is told:
A horse can trot, for all he's old.

From the *Atlantic Monthly* July 1876 pages
44-48 and *Hub* August 1876 pages 180-181.

Life Sketches of Bill Brazen, the Fast Young Man.
*New York Coach-maker's Magazine*, December 1858, page 140–January 1859, page 160–
March 1859, page 200.

New York.–The Trail of Speed Between Miss Elsa VonBlumen, on a Bicycle, and the
Trotting Mare "Hattie R," at Rochester. From a sketch by Burt Miller.
The race provided enjoyment for a large crowd of spectators and seemed ending in favor of
Miss VonBlumen's bicycle.
*Frank Leslie's Illustrated Newspaper*, June 18, 1881 pages 265 & 267.

A Horse Trot.–Drawn by Paul Frenzeny.
*Harper's Weekly* August 20, 1881, page 564.

Pennsylvania.–Annual Exhibition of the Arts and Industries of Pittsburgh.
From a sketches by L. L. Roush. The original fair grounds was started in 1875 and
reorganized in 1877, and it consisted of half-mile track that for the first time used electric
lighting in 1881 for evening races.
*Harper's Weekly* November 5, 1881 page 165 & 167.

Great Trot At Fleetwood [ New York] Between Jay-Eye-See and St. Julien.–Drawn by Gray-
Parker. *Harper's Weekly*. October 13, 1883, p. 652.

Note: Gray-Parker (Clarence Gray Parker) was a noted graphic illustrator of the times
specializing in horses. He was born and grew up in France to English parents. He married  Mary
Louisa Flemming (died May 18 or 19th, 1890) they had a son & daughter and lived in Jersey City,
New Jersey. Clarence Gray Parker died around the 23 of January 1910.

142

At the Start–Receiving Warning From the Judge.
Scene at Fleetwood Park Race-course [New York].
*Harper's Weekly* September 21, 1895 page 893.

Last Look Over.
Scenes at Fleetwood Park Race-course [New York].
*Harper's Weekly* September 21, 1895 page 893.

Whirlwind Trio. Empire City Park, September 6th, 1899. Courtesy of Martin Auction.

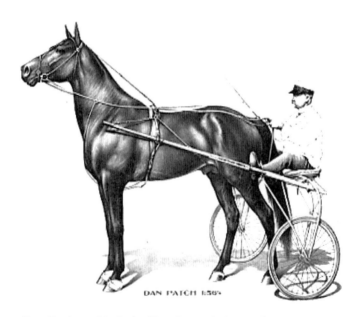

From Trotting and the Pacing Horse In America by Hamilton Busbey, 1904.

ALABAMA
Birmingham, Montgomery, Selma

ARKANSAS
Rogers

ARIZONA
Phoenix

BRITISH COLUMBIA
Victoria

CALIFORNIA
Hanford, Los Angeles, Marysville, Rocklin, Sacramento, Salinas City, San Francisco, Santa Ana, Santa Rosa, Woodland

COLORADO
Canon City, Colorado Springs, Denver, Fort Collins, Grand Junction, Greeley, Lamar, Loveland Pueblo

CONNECTICUT
Berlin, Branford, Bridgeport, Collinsville, Danbury, Granby, Hartford, Meriden, New Milford, Newtown, Norwich, Putnam, Rockville, Simsbury, Stafford Springs, Suffield, Torrington, Willimantic

DELAWARE
Wilmington

DISTRICT OF COLUMBIA
Washington

GEORGIA
Augusta, Macon, Rome

IDAHO
Blackfoot

ILLINOIS
Aledo, Anna, Assumption, Atlanta, Aurora, Avon, Belvidere, Bradford, Bushnell, Camargo, Cambridge, Carlinville, Carmi, Carrollton, Charleston, Clinton, Decatur, Delavan, El Paso, Fairbury, Farmer City, Galesburg, Griggsville, Joliet, Joslin, Kankakee, Kewanee, Knoxville, LaSalle, LeRoy, Lewiston, Libertyville, Macomb, Martinsville, Mendota, Monticello, Morrison, Mount Caroll, Mt. Sterling, Olney, Oregon, Ottawa, Paris, Pekin, Peoria, Princeton, Quinsy, Robinson, Sandwich, Saybrook, Springfield, Sterling, Streator, Urbana, Watseka, Wheaton, Woodstock, Wyoming, Yorkville

IOWA
Alta, Anamosa, Atlantic, Audobon, Avoca, Bedford, Bloomfield, Britt, Burlington, Cedar Rapids, Charles City, Clinton, Columbus Junction, Coming, Creston, Decorah, Des Moines, DeWitt, Donnellson, Dows, Dubuque, Eldon, Eldora, Elkader, Fairfax, Fairfield, Fonda, Forest City, Greenfield, Grinnell, Guthrie Center, Hamburg, Hampton, Harlan, Indianola, Iowa City, La Porte City, Malcolm, Manchester, Maquoketa, Marengo, Marion, Marshalltown, Mason City, Milton, Missouri Valley, Mt. Pleasant, National, New Hampton, New Sharon, Newton, Onawa, Osage, Red Oak, Rock Rapids, Rock Valley, Sac City, Sheldon, Shenandoah, Sioux City, Sutherland, Tipton, Toledo, Victor, Wapello, Waterloo, Waverly, Webster City, West Liberty, West Point, What Cheer, Wilton Junction, Winfield, Winterset

KENTUCKY
Cynthiana, Erlanger, Guthrie, Lexington, Uniontown

LOUISIANA
Shreveport

MAINE
Andover, Bangor, Belfast, Bethel, Blue Hill, Bridgeton, Canton, Cherryfield, Cornish, Damariscotta, East Sabago, Exeter, Farmington, Freeport, Fryeburgh, Gorham, Hartland, Lewiston, Lincoln, Livermore Falls, Madison, Monroe, New Glouster, Newport, Patten, Phillips, Pittsfield, Presque Isle,

Readfield, Regina, Rumford Falls, Skowhegan, South Paris, South Windsor, Topsham, Union, Unity, Waterville, West Cumberland

## MANITOBA
Brandon, Carberry, Killarney, Neepawa, Portage La Prairie, Winnipeg

## MARYLAND
Baltimore, Cumberland, Easton, Frederick, Hagerstown, Pocomoke City, Rockville, Timonium, Tolchester Beach, Upper Marlboro

## MASSACHUSETTS
Amherst, Barnstable, Barre, Brockton, Charlemont, Clinton, Dorchester, Great Barrington, Greenfield, Marshfield, Middleboro, North Adams, North Hampton, Oxford, Palmer, Readvilie, South Framingham, South Weymouth, Spencer, Sturbridge, Taunton, Worcester

## MINNESOTA
Albert Lea, Austin, Bird Island, Hamline, Hibbing, Howard Lake, Hutchinson, Madelia, Marshall, New Ulm, Park Rapids, Preston, Rochester, St. James, St. Peter, Sauk Center, Stillwater, Thief River Falls, Tyler, Windom, Worthington

## MISSISSIPPI
Columbus, Jackson

## MISSOURI
Bowling Green, Brookfield, Butler, Girardeau, Carthage, Chillicothe, Columbia, Green City, Hamilton, Higginsville, Holden, Independence, Iron Mountain, Joplin, Kahoka, La Plata, Maitland, Milan, Marshall, Memphis, Mexico, Moberly, Monroe City, Oran, Platte City, St. Joseph, Sedalia, Springfield, Trenton, Warrensburg

## MONTANA
Bozeman, Butte, Great Falls, Helena, Kalispel, Livingston, Missoula

## NEBRASKA
Albion, Auburn, Battle Creek, Beatrice, Benkleman, Clay Center, Fremont, Friend, Geneva, Hastings, Lincoln, McCook, Madison, Neligh, Nelson, Norfolk, O'Neil, Osceola, Pierce, Randolph, Salem, Stanton, Tekemah, Tilden, Wahoo, Wayne, Wymore

## NEW BRUNSWICK
Chatham, Frederickton, Moncton, St. John, Sussex, Sydney, Woodstock

## NEW HAMPSHIRE
Claremont, Concord, Greenfield, Lancaster, Littleton, Nashua, Rochester

## NEW JERSEY
Bordentown, Bridgeton, Flemington, Freehold, Hightstown, Hohokus, Manasquan, Mt. Holly, New Brunswick, Plainfield, Salem, Trenton

## NEW MEXICO
Albuquerque

## NORTH CAOLINA
Charlotte, Fayetteville, Greensboro, Raleigh, Winston-Salem

## NORTH DAKOTA
Buffalo, Carrington, Casselton, Cooperstown, Courtenay, Fargo, Grand Forks, Granville, Harvey, Jamestown, Kinsel, Langdon, Leeds, Mayville, Minot, New Rockford, Page, Valley City, Wahpeton

## NOVA SCOTIA
Halifax

## NORTHWEST TERRITORY
Calgary, Edmonton, Indian Head, Moose Jaw Quappelle, Wolseley

## OKLAHOMA
Blackwell, Jefferson, Newkirk

## OKLAHOMA TERRITORY
Enid

## ONTARIO

Barrie, Bothwell, Brockville, Brussels, Chatham, Cobourg, Eganville, Hamilton, Listowell, London, Orangeville, Ottawa, Prescott, Preston, Seaforth, Stratford, Toronto, Windsor, Wingham

## OREGON

Baker City, Salem

## PENNSYLVANIA

Dubois, Erie, Greensburg, Hallstead, Hanover, Holmesburg, Honesdale, Hughesville, Imperial, Indiana, Johnstown, Kittanning, Kutztown, Lebanon, Lewisburg, Manoa, Mercer, Meyersdale, Middletown, Milton, Monongahela, Mount Morris, Narberth, Nazareth, New Castle, Newport, Morristown, Oil City, Oxford, Philadelphia, Phoenixville, Port Royal, Pottstown, Pulaski, Reading, Rimersburg, Scranton, Shrewsbury, Stoneboro, Stroudsburg, Titusville, Towanda, West Chester, Wilkes Barre, York, Youngwood

## QUEBEC

Bedford, Montreal, Sherbrooke, Three Rivers

## RHODE ISLAND

West Kingston, Woonsocket

## SOUTH DAKOTA

Aneta, Armour, Ashton, Flandreau, Huron, Madison, Mitchell, Plankington, Platte, Watertown

## TENNESSEE

Columbia, Knoxville, Nashville, Shelbyville, Winchester

## TERRITORY OF IDAHO

Ardmore

## TEXAS

Beaumont, Bowie, Corsicana, Dallas, Denison, Fort Worth, Gainesville, Houston, San Antonio, Taylor

## UTAH

Ogden

## VERMONT

Barton, Bellows Falls, Bradford, Brattleboro, Fair Haven, Middlebury, Morrisville, Newport, Northfield, Rutland, St. Johnsbury, Sheldon Junction, South Wallingford, Tunbridge, Windsor, Woodstock

## WASHINGTON

Colville, North Yakima, Spokane, Walla Walla

## WEST VIRGINIA

Belington, Buckhannon, Clarksburg, Elkins, Huntington, New Martinsville, Pennsboro, Point Pleasant, Weston, Wheeling

## WISCONSIN

Appleton, Antigo, Ashland, Augusta, Baraboo, Beaver Darn, Berlin, Black River, Bloomington, Boscobel, Chilton, Chippewa Falls, Darlington, De Pere, Elkhorn, Elroy, Everett, Fon du Lac, Galesville, Gays Mills, Hillsboro, Jefferson, Kenosha, Kilburn, LaCrosse, Lancaster, Madison, Manitowoc, Marshfield, Mauston, Menomonie, Merrill, Milwaukee, Mineral Point, Monroe, Neillsville, New London, Osconto, Oshkosh, Platteville, Plymouth, Portage, Reedsburg, Rhinelander, Rice Lake, Richland Center, Sparta, Stevens Point, Tomah, Viroqua, Watertown, Wausau, Wautoma, Weyauwega

**ADVERTISEMENT FOR CUSHION PADS**

# Four-wheeled

# Racing Sulky

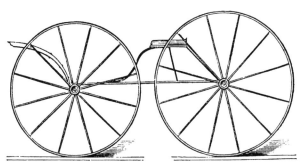

No. 221.–Skeleton Wagon.
Lawrence, Bradley & Pardee, New Haven, Connecticut, catalog
1862. Made to weigh from 75 to 135 lbs.

# Four Wheeled Racing Sulky

## FOUR WHEELED RACING SULKY or SKELETON WAGON.

From the book Drivers Up by Dwight Akers published in 1947 "Racing to vehicles was of two sorts--"in harness," that is to sulky, and "to wagon," that is to a four-wheeled vehicle. On the average, races "to wagon" were estimated to be three seconds to the mile slower than races to sulky. This difference was made use of in arranging handicaps. Not only were there races of sulky or wagon against saddle, but races of wagon against sulky, occasionally of a team against a single horse. Since matches were also contested in heats that ranged in distance from one to four miles, the racing calendar of early days was a more varied one than that of the present.

For use in wagon races, the carriage makers perfected a vehicle of skeleton design. In [June 15,]1844, Ripton appeared on Beacon track [Beacon Course, Hoboken, Hudson County, New Jersey] harnessed to a wagon of marvelous lightness--"the lightest, strongest, and handsomest we ever saw. It was manufactured expressly for Ripton who goes in it today in his match for $1000 a side, with Confidence, who goes in a sulky. This wagon when it was first turned out weighed less than seventy pounds, but having been painted, strapped and ironed extra, for hard service, its weight now is seventy-four pounds. It is from the manufactory of J. H. Godwin, of 114 Elizabeth street, one of our best builders, and though light as a feather, it is made of such excellent materials as to be capable of carrying two persons without straining. Its spokes are so thin, long and numerous, and its body so fragile and light, that it looks for all the world like an over-grown Daddy Long Legs, or a gigantic spider." *Spirit of the Times; A Chronicle of the Turf, Agriculture, Field Sports,...* June 15, 1844, page 186.

Ripton's wagon was a credit not only to the builder's ingenuity but to a reinsman's cleverness in "out-smarting" his opponent. His four-wheeled "Daddy Long Legs" actually weighed less than his rival's two-wheeled cart. By a stroke of genius, Driver George Young had wiped out the handicap imposed on his horse. The invention, however, did not start a new fashion in wagons. On most courses the rules of wagon racing called for a vehicle weighing not less than two hundred and fifty pounds. Races such as Ripton's, to lighter vehicles, were not recognized as standard performances."

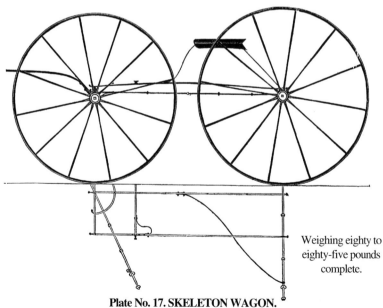

Weighing eighty to eighty-five pounds complete.

**Plate No. 17. SKELETON WAGON.**
*New York Coach-Maker's Magazine* October 1859 page 87.

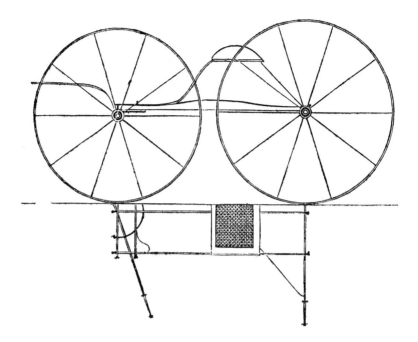

**Plate No. 23. CAFFREY'S SKELETON TRACK WAGON.**

*Coach-Makers' International Journal.* March 1869, page 85.

This draft was kindly furnished by Mr. Caffrey, who has established a wide reputation for first-class light work. A visit to his factory, in Camden, New Jersey, opposite Philadelphia, will be sufficient to convince any one that he builds as light work, (if not the lightest,) as can be found in the country. Using nothing but first-class stock, in every part of the vehicle, his work stands well, and, of course, gives good satisfaction. An admirer of fast horses, and driving a great deal himself, he more readily detects any imperfections in his wagons. This, we think, will account, in a great measure, for the superiority of his work.

Dimensions: Seat, 13 by 20 inches in cane bottom, silver rail each side as shown by draft. Spars set 20 inches apart from out to out, 1 inch square, arched 1 inch, ¾ by ⅝ at ends. Double perches, ⅝ by ¾ length, 53½ inches. Hubs 6½ by 3⅛. Front band: 2¼; Back: 2½. Spokes: ½ inch by 1⅟₁₆ths. Depth of. rim: ⅞. Tire: ¾, No. 12 steel. Axle: ¾ steel, 6½ arm. Wheels: 3 feet 11 and 4 feet 1. Track; 4 feet 4.

The half of top view shows a single perch. We would prefer the double perches. They are being built either style to suit the purchaser: The head bar to which the spars are clipped are ¹⁵⁄₁₆ths by 1¼ in centre, ¾ by ⅟₁₆ths at ends. The toe bar is 1 inch square in the centre, ¾ at the ends. Perches: not plated; front bed arched 1 inch; back, 1⅜.

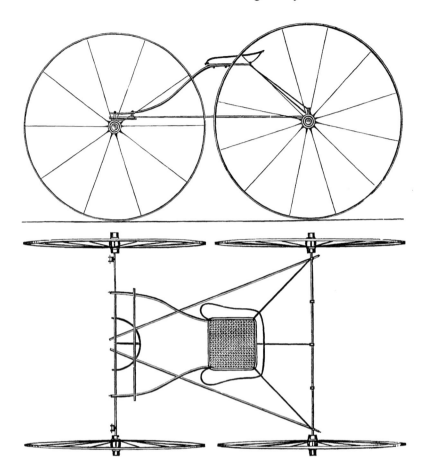

**SKELETON WAGON, WITH SIDE AND TOP VIEWS.**

Built by E. W. Smith, New York, New York.

*Hub* May 1872 page 38.

We are indebted to Mr. E. W. Smith, successor to S. E. Bates, Broadway and Forty-seventh street, for these drawings of a skeleton wagon of his make. Its construction is different from other patterns, inasmuch as it requires only three iron stays to the seat, instead of seven, as usual. Mr. Smith has not patented his device, and it is open to the trade.

Our top view shows the two perches and the hickory risers in front of seat; also the three iron stays from the latter to hind axle-bed. The fifth-wheel has thirteen inches diameter, and consists of a single plate only, with supports on the axle-bed.

The weight of skeleton wagons is from seventy-five to eighty pounds.

Dimensions: Wheels, 3 ft. 11 x 4 ft. 1 in. Track, 4 ft. Axles, 5/8 for shafts only, and ¾ for pole and shafts. Hubs, 3¼ x 6 in. Spokes, ⅞ in. Rims, ¾ x ⅛ in. steel.

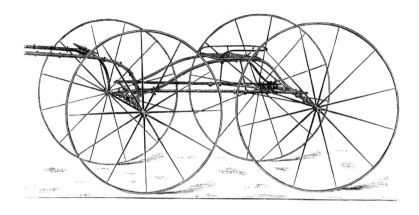

**Plate No. 40. JONES'S FIFTY-NINE-POUND SKELETON-WAGON.**

Exhibited by Phineas Jones & Co., Newark, New Jersey.

*Hub* July 1876, page 124 also *Carriage Monthly* July 1876 pages 83 & 85.

Phineas Jones & Co., of Newark, New Jersey, are not carriage-builders, but their business in wheels and wheel stock has long been identified with the carriage trade in this country, and at the Centennial they take a seat on the same bench with the carriage-builders, by exhibiting a Skeleton-wagon and Sulky, which show very creditably their make of wheels, and several new specialties which they are introducing to the market.

The chief novelty of the Skeleton-wagon, herewith illustrated, consists in combining with the reach two bent hickory supports to the seat, which are so formed as to produce a brace in two ways, or both laterally and vertically; and, by this construction, dispensing with the numerous iron braces ordinarily used, and also with the reaches, as the side-bars themselves form the reaches. The side-bars and bent supports to the seat are rigidly connected at the ends, and form a truss work for the support of the seat. The advantages claimed for the above-named construction over that of the ordinary sulky, are less weight (by about 10 lbs.), less expense, greater simplicity and grace, and greater strength.

Weight of the Skeleton--wagon exhibited: weight of all the wood-work, excepting the wheels, but including the seat, 9¾ lbs.; total weight of job, 59 lbs. Finished in the white, with a single coat of varnish.

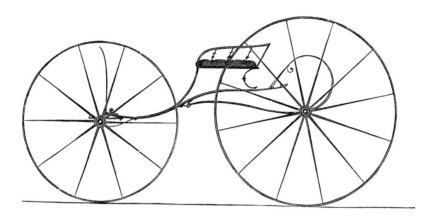

**Plate No. 6. NEW-HAVEN C-SPRING BUGGY.**
Drawn by C. A. Lines, with B. Manville & Co., New Haven, Connecticut.
*Hub* April 1877.

Our illustration has been reproduced fac-simile from a pen-and-ink drawing, in half-inch scale, sent us by Mr. Charles A. Lines, with B. Manville & Co., of New-Haven, Ct., who has also kindly furnished the following description of its construction and proportions. It is drawn in half-inch scale. You will see in the drawing the manner in which the two bars are joined together. The seat rests on iron risers, the front riser following the sweep of the bar: Height of wheels, back, 48 inches; front, 44 inches. Distance from center to center of wheels, 55 inches. Distance from ground to bottom, 24 inches. Leg-room, 26 inches. Seat from ground, 42 inches. Dasher, 16 inches. Seat to side-bar, 6 inches. Distance between bar and back end perch, 10 inches. The C-spring is open 12 inches. An elliptic spring can be used in place of the C-spring on this wagon, if preferred. Felloes, ¾ inch. Hubs, 2½ inches. Axletree, steel, 1 inch square. Seat-room, 16 inches. Loop-irons, connecting with front and back spring, ⅛ inch, full width of side-bar; bar rounded on top, tapering at each end, being stronger at the point where the coupling is fastened. Seat-risers, front, ³⁄₁₆; ¾ wide; back, ⅜ round. The double curve bar is of hickory, and the two sides are connected by a small iron bar near the joint where the C-spring is attached to the bar. The perch is of iron or steel; width, 1 inch, and rounded on top, and ½ inch thick, tapering forward to connect with the coupling. The C -spring is bolted on to this perch. The front spring is half elliptic, the bar being secured the same as in all skeleton-wagons. The front riser to the seat is designed to follow the curve of the bar, and is bolted through to secure both the riser and the bar on the under side of the wooden bar. The back riser may be made to suit the taste. It is drawn with a curve. Width of seat, 3 feet. Track, 5 feet.

Trimming.--Patent-leather dasher and seat-fall; cushions, black enameled leather. Shafts, trimmed.

Painting.—Light canary yellow fine-lined with black. Hub-bands, black.

### SIDE-BAR TROTTING WAGON.
*Carriage Monthly* August 1877, page 82.

This fashion plate presents a drawing of a light, tasty, easy-riding vehicle for fast driving over country roads, much superior to the "Buck-board," and not much heavier, but, perhaps, a trifle advance in cost.

The body-sills should be of superior second-growth ash or white oak, ⅞ by 2 inches. The dash-foot should form the angle shown in the drawing, to which the foot-rail should be welded. This lower opening may be covered with poor grade of patent leather, or with harness leather.

The seat is stayed with iron braces, fastening on the sills. Seat-rail is of iron.

Dimensions.–Width of body: 24 inches; seat-frame: 27 inches; wheels: 3 feet 8 inches and 4 feet; hubs: 3 by 6 inches; spokes: ⅞ inch; tire: ¾ inch wide; springs: half elliptic; axles: ¾ inch steel; carriage part: best Eastern hickory or lance-wood; track: 4 feet.

Painting.–Pure medium green; irons black, striped with fine line of dark French carmine.

Trimming.–Cushion leather.

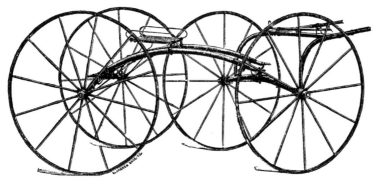

SKELETON WAGON built by S. Toomey & Co., Canal Dover, Ohio.
From Life with the Trotters by John Splan 1889.

COLT BREAKER.–Built by Biddle, Smart & Co.
*Hub* March 1894 page 968.

LADY EMMA, GEORGE WILKES, and GENERAL BUTLER: Trotting for a Purse of $1000 Mile Heats, Best 3 In 5. Published by Currier & Ives, 1865. From the Print Collection of the Library of Congress.

The Celebrated Trotting Stallion ETHAN ALLEN In Double Harness, With Running Mate: Driven by Dan Mace, Trotting Against Dexter to Sulky On the Fashion Course, Long Island, June 21st 1867, Winning In Three Straight Heats In the Unparalled Time of 2:15 2:16 2:19. Published by Currier & Ives, 1872. From the Print Collection of the Library of Congress LC-USZC2-2059 (color film copy slide).

Plate 9

The Trotting Gelding BILLY D. With Running Mate: Owned by J. B. Barnaby, Driven By John Murphy. Artist J. McAuliffe, published by Currier & Ives, 1881. From the Print Collection of the Library of Congress LC-USZC2-3478.

The Trotting Gelding FRANK With J. O. NAY, His Running Mate: As They Appeared at Prospect Park Long Island, Nov. 15th, 1883, Driven by John Murphy. Published by Currier & Ives, 1884. From the Print Collection of the Library of Congress LC-USZC2-3479.

Plate 10

Famous American Trotting-Horse, TACONEY.
*Ballou's Pictorial Drawing-Room Companion* April 10, 1858 page 236.

Trotting On the Milldam, Boston.
*Ballou's Pictorial Drawing-Room Companion* February 12, 1859, page 105.

Scene In the Trotting Park, South End, Boston.
*Ballou's Pictorial Drawing-Room Companion* August 13, 1859, page 112.

George M. Patchen, the "Champion Trotting Stallion."
From *Lawrence, Bradley & Pardee* catalog of 1862.

# ROAD RIDERS

# AND

# SPEED WAGONS.

# Road Riders

## "ROAD RIDERS."

Road Riding became a fashionable sport and a favorite recreational sport of many with the major cities accommodating these Road Riders with special speed-ways for the driving of fast trotters. Harness racing had started by owners of fast trotters racing on the public highways, and then when it became an organized sport professional reins-men were employed to drive in the races. Peter Welsh in his book gives credit to Robert Bonner as one of the leading men who made Road Riding a popular pastime when in May 1862 Bonner driving Lady Palmer and Flatbush Mare to a fast wagon made the mile in 2:12 and later driving his matched pair to two miles in 5:01 1/4. Robert Bonner first started the Road-riding movement in 1856, and throughout his life he became the the owner of many fine fast trotters, condemning the practice of betting as an evil he, devoted his life to improving the harness horse, enjoying the pleasures of the road, and protesting the over-commercialization of this American pastime.[1]

Prominent among the early riders were Commodore Vanderbilt, Robert Bonner, Frank Work, William H. Vanderbilt, Shepherd F. Knapp, George B. Alley, Charles H. Kerner, and William Turnbull. Commodore Vanderbilt's pair were Post Boy and Plow Boy, and the spirit of rivalry between Bonner and Vanderbilt grew more intense with the years, and their respective friends caught the fever. Later John D. Rockefeller, William Rockefeller, Frank Work, William H. Vanderbilt, T. C. Eastman, and C. J. Hamlin were carried forward by the torrent, and the road-riding movement was at its zenith.[2]

## THE GREATER BOSTON SPEEDWAY.
### *Harper's Weekly* March 19, 1898, page 285.

The (Boston) Metropolitan Park Commission in including in its scheme of park improvement for Greater Boston remarkably complete provisions for speeding purposes. An important feature of this metropolitan scheme is the reclamation of the scenery of the Charles River by converting its waters and shores into a continuous chain of pleasure-grounds. The banks of the stream at one point offered an ideal site for a speedway. A plan for the work was prepared by the landscape architects, Messrs. F. L. and J. C. Olmsted, and its execution is now in hand. The scheme is admirably complete in meeting all the requirements of the case, with provisions for public enjoyment of the spectacle as well as for the convenience and safety of the participators.

The plan comprises two speedways, in fact--one for horses and the other for bicycles. The location is central, being in the Brighton district of Boston, just across the river from Cambridge, and easily accessible by parkways or other good roads from all parts of Greater Boston. The famous Longfellow Meadow, celebrated in the poet's verse, and the chief feature in the landscape from the historic Longfellow homestead, is traversed by the speed way and its approaches. Being but a short walk from Harvard, it will be a favorite resort for the university students, with whom the bicycle-track will be especially popular. The speedway, indeed, is a great extension of an already important athletic centre. The Harvard athletic ground, Soldiers' Field, presented to the university by Mr. Henry L. Higginson, adjoins it, as does the North Brighton Play-Ground, and the Harvard boat-house is across the river, close to the Boylston Street bridge. From the North Brighton Play-Ground a subway passing beneath the speedway connects with a great ball-field on the bank of the river.

---

1. Welsh, Peter C. *Track and Road: The American Trotting Horse*...Washington, DC : Smithsonian Institution Press, p. 106.

2. Busbey, Hamilton. *Trotting and the Pacing Horse In America*. New York, NY : Macmillan Company, 1904, pp. 296-300.

# Road Riders

The speedway is approached and bordered by a parkway drive. This road, where it parallels the speedway; is sixty feet wide, to allow space for the return of the speeders from the finish to the start, speeding being permissible only in one direction. A row of trees in a ribbon of turf separates the drive from the speedway, which is fifty feet wide. Instead of being crowned, the speedway slopes slightly from one side to the other, counteracting the effect of the long, easy curve. The course is a mile from start to finish. At the end of the mile is a concourse, and the speedway track continues in-a long "run over," so as to slow the horses before turning into the driveway.

Next to the horse-speedway is it's double bicycle-track. The two tracks, each twenty feet wide, are separated by at hedge occupying space five feet wide. Like the horse-speedway, these tracks are also sloped slightly from the outer side of the curve to the inner. This gives a mile on a long, easy curve, practically a "straightaway." At the end of the mile, however, the bicycles, instead of swinging into the return drive, like the horses, keep on, the track making a gradual loop and returning upon itself. This gives a continuous course of two and a quarter miles, with "corners" at the loop similar to those of a one-third mile track. To avoid interference with those on the track the start is placed on a siding, and subways give access to the space within the track. A lavatory is located within convenient access of the start, and will be appreciated by users of the track.

The edge of the river is followed by a broad promenade. Rows of trees separate the bicycle-track from the horse-speedway and from the adjacent walk. All these ways with the exception of a portion of the boundary road that will be faced by houses, have a grade just above the marsh-level, and are protected front high tides in the river by a temporary dike along the line of the promenade. With the enactment of expected national and State legislation, a dam lower down stream will keep out the salt water, and enhance the beauty of the river by maintaining an even level of fresh water. Neither the horse-speedway nor the bicycle-course will take the place of the ordinary racing-track, since all parts of the course will not be visible from any one point. But a free and public place for these popular sports will be an important feature in the scheme of out-door recreation furnished by the extensive and varied pleasure-grounds of the New England metropolis.

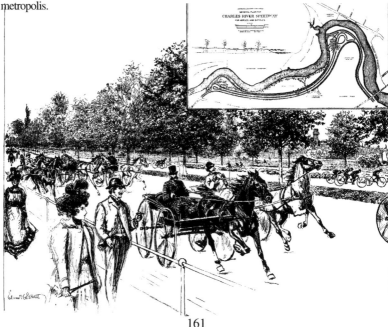

# Road Riders

## FIRST SPEEDWAY PARADE.

*Hub* June 1900, 124.

The first speedway parade held on May 5, 1900 by the Road Drivers' Association of New York City was six miles of roadsters. This first parade in which 800 horses participated was accredited with having given the lovers of the horse a rare treat, as never before was there such a gathering of speedy horses in light harness and before light wagons. The projectors of the movement had anticipated a goodly number, and when they issued their official catalogue the numbers ran almost up to 600, but on the day of the parade fully 200 more were in line. When we take into consideration the fact that this parade was for roadsters, and that more than 350 had records of less than three minutes, while there were hundreds without records that none but those having the lowest would care to contest, we can form some idea of the feeling to this city regarding the light roadster. Those who feared that the day of the American trotting horse had passed must have rejoiced at the sight of so many hundreds of fleet beautiful animals, while the builder of light carriages could go to his home after the parade satisfied that the light carriage, the typical American vehicle, that has no counterpart elsewhere, would retain its place, and the demand for it would increase for years to come, no matter how great the call for the motor vehicle.

The revival of this great sport in New York is due to the building of the speedway, as a road set aside where gentlemen can speed their horses without interference from heavy vehicles of any kind, whether motor or horse drawn, and where the ever-in-the-way bicycle cannot enter. The demands of the times call for street cars, and in every city the residence avenues and streets, as well as those devoted to business, are given over to railway companies, and pleasure driving on them is no longer possible. The park drives and a few boulevards offer opportunities for heavy pleasure vehicles, where horses are driven at moderate gaits, but where speeding is impossible. This condition of things did much to discourage fast driving, but lovers of the roadsters in New York succeeded in getting a speedway built for their use, and immediately the demand was revived for fast roadsters, light vehicles, and harness. How great this demand has become can be judged from the success of the first road drivers' parade.

The original plan contemplated the forming of the parade at the north end of Central Park, but as the entries increased this was abandoned, and it was decided to start at Seventy-second street and Riverside Drive, the different divisions to form in the side streets. For an hour before the start there moved on the upper West Side streets a panorama of fleet horses, one man road wagons, standard style, bike wagons of the new school, side bar buggies, carrying two persons, and other light vehicles running on their solid rubber or pneumatic tires as noiselessly as the summer wind. The air was cool and bracing, and the spirited animals seemed to enjoy the sport as well as the drivers and sightseers. Owing to the American disposition to be in the lead there was some confusion as to position at the start, but long before entering the speedway all were in line, and jogging along at a slow trot, showing the beautiful forms of the horses and the perfection of the light road rig. He would be a stoic indeed who could not see beauty at every step of the six mile procession, or, would wish that so marked a feature of American out-of-door life be done away with, nor will it be, so long as man's, admiration of man's best friend continues.

Those who give preference to the mechanical motor will have ample opportunities to indulge in speeding the automobile, without clashing in the least with the horseman's favorite. Both sports may be enjoyed, and as the foolish antagonism is removed the possibilities of rational sport will be increased.

It is seldom that a parade brings out such an army of sightseers. As it was, the sidewalks and points for observation along the entire line of parade, from Seventy-second street to the north end of the speedway, a distance of about seven miles, were thronged with spectators, the parade itself being nearly six miles long. It is true that all of the horses in the parade were not

The King of the Road: DEXTER Driven by His Owner Mr. Robert Bonner of the New York Ledger at Prospect Park Brooklyn August 31st 1869, Trotting a Mile to Road Wagon, Weighing With Driver 319 lbs. In the Unprecedented time of 2 Minutes 21 3/4 Seconds. Published by Currier & Ives, 1866. From the Print Collection of Library of Congress LC-USZC2-3427 (color film copy slide).

The Celebrated Trotting Team EDWARD and SWIVELLER, owned by Frank Work Esq., New York: Winning Their Match for $1,000, Against Time 2:20 to Wagon, driven by John Murphy. At the Gentlemen's Driving Park, Morrisania, New York, July 8th, 1882. Published by Currier & Ives, 1882. From the Print Collection of the Library of Congress LC-USZC2-3342 (color film copy slide).

Plate 11

Mr. William H. Vanderbilt's Celebrated Team SMALL HOPES and LADY MAC:
Driven By Their Owner to Road Wagon, Time 2:23. Published by Currier & Ives, 1878. From
the Print Collection of the Library of Congress LC-USZC2-3443 (color film copy slide).

The Celebrated Trotting Mares MAUD S. and ALDINE, As They Appeared June
15th 1883: At the Gentlemen's Driving Park, Morrisania, New York Driven by Their Owner,
William H. Vanderbilt, Esq. Published by Currier & Ives, 1883. From the Print Collection of
the Library of Congress LC-USZC2-3340 (color film copy slide).

Plate 12

owned by New Yorkers, but the fact that Philadelphia, Buffalo, Hartford and other cities each contributed speedy roadsters shows how far reaching the feeling is in favor of the trotter, and emphasizes the statement that the roadster never before stood so high in the estimation of gentlemen drivers, and that there are scores of cities where speedways could be built, to the advantage of the horse raiser and trainer, the carriage builder, the harness maker and the gentleman driver.

Dr. H. H. Kane, the president, and the other officers, as well as the members of the Road Drivers' Association, are to be congratulated on the success of the first annual parade. It will be useless to attempt to enumerate the horses, but we can say without fear of contradiction that never before was there such a collection of equine beauties, such an array of light, graceful vehicles and thread-like harness, or such crowds of interested spectators to view and applaud the American gentleman's most delightful and exhilarating pastime. Thanks to the projectors of the speedway, and to the men who as an association gave the opportunity to show to the world that the horse and light carriage hold a place from which they cannot be driven by mechanical appliances, no matter how perfect or beautiful the automobile may become, and that there is room for all, and the Hub hopes to be able to report more speedways, more horse shows, more automobiles, as all tend to make life more and more beautiful, and to contribute to the health, wealth and prosperity of our people.

Plate No. LV. SPEED WAGON.
*Hub* July 1900.

On the Road.
*Harper's Weekly.* July 10, 1858, page 440.

"The Best Time On Record."–Mr. Bonner's Celebrated Team, LADY PALMER and
FLATBUSH MAID.
*Frank Leslie's Illustrated Newspaper* July 5, 1862, page 213.

New York City.–Mr. W. H. Vanderbilt Speeding His Fast Team, "SMALL HOPES" and "LADY MAC," on the Fleetwood Track.
*Frank Leslie's Illustrated Newspaper*, December 1, 1877, page 213, and
*Frank Leslie's Popular Monthly,* November 1885, page 540.

Rival Teams–Mr. Work's "DICK SWIVELLER" and "EDWARD," and Mr. Vanderbilt's "EARLY ROSE" and "ALDINE." Drawn by P. Frenzeny.
*Harper's Weekly* October 14, 1882, page 644.

John H. Shults's Pair of Pacers--GOLD LEAF, Record 2.11¾, and ARROW, Record 2.13¼ .
*Harper's Weekly* (Supplement) May 30, 1891 page 394, and May 23, 1891.

ARAB, Record 2.15, and MILL BOY, Record 2.26, Owned by John Shepard, Boston.
*Harper's Weekly* (Supplement) May 30, 1891 page 393, and May 23, 1891.

JACK, Record 2.12¼ , and PILOT H., Record 2.29½.
*Harper's Weekly* (Supplement) May 30, 1891 page 394, and May 23, 1891.

John D. Rockefeller's Pair--MIDNIGHT, Record 2.18¼ , and FLASH, Record 2.19½
*Harper's Weekly* (Supplement) May 30, 1891 page 393, and May 23, 1891.

# SPEEDING WAGONS or ROAD WAGONS.

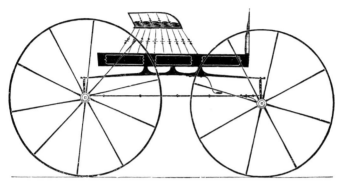

Plate 24. **TROTTING BUGGY.**
*New York Coach-maker's Magazine* December 1858 page 130.

Trotting Buggy made by E. Chamberlin, Troy, New York. It is made as light as 160 lbs.--from 160 to 210 lbs. The outside spindles are made of three-eighths iron, with a collar in the centre to represent a spindle, and the foot of the rod sets on the sill of the body, the same as the brace from the seat of a skelton wagon. The sides of the box do not connect at all with the iron legs, so that there is no strain from the seat upon the body at all. The ironlegs can be plated or japanned. The wood-spindles are place in the top of the box, and run up into the edge of the seat panel, outside of the iron legs that run across the bottom of the seat-frame.

Plate III. **ROAD WAGON.**
*New York Coach-maker's Magazine* June 1860 page 9.

Road Wagon as made in Boston, Massachusetts. The front of the body is dropped a little, in order to give all the room possible for the legs consistent with a narrow panel. The sweep of the seat-rail is somewhat antiquated, but is well adapted to this kind of body when lightness of appearance is studied.

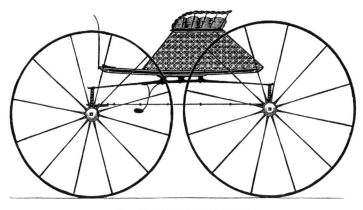

Plate III. **TROTTING BUGGY.**

*New York Coach-maker's Magazine* June 1860 page 9 & February 1859 page 172.

This buggy, when finely got up, makes one of the neatest kind of pleasure-wagons ever constructed. The boot of this example is cane-work, and in connection with a varnished wood body, makes a tasty job.

The seat rail maybe finished in a special way by first having the seat rail rounded and smoothed by the wood-workman, before it is put on the seat. When it reaches the trimmer's shop, where it is laced unpainted, the trimmer winds a cord, about one-fourth of an inch large, around the rail, say, so as to have about three-fourths of an inch space between the cord, all around the seat. This done, he next takes a strip of patent leather, a trifle wider than is necessary to go around the rail (as there must be a little allowance for shrinkage), and having supplied the flesh side of the leather with paste, draws it moistened around the rail, and "whips" it on the under side, far enough on the inside to avoid the seam being seen when the seat is hung up. The next operation, after "whipping," is to wind a cord around the leather in such a manner as to have this cord bind the leather to the rail close to the cord put on at first, at both edges, where it should be permitted to remain until the pasted leather gets perfectly dry. Afterwards, this last cord is to be taken off, when the rail will present the appearance we have endeavored to show in our illustration. .

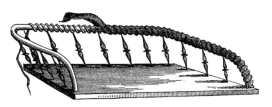

Plate XXXIX. **CLIPPER BUGGY.**
*New York Coach-maker's Magazine* April 1861 page 211.
Clipper Buggy as made by Brewster & Co., New York, New York. Draft by I. W. Britton.

Plate 32. **HALF-SPRING NO-TOP TROTTING WAGON.**
*Hub and New York Coachmaker's Magazine* July 1871 page 62.

The pillar on seat is quite novel; only the molding the expressed in white, and to set the pillar before it deeper, say ¾ inch. The one molding which we carry around the body relieves and lightens it. Dimensions: Width of body 24 inches; Hubs, 5 ⅞ x 3 inches; Spokes, ¾ inch; Springs, 2 plates, 1¼ inch; Wheels, 3 feet 10 inches and 4 feet 2 inches.

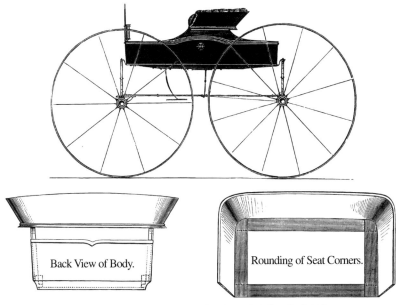

Back View of Body.

Rounding of Seat Corners.

Plate 92. **NEW YORK PIANO BOX NO-TOP WAGON.**
*Hub* March 1874 page 382.

    The body is slightly curved top line for the box. After the panels are on, the design is produced by very thin moldings of a half-oval or half-diamond shape. Care should be taken that the curvature is not too high. From 1½ to 1¾ inches is about right. The principal dimensions are: Wheels, 3 feet 10 inches and 4 feet 1 inch; Spokes, 1³⁄₁₆ inch; Hubs, 3¼ x 6 inches; Axles, ¾ inches.

    **SPEEDING-WAGON** by J. L. H. Mosier (Foreman at Brewster & Co.)
*Hub* April 1879, page 9.

    A vehicle calculated for fast driving--not racing-should be so constructed as to avoid all lateral and swaying motion, and this can not be accomplished by using full elliptics, for these, if set transversely to the body, or parallel with the axles, would, in speeding, produce not only a vertical, but a lateral motion, as indicated by Fig. K, in which 25 shows the spring, and dotted lines 26, 26 the direction of the motion imparted. We would also have the side motion indicated by Fig. L; 27 section of body, and the dotted lines 28, 28 the motion imparted. These two motions, combining, would retard speed to a marked degree. To overcome these retarding motions, without altogether giving up the quality of elasticity, we generally apply, in place of elliptics, two flat half-elliptic springs, placed in the same way, and connect these two half-springs by elastic wooden side-bars, on which we suspend the body. There are other patented combinations, in which steel side-springs are used in place of one in combination with the wooden bars, and which are preferred by some. The Dexter spring is an example of this kind.

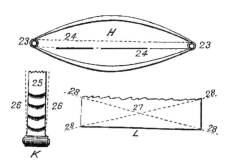

### PNEUMATIC TIRED BUGGY.

*Hub* April 1895 page 69.

It is asserted that the draught of a vehicle is reduced from thirty to fifty per cent by the use of ball-bearing axles. It is readily seen from this how much is added to the speed and running quality of a carriage, not to mention the great relief afforded the horse, which is a matter worthy of consideration by every humane driver.

Any rider will appreciate the luxury of riding in a vehicle fitted with elastic tires. The solid rubber tire has been used for a number of years to a limited extent, confined almost exclusively to heavy vehicles, cabs, coupes, broughams, etc. The chief advantage of a solid rubber tire is that it renders the vehicle less noisy. It does not add to the ease and comfort of riding to the same extent as the pneumatic or cushion tire. The drawback to the pneumatic tire is its liability to puncture, and this objection is, of course, a serious one on ordinary country roads. For smooth pavements, especially asphalt, this style of tire is unequaled. But by far the most practicable tire for road use is the cushion, which embodies the durability of the solid tire with much of the resiliency of the pneumatic. A vehicle fitted with ball-bearing axles and cushion tires is as much superior to the ordinary carriage as the latter is to the lumber wagon. The increased comfort to the rider is not the only benefit resulting from this combination, but the life of the vehicle is prolonged by, relieving it of the strain that accompanies the use of a rigid steel tire.

The Michigan Wheel Company, of Lansing, Michigan, confine themselves exclusively to the manufacture of ball-bearing rubber tired carriage wheels. They furnish all kinds of vehicle wheels, fitted with either cushion or pneumatic tires, and with or without ball-bearing axles. Their wheels have been thoroughly tested during the past two years and have given the best of satisfaction wherever used. If you wish to thoroughly enjoy driving, send your wheels to them and have them fitted with ball-bearing axles and cushion tires. You will find that you are more than repaid for the extra cost in the comfort and pleasure of riding, and in the prolonged usefulness of your horse and vehicle. These rubber tires will last two years, and in the end it is a matter of economy to have a good vehicle fitted with rubber tires. The Michigan Wheel Company, of Lansing, Michigan. will furnish any additional information desired, together with catalogue and price list.

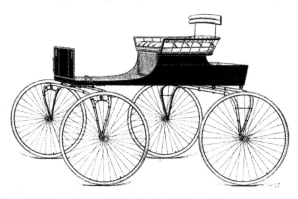

**SPEEDING WAGON, WITH CUT DOWN FRONT.**

*Hub* July 1900, page 150.

Plate No. 473. Illustrates one of the lightest styles of speeding wagons. The body is attached to the gear without springs or side bars. Stirrups are placed outside of the body at the front, for the driver's feet to rest in.

Dimensions of Woodwork.–Body. Length, 54 inches; width across top, outside, 16 ½ inches; across bottom, 16 inches. Width of seat across top, 21 inches; across bottom, 18 inches. Wheels, wire. Height, front, 28 inches; rear, 28 inches. Tires, 1 ½ inches pneumatic. Track, 3 feet 10 inches. Distance between center of axles, 43 inches.

Painting.–Body, black, without striping. Gear, coach red. Steps, etc., black. Trimming, cushion and back rest, gray whipcord.

**SPEEDING WAGON, WITH SKELETON SEAT RISER.**

*Hub* July 1900, page 150.

Plate No. 474 illustrates a wagon with low side panels and a cut-down front, the seat being set upon a wood riser in front and iron legs at the back. The seat is a bent rail spindle.

Dimensions of Woodwork.–Body, length, 53 inches; width across outside, 15 inches. Width of seat across top, 20 inches; across bottom, 17 inches. Wheels, wood hub. Height, front, 28 inches; rear, 30 inches. Hubs, length, 5 inches; diameter at center, 2 ½ inches; front end, 1¾ inches; back end, 2¼ inches. Size of spokes, ¾ inches. Number of spokes, 12 and 12. Stagger, ¾ inches. Depth of bands, front, 1 ½ inches; back, ⅝ inches. Distance between center of axles, 47 inches. Tires, 1½ inches, pneumatic. Track, 3 feet 10 inches outside.

Painting.–Body, dark green. Gear, orange, striped black. Trimming, maroon cloth.

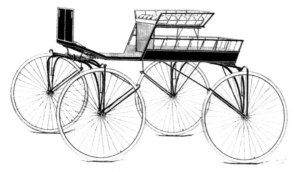

**SPEEDING WAGON, WITH SPINDLE BODY AND SEAT.**

*Hub* July 1900, page 150.

Plate No. 475 illustrates a sppeding wagon with the body made up with a row of spindles all around back of the front seat post, the seat being made up in the same style. The seat riser panel is done away with, and the seat is supported by the two posts and iron legs.

Dimensions of Woodwork.–Body, length, 54 inches; width across top, outside, 15 inches; across bottom, 14 inches. Width of seat across top, 19 inches; across bottom, 16 inches. Wheels, wire. Height, front and rear 28 inches. Tires, 1½ inches, pneumatic. Track, 3 feet 8 inches, outside. Distance between center of axles, 45 inches.

Painting.–Body, black, fine lined with red. Gear, carmine and black. Trimming, whipcord.

**SPEEDING WAGON WITH CORNING BODY AND SKELETON RISER.**

*Hub* July 1900, page 150.

Plate No. 476 illustrates a speeding wagon with body after the "Corning" form, but without seat riser panels. The body is hung upon side bars and cross springs. The seat is made up like a coach seat, only that the rail is much lighter.

Dimensions of Woodwork.–Body, length, 55 inches; width across outside, 16 inches; width of seat outside, 18 inches. Wheels, wood hub. Height, front 28 inches; rear 30 inches. Hubs, length, 5 inches; diameter at center, 2½ inches; front end 1¾ inches; back end, 2 ¼ inches. Size of spokes, ¾ inches. Number of spokes, 12 and 12. Stagger, ¾ inches. Distance between center of axles, 54 inches. Tire, 1 ½ inches, pneumatic. Track, out-side 3 feet 10 inches.

Dimensions of Ironwork.–Springs, 18 inches long between centers of heads, with 2 ½ inches opening on main leaf. Width of steel 1¼ inches. Number of plates, 4. Thickness, No. 5 steel.

Painting.–Body, dark lake. Gear, coach red and black. Trimming, maroon cloth.

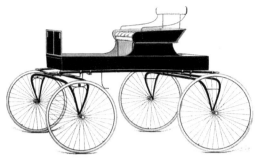

## SPEEDING WAGON, WITH LOW SIDE PIANO BOX BODY.
### *Hub* July 1900, page 150.

Plate No. 477 illustrates a speeding wagon with low side piano box body, suspended on side bars and cross springs, the seat being a solid panel the same as te regulation road wagon. The gear has wire wheels, with pneumatic tires.

Dimensions of Woodwork.–Body, length, 54 inches; width across top, 14 ½ inches; across bottom, 14 inches. Width of seat across top, 20 inches; across bottom, 16 inches. Wheels, wire, height, front, 26 inches; rear, 28 inches. Distance between center of axles, 49 inches. Tires, 1 ½ inches, pneumatic. Track, outside, 3 feet 8 inches.

Dimensions of Ironwork.–Springs, 17 inches long between centers of heads, with 2 inches opening on main leaf. Width of steel, 1¼ inches. Number of plates, 3. Thickness, No. 5 steel.

Painting.–Body, black, no striping. Gear, carmine and black. Trimming, whipcord.

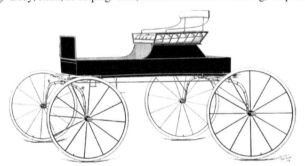

## SPEEDING WAGON, WITH PIANO BODY AND STICK SEAT.
### *Hub* July 1900, page 150.

Plate No. 478 illustrates a speeding wagon with low side piano body and plain spindle seat, suspended on a skeleton gear and wood wheels.

Dimensions of Woodwork.–Body. Length, 52 inches; width across top, 18½ inches; across bottom, 18 inches. Width of seat across top, 22 inches; across bottom, 19 inches. Wheels, wood hub. Height, front, 28 inches; rear, 30 inches. Hubs, length, 5 inches; diameter at center, 2 ½ inches; front end, 1¾ inches; back end, 2¼ inches. Size of spokes, ¾ inches. Number of spokes, 12 and 12. Stagger, ¾ inches. Depth of bands, front, 1½ inches; back, ⅝ inches. Distance between center of axles, 55 inches. Tire, 1 ½ inches, pneumatic. Track, 4 feet outside.

Dimensions of Ironwork.–Springs, 20 inches long between centers of heads, with 2 ½ inches opening on main leaf. Width of steel, 1¼ inches. Number of plates, 4. Thickness, No. 5 steel.

Painting.–Body, dark green. Gear, green and black. Trimming, green cloth.

### THE SPEED WAGON.

*Hub* August 1900, page 204.

Within five years there will hardly be a large city that will not have its "speedway," and the popularity of the speedy roadster will be greater than ever before. Just how many styles of speeding wagons there are in the market we cannot say, but twenty-five would be a low estimate for this year, if we consider the different gears and the styles of bodies. That this number will be increased next year none can doubt, and it is advisable for all who contemplate the building of these vehicles to study well their wants, and if the desired conditions cannot be obtained otherwise we advise the purchase of some one of the patented gears that have proved satisfactory, in preference to wasting time and money in efforts to get out one of these without a full knowledge of the real peculiarities. The conditions required are light weight, great stability and perfect set and balance of axles. Some of the patented vehicles meet these requirements while others are faulty, notably when pneumatic wire wheels are used. One noticeable fault is the jumping motion of the front wheels, while the rear wheels run perfectly steady. That this is due to faulty construction is proven by the fact that there are others of like weight that run perfectly steady.

The lightest vehicles are without springs. In some they weigh but sixty- five pounds, while there are few that go above seventy-five pounds. To accomplish these results the bodies are lightened as much as possible. The width of the bodies ranges from 14 to 18 inches on the bottom. They are 4 feet 3 inches to 4 feet 7 inches long, with the seat set back so as to allow for 28 inches room from the front of the seat bottom to the toe bar. This throws the seat back farther than common, but is necessary, as the seats are set low, in no case-exceeding 12 inches from the top of the seat bottom to the bottom board of the body. The body panels are cut low. Where the panels are of uniform depth they are cut as low as 5 inches and seldom deeper than 6½ inches. The cut down fronts will be as low as 2 inches, and the panel back of that 5 to 6 inches deep. The bracket front, after the style of the "coal box" of years past, is about ½ inches deep, and the main panel 4 ½ to 5 inches deep. To further lighten the bodies the back ends of some are cut down to 2 inches at the back corner.

Great care is necessary in the construction of the bodies; those that are hung without springs require substantial sills, as the suspension is at the ends and there is no central support of any kind. Then, too, the bottom board forward of the seat must be full ½ inch thick, and well secured, as there are times when the driver is compelled to throw extra weight upon the bottom. From a point 6 inches back of the front edge of the seat frame the bottom boards need not be more than ¼ of an inch thick. Stay the seats well by braces from the sills, so placed that they will act as side, rear and front stays.

A body built for cross springs does not require as heavy sills as one hung on the ends, as the cross bars for the springs are set several inches from the end of the body, and there is less pressure between the supports, but even these must be sufficiently strong to withstand the strain, as it falls mainly upon them. The low, thin side panels add but little to the strength.

As will be noticed by examining those published last month, there is a marked difference in the wheels; in some cases the wire wheels of uniform height are used, in others they are of wood of uniform height. In others we have those of different sizes, the front wheels being two inches lower than the back, this difference being observed in both the front and rear wheels. The fact of these existing, differences proves conclusively that builders have not yet settled on any one style or hang of body or gear. Those who have given special attention do not agree, and scarcely any two follow the same rules.

The one danger that is most to be feared is in the direction of extreme lightness. This is twofold in its results: First, it endangers life, and secondly, it interferes with the steady movement so necessary to the speed of the horse. Naturally, where such great reduction is made in weight the best materials must be used, and the best mechanical speed employed in the construction. Fortunately we have the desired material, and in time we will learn which is best, the use of metal only for the gears, or the combination of wood and metal. In the meantime the *Hub* will watch the development of these light vehicles, and keep its readers informed as to the situation.

Plate No. 560. **SPEEDING WAGON.**
*Hub* June 1902 page 91.

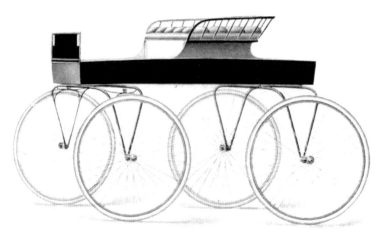

**MULHOLLAND RACING WAGON.**
*Hub* December 1905, page 331.

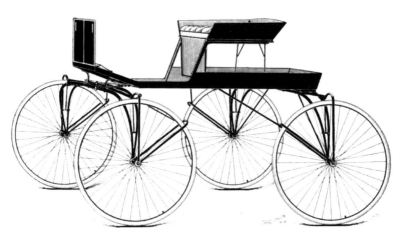

Plate No. 657. **SPEEDING WAGON.**
*Hub* May 1907, page 52.

# AMATEUR DRIVING CLUBS.

### NEW YORK DRIVING CLUB.
*Hub* May 1886 page 114.

Six years ago [1880], when the value of fast roadsters owned in New York City amounted to millions of dollars, David Bonner, Shepherd F. Knapp, Alexander Taylor, Jr., Jason Miller, N. L. Hunting, and Mr. T. C. Eastman (the first President), discussed the formation of a club of gentlemen interested in driving and in the development of the trotting horse. The idea spread rapidly, and resulted in the organization of the Gentlemen's Driving Association of New-York, now named the New York Driving Club. Within a very short time the list of members numbered more than five hundred, including Robert Bonner and his three sons, Capt. Jacob H. Vanderbilt, W. H. Vanderbilt, Frederick Vanderbilt, David Bonner, Joseph Harper, George B. Alley, Frank Work, H. W. T. Mail, Louis L. Lorillard, A. Newbold Morris, W. H. Fearing, S. W. Cadwell, Hermand and George G. Clausen, Isidor Cohnfeld, Peter Doelger, J. H. DeMott, Alfred de Cordova, C. F. Woersihoffer, Nathan Strauss, Leland and Charles Stanford, W. W. Webb, W. H. Young, William Turnbull, Starin Myndert, J. T. Souter, George J. Gould, Hugh J. Grant, W. H. Gunther, J. G. Coster, A. Wright Sanford, William Rockefeller, Henry and Simon Selligman, A. S. Peabody, Jordon L. Mott, J. R. Keene, Edward Kearney, W. H. Hollister, I. L. Humphreeville, M. B. Brown, J. L. and J. H. Barclay, J. E. Alexandre, Lawrence Kip, W. C. Floyd Jones, Peter Moller, G. P. Morosini, F. C. Moulton, and others. In due time the association secured the old Fleetwood track and grounds in Morrisania, and thousands of dollars were spent in improvements. The club house is on a bluff overlooking the entire track. More horse talk has taken place here and more trotters have been watched in hotly contested races and brushes, than from any other point in the world, and many visitors of note have shared this pleasure.

W. C. Fair's b.m. Gold Leaf Maid.
From Year Book--Gentlemen's Driving Club of Cleveland, 1900.

179

# Speeding Wagons

Eddrea,     Mazel,     Anton,     Garletta.

M. A. Bradley,     D. R. Hanna,     H. M. Hanna,     C. F. Emery.

"THEY'RE OFF." *Year Book--Gentlemen's Driving Club of Cleveland,* 1900.

## GENTLEMEN'S DRIVING CLUB OF CLEVELAND.

May 25, 1895, the Gentlemen's Driving Club of Cleveland was organized, with William Edwards as honorary president; C. E. Grover, president; and Frank Chamberlin, secretary. Its object was matinee racing to road wagons, and although it was not the first club of the kind, it quickly took higher rank than any other club built on similar lines. It has a large and important membership, and as horses famed for speed contest for ribbons and cups, the races are attended by thousands. The members of the club are amateurs, and an amateur is defined "as a man who has not accepted wages or hire for his services as a trainer or driver. Any individual club member who competes for the first, or against professional, except in such events as are especially arranged for amateurs, after May 1, 1901, shall forfeit his amateur standing."

The officers of the club at this time are: honorary president, H. M. Hanna; president, H. K. Devereux ; vice-president, D. R. Hanna; secretary-treasurer, F. L. Chamberlin. The Gentlemen's Driving Club of Boston was organized in January, 1899, and the officers at this time are: president, Albert S. Bigelow; vice-presidents, Peter B. Bradley, John E. Thayer, J. Malcolm Forbes; treasurer, Frank G. Hall; secretary, T. L. Quimby. At a meeting held in New York, in November, 1890, the League of the American Driving Clubs was organized, with the clubs of Boston, Chicago, Cleveland, Pittsburg, and Syracuse in membership, to which have been added Columbus, New York, and Memphis. The officers of the league are: president, H. K. Devereux; vice-president, Harry Darlington; secretary-treasurer, T. L. Quimby. Horace White and C. K. G. Billings are prominent among the directors. Many thousands of dollars are spent each year for horses to compete for badges of honor at the amateur meetings, and lovers of the light-harness horse hope that amateur racing to road wagon has come to stay.[1]

1. From Busbey, Hamilton. *Trotting and the Pacing Horse In America.* New York, NY : Macmillan Company, 1904, pp. 301-302.

# Speeding Wagons

## THE BY-LAWS.
### ARTICLE I.
### NAME.

This Association shall be known as the Gentlemen's Driving Club of Cleveland.

### ARTICLE II.
### OBJECT.

This Association shall have for its object the providing of pleasure for its members, by giving and controlling friendly contests of speed, and the promotion of social intercourse among its members.

### ARTICLE III.
### OFFICERS.

SECTION 1. The officers shall consist of a President, Vice-President, Secretary and Treasurer, and a committee of six members of the Association who, together with the President, Secretary and Treasurer, shall constitute an Executive Committee; also a committee composed of three members of the Association who shall act as a Committee on Races, all of whom shall be elected at the regular annual meeting and serve for a term of one year, and until their successors are elected. The duties of the Secretary and Treasurer may be discharged by one and the same person. The Vice-President may discharge the duties of the President in his absence.

SEC. 2. All officers shall be elected by ballot except for the first year, when they may be elected by a viva voce vote. A majority of votes cast shall be required To elect.

### ARTICLE IV.
### APPLICATIONS FOR MEMBERSHIP, INITIATION FEES AND DUES.

SECTION 1. Any person, whose principal place of business is in Cleveland and who is an amateur driver, applying for admission to membership must be endorsed as recommended by two members of the Club and approved by at least six members of the Executive Committee.

SEC. 2. After the applicant shall be approved by the Executive Committee he may become a member of the Club upon the payment of twenty dollars ($20.00), as an initiation fee, which fee shall include all dues to the next annual meeting.

SEC. 3. The annual dues of the Association shall be fifteen dollars ($15.00), and payable in advance at the annual meeting. A member failing to pay his dues for three months, shall be liable to have his membership forfeited at any subsequent meeting of the Executive Committee by a two-thirds vote of the members present.

SEC. 4. There shall be a non-resident list, admission to which and dues shall be the same as prescribed for resident members. In order to be eligible to non-resident membership of these club members shall be required to keep their horses in the city of Cleveland for three months during the matinee season, subject to the rules of the club and programming of the horses by the Race Committee. Non-resident members shall have all the privileges of resident members except that they shall not hold office or vote.

SEC. 5. Any person who has ever driven or ridden any trotter or pacer not actually owned by himself in any public event or race other than such as are specially arranged for amateurs; or any person having trained, driven or ridden any trotter or pacer for hire or who has received any compensation for such service other than the purse, stake or wager, shall be deemed a professional.

### ARTICLE V.
### MEETINGS.

SECTION 1. Annual meetings of the members of this Club shall be held at a place appointed by the President, on the first Monday in April in each year. Regular meetings shall be held after the annual meeting at such times as may be agreed upon, and special meetings may be called by the President at any time, and upon the request of the Executive Committee, and the President shall call a special meeting upon the request in writing of any five members of the Club.

SEC. 2. Ten members shall be required to constitute a quorum for the transaction of business.

## ORDER OF BUSINESS.

1. Reading of Minutes. 2. Election of Officers. 3. Report of Treasurer. 4. Report of Committee. 5. General Business.

## ARTICLE VI.
## TRIALS OF SPEED.

SECTION 1. All meetings and contests shall be conducted under the rules of the National Trotting Association, of which this Club is a member-except wherein the same conflict with the By-Laws and rules of this Club.

SEC 2. The members of this Club are requested to meet at such times and place as may be designated by the Race Committee, the occasion being for pleasure driving and trials of speed.

SEC. 3. All regular events in harness must be to four-wheeled road wagons.

SEC. 4. Only members of the Club shall be allowed to drive in regular events; but there may be special events arranged for by the Race Committee in which other than members may participate. All horses entered or contesting in regular events must be owned by members of the Club. While any member may drive another member's horse, the interests of this Club and the pleasure of its members will be better served should each horse be driven by its owner. It is therefore the desire of the Club that the driving should not drift into the hands of a few members, but that special efforts should at all times be made by every member to do his own driving.

SEC. 5. All participants in a race, or members of the Club upon the ground, shall be under the immediate supervision and control of the judges, whose orders must be respected or obeyed, and any breach of the same on the part of the member participating shall be subject to such penalties as hereinafter named.

## ARTICLE VII.
## PENALTIES AND FINES.

SECTION 1. Any offending member, or his horse, or both, may be suspended from participating in races given under the auspices of this Club for such a length of time as the judges may designate, either for foul driving, or other causes.

SEC. 2. Any member guilty of ungentlemanly conduct at the meetings of the Club, or a violation of the rules of this Club, shall be subject to fine or expulsion by a two-thirds vote of the Executive Committee.

## ARTICLE VIII.
## POOL SELLING.

SECTION 1. No pool selling or book making of any kind shall be allowed on the grounds during the meetings of this Club.

## ARTICLE IX.
## JUDGES.

SECTION l. The Race Committee shall appoint three members of the Club to act as judges and timers for each meeting. The President, however, may always act as exofficio in the judges' stand, and if any member is dissatisfied with the rulings or findings of the judges he may appeal to the Executive Committee, not interested in the controversy, who shall investigate the same, and their decision in the matter shall be final.

## ARTICLE X.
### SPECTATORS.

SECTION 1. No person will be admitted to the private boxes at the meetings of this Club, except members and others holding tickets of admission, and such persons who are introduced by members.

SEC. 2. Tickets of admission shall be issued to each member for the meetings by the Executive Committee, and can be procured from the Secretary. The member will be held responsible for the conduct of persons gaining admission.

## ARTICLE XI,
### OBSERVANCE OF RULES.

It shall be the duty of each member to see that the rules of this Club are rigidly enforced, and any violation of the same on the part of a member, or any conduct unbecoming a gentleman shall subject such violator to an expulsion, suspension or a public reprimand by the President of the Club.

## ARTICLE XII.

Upon one month's notice previously given in writing by two-thirds of the members present at any regular or special meeting the foregoing articles of the association may be altered or amended by a two-thirds vote of those present at any subsequent meeting,

## RULES.
### I.
### ENTRIES.

All requirements of the National Trotting Association with reference to the making of entries by the owners or agents are by necessity of the nature of this organization waived. The Race Committee shall arrange and make up the races, classifying the horses and have programs of the same printed.

### II
### DRAWING HORSES.

Each member scheduled for a race will be provided weekly with a program of the events for the current week, and it shall be his duty to notify the Secretary on or before ten o'clock a. m. of the day of race if it is his intention not to start. For violation of this requirement a fine of not less than $2.00 and not more than $5.00 will be imposed by the judges, unless there be a valid excuse, such as absence from city or other satisfactory cause.

A horse can also be drawn before starting, at the post, or during the race by consent of the judges for proper cause, such as lameness, sickness of horse or driver, etc. The judges have sole power of deciding whether the cause is sufficient to warrant such withdrawal.

### III
### CHANGE OF PROGRAM.

After the program of races leaves the hands of the Race Committee no horse will be permitted to start in any regular event in which he has not been named.

In case, however, there shall only two starters appear in any race the judges shall have the power to declare said race off and substitute a new race, which shall be placed last on the program. The starting in such race shall not be compulsory but by mutual agreement between judges and members.

### IV.
### WEIGHT.

There shall be no limitation with regard to weight of drivers in regular events.

# Speeding Wagons

## V.
### AWARD OF RIBBONS.

In every regular event there shall be a blue ribbon awarded to the winner thereof. Should there be three or more starters the second horse shall be awarded a red ribbon, and should there be four or more starters the third horse shall be awarded a yellow ribbon.

## VI.
### AWARD IN CASE OF WALK-OVERS.

There shall be no ribbon awarded in case of a walk-over unless the horse starts to beat club championship time, and succeeds in so doing.

## VII.
### AWARD IN CASE OF TIES.

In case of ties for places in races it shall be optional with the owners to decide by lot, or by the positions of the horses tieing in future events. If mutual agreement cannot be arrived at, the position shall be decided by lot in the presence of the judges.

## VIII.
### DISTANCE AND LAYING UP.

There shall be no distance, but no member shall be permitted to "lay up" a horse except in cases of accident Any member found guilty by the judges of "laying up" shall be promptly ruled out of the race.

In such cases where a horse has lost a hopeless amount of ground by a break, he must be driven from the point where he regains his stride to the wire at least as fast, as the contesting horses.

It is understood by this rule that a member is not expected to punish and exhaust his horse in what is plainly a vain effort to recover ground lost by a break, but it also intends to prevent absolutely any "laying up."

If a horse, by simply breaking and not by reason of some accident or foul, is, in the opinion of the judges, over 150 yards behind at the finish of any heat he may be disqualified from competing in subsequent heats of the same event.

## IX.
### CALLING HORSES-TIME.

After calling the horses for any event they shall be in front of the judges' stand in ten minutes ready for the start, and any member not on hand within that time limit, unless in case of breakage of harness or some other valid reason, notice of which must be sent to the judges at once, shall be either disqualified and not allowed to start, or be subject to a fine of $5.00, or both, in the discretion of the judges. This requirement exists at the start of a race and also for subsequent heats in the race.

## X.
### HORSES ELIGIBLE TO START.

A race once started none but the original starters shall continue in it and in case a horse that has participated in a race fails to appear at the score in time to be sent away with the others, he shall not be permitted to start in subsequent heats.

## XI.
### UNRULY HORSES.

When a horse that is unruly at the score shall have been directly responsible for three recalls the judges shall start the remainder of the field without reference to such offending horse.

## XII.
### ACCIDENTS.

The breaking of a vehicle, or harness, or casting of a shoe shall be considered unavoidable accident, and the judges may give sufficient time for repairs. The judges to decide what is a sufficient time.

# Speeding Wagons

Should an unavoidable accident happen after the word go is given the horse shall be driven over the course as fast as the driver considers it safe to proceed. Should he be compelled to stop he must at once return and report the accident to the judges. Should they consider him no way at fault they may permit him to start in subsequent heats.

## XIII.
## SCORING.

All drivers shall use their best efforts to secure an even start with as little scoring as possible. They are required to strictly obey the directions of the judges in scoring by any horse chosen under penalty of a fine or disqualification from the race. They must stop their horses as soon as possible after a recall and jog back to the starting place for another score.

Those having outside positions should jog back on the inside of the track, those having inside positions on the outer side so that all may have sufficient room to turn together.

In meeting approaching vehicles on the track always keep to the left.

## XIV.
## ALTERNATING OF RACES.

Heats in three races may be alternated. The limit of time between heats shall not be less than fifteen minutes unless by mutual agreement.

## XV.
## POSTPONEMENT AND CHANGE OF PROGRAM.

The judges shall have the power to declare on any races, or to change the same from mile heats to a mile dash. They can also declare finished any race at any time for cause.

No races once started shall be postponed as unfinished.

## XVI.
## HOPPLES.

No horse wearing hopples will be permitted to start in regular events of this club.

## XVII.
## PLACE FOR COOLING OUT.

All competing horses shall be cooled out in the cooling-out shed under penalty of fine or disqualification.

## XVIII.
## POWER OF JUDGES TO REMOVE DRIVERS.

Should the judges consider any driver unfit to drive for any cause, at any time, they may substitute another driver.

## CUPS, RIBBONS AND PRIZES-RULES GOVERNING AWARDING OF SAME.
## I.

After each regular matinee season and at a time and place fixed by the Race Committee, there shall be a meeting of the members of the Club for the purpose of awarding the cups, ribbons and prizes won during the season.

There shall be two silver cups known as the Club's Championship Cups for horses competing in not less than three meetings during the season.

These cups shall be awarded each season, one to the trotter and one to the pacer making the fastest time to road wagon for that season. The names of the members, horses and year shall be engraved on the cups successively, and they shall be held for one year by the members winning them. These records must be made at a regular meeting of the Club except in case of tie records. In event of tie there shall be a special meeting called to decide the tie.

The horse winning at the special meeting shall be entitled to the cup, unless the record as tied be lowered at said meeting, in that case the cup shall go to the horse making the record-unless the winner of the race should again tie the record as reduced.

In case of only one horse appearing to contest for the cups at any regular meeting the

# Speeding Wagons

owner shall at his request be permitted to start against time—time in this case being the then existing Club record for that season and a contestant as against the horse. He shall also be allowed a prompter should he desire one. The judges must announce before starting, the conditions existing, and the fact of the horse going against time. The horse in each case shall be allowed two trials or heats, but need not go more than one. There shall be no recall after the word is given.

The two silver cups presented to the Club by Mr. F. N. Reed shall be known as the Reed Championship Cups. They shall be awarded each year one to the trotter winning the greatest number of heats in time from 2:17 to 2:24, and one to the pacer winning the greatest number of heats in time from 2 :15 to 2 :22, both inclusive ; provided

FIRST. That should either the trotter or the pacer winning the greatest number of heats during any one season, in the time as specified, prove to be the one winning the Club's Championship Cup then the Reed Championship Cup shall be awarded to the horse winning the second greatest number of heats in the time as specified.

SECOND. That should there be a tie either of two or more horses for either cup then the cup shall be awarded to the horse whose winning heats in the time as specified shall average the fastest. In case there should still be a tie in fastest average of heats in time specified, then the horse entitled to the cup shall be decided by lot by the owners of the horses tieing.

THIRD. That any horse winning these cups any one season must have started at least five times during that season at the Club's meetings.

FOURTH. That only performances in regular events and at regular meetings of the Club shall be recognized.

These cups are to be awarded each season for the performances as indicated that season and shall be held by the members winning them for one year.

The names of the members winning the cups shall be successively engraved on the cups, together with the names of the horses and year. In case of a tie, where final award must be decided by lot, as stated, the names of both members and horses tieing shall be engraved on the cup. *From Year Book of the Gentlemen's Driving Club of Cleveland. Conataining Complete Summaries Of All Performances To Road Wagon, An Alphabetical List of Horses With Road Wagon Records of 2:30 or Better, Alphabetical List of Horses With Slow Records, List of Members, List of Horses, By-laws and Rules. 1897.* (from the Library of Congress)

**SPEEDING WAGON.**
*Hub* August 1900, page 198.

**SPEED WAGON.**
*Hub* Circa 1900.

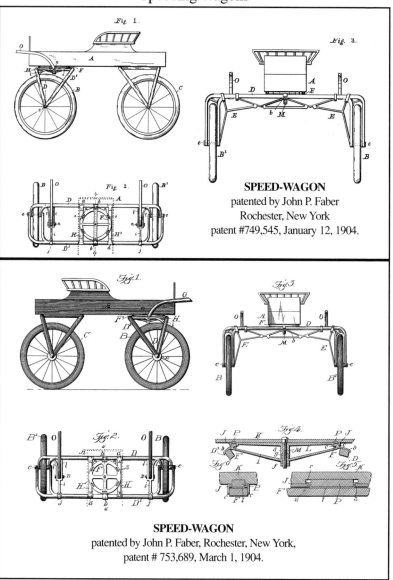

**SPEED-WAGON**
patented by John P. Faber
Rochester, New York
patent #749,545, January 12, 1904.

**SPEED-WAGON**
patented by John P. Faber, Rochester, New York,
patent # 753,689, March 1, 1904.

# BIBLIOGRAPHY.

Akers, Dwight. *Drivers Up the Story of American Harness Racing*. New York, NY : G. P. Putnam's Sons, 1947.

An Old Sulky. *Hub* Vol. 39 No. 9 (December 1897), page 649. Note: Report of sulky made in 1756, in the Philadelphia area.

Busbey, Hamilton. *Trotting and the Pacing Horse In America*. New York, NY : Macmillan Co., 1904.

Coates, Henry Troth; Fleming, George. *A Short History of the American Trotting and Pacing Horse*. Philadelphia, PA : Coates & Co., 1901. 5 editions.

Dimon, John. *American Horses and Horse Breeding. A Complete History of the Horse From the Remotest Period In His History To Date. The Horseman's Encyclopedia and Standard Authority On Horses, Embracing Breeds, Families, Breeding, Training, Shoeing, and General Management. The Modern and Practical Horse Doctor On the Cause, Nature, Symptoms, and Treatment Of Diseases Of All Kinds*. Hartford, CT : J. Dimon, 1895.

Evolution of the Sulky. *Hub* Vol. 41 No. 9 (December 1899), page 388.

*Famous American Trotting Horses. Being Full Page Portraits of the Celebrities of the American Turf, Past and Present, With Short Notices of Their Performances*. Philadelphia, PA : Porter and Coates, 1877. Note: Line illustrations of: Mac; Tacony; Blackwood, jr.; Governor Sprague; Smuggler; Lula; Goldsmith Maid.

*Gentlemen's Driving Club of Cleveland. Year Book of the Gentlemen's Driving Club of Cleveland. Conataining Complete Summaries Of All Performances To Road Wagon, An Alphabetical List of Horses With Road Wagon Records of 2:30 or Better, Alphabetical List of Horses With Slow Records, List of Members, List of Horses, By-laws and Rules*. Cleveland, OH : Gentlemen's Driving Club of Cleveland, 1897. (from the Library of Congress)

Herbert, Henry William. *Frank Forester's Horse and Horsemanship of the United States and British Provinces of North America*. New York, NY : Stringer & Townsend, 1857. 11 editions.

Humphrey, John H. *Roman Circuses : Arenas for Chariot Racing*. Berkeley, CA. : University of California Press, 1986.

Linnehan, John William, 1860-; Cogswell, Edward E. *Driving Clubs of Greater Boston*...edited and complied...Boston, MA : Press of Atlantic Printing Company, 1914. (Library of Congress). Note: Lots of photos.

McCully, Charles Arnold. American Roadsters and Road Riders. *Harper's Weekly* May 30, 1891, pages 393-396. Note: Gives a description of several popular teams of horses of the times. Illustrated is: John D. Rockfeller's Pair.--Midnight, and Flash; Arab and Mill Boy owned by John Shepard, Boston; Jack and Pilot; John H. Shult's Pair of Pacers--Gold Leap and Arrow.

Nancy Hanks. *Hub* Vol. 34 No. 6 (September 1892), page 202.

Porter, William Trotter. *Spirit of the Times*. New York, NY William Trotter Porter, published from 1837-1861; Published 1868-1892 by E. A. Buck; 1831-1832 as *Spirit of the Times & Life In New York*, by Porter & Howe; 1835-1837 as *New York Spirit of the Times* by William Porter.

Pneumatic Sulky. *Hub* Vol. 34 No. 7 (October 1892), page 247.

Rival Teams. *Harper's Weekly* October 14, 1882, pp. 644 & 646.

Sherman, I. A. Success of the Pneumatic Sulky-tire. *India Rubber World* Vol. 6 No. 6 (September 15, 1892), page 359. Note: States that the Boothroyd, rubber tire was used.

Slobody, Evelyn and Lawrence; Pines, Philip A. *Currier & Ives Present Trotting, the National Pastime Of Early America : A Pageant Of Their Horse Prints From 1840-1895.* New York, NY : Benson Press, 1984. Note: Prints in the collection of the Harness Racing Museum and Hall of Fame, Goshen, New York.

Splan, John. *Life With the Trotters.* Chicago, Ill.: H. T. White, 1889.

Sullivan, George. *Harness Racing.* New York, NY. : Fleet Press Corporation, 1974.

Wallace, John Hankins. *Wallace's Monthly.* New York, NY : Benjamin Singerly, 1875-1894.

Walsh, J. H.; Fleming, George; Harvey, Ellwood; Coates, Henry Troth; and others. *Every Horse Owners' Cyclopedia: the Anatomy and Physiology of the Horse...The American Trotting Horse, With Suggestions On the Breeding and Training of Trotters, by Ellwood Harvey. A Short History of the American Trotting Turf, and Tables of Trotting and Pacing Performances , by Henry T. Coates....* Philadelphia, PA : Porter & Coates, 1882.

Welsh, Peter C. *Track and Road: The American Trotting Horse A Visual Record 1820 to 1900 from the Harry T. Peters America On Stone Lithography Collection.* Washington, DC : Smithsonian Institution Press, 1967.

Wheels and Rubber Tires. *Hub* Vol. 38 No. 1 (April 1896), page 50.

Woodruff, Hiram Washington. *The Trotting Horse Of America How To Train and Drive Him: With Reminiscences of the Trotting Turf.* New York, NY : J. B. Ford, 1868. 16 editions.

Youatt, William. *The Horse, ...Together With A General History Of the Horse; A Dissertation On The American Trotting Horse, How Trained and Jockeyed, An Account Of His Remarkable Performances; and An Essay On the Ass and the Mule.* published by Leavitt & Allen, New York, [1843]. numerous editions and variations of this title first published in 1833.

OTHER ILLUSTRATIONS NOT IN THIS BOOK.

Great Horse Show at Springfield, Massachusetts–The Cavalcade Passing the Judges Stand. *Frank Leslie's Illustrated Newspaper* October 2, 1858 pages 278-279.

Agricultural Fair At Manchester, New Hampshire. *Ballou's Pictorial* October 13, 1855 pages 236-237.

Indiana State Fair at Terre Haute. *Harper's* Weekly November 2, 1867 pages 696-697.

Great Fair of the St. Louis Agricultural and Mechanics Association. *Frank Leslie's Illustrated Newspaper* November 8, 1856, page 341. (Trotting Horse in Sulky).

Great Fair at St. Louis. *Frank Leslie's Illustrated Newspaper* November 15, 1856, page 365. . (Trotting Horse "Young St. Lawrence" in Sulky).

## UNITED STATES HARNESS RACING TRACKS

Balmoral Park
26435 South Dixie Highway
Crete, Illinois 60417

Bangor Raceway
100 Dutton Street
Bangor, Maine 04401-0614

Batavia Downs
8315 Park Road
Batavia, New York 14020

Player's Bluegrass Downs
150 Downs Drive
Paducah, Kentucky 42001

Buffalo Raceway
5600 McKinley Parkway
Hamburg, New York 14075

Cal-Expo (California State Fair & Exposition Grounds, Sacramento)
2335 American River Drive
Suite 406
Sacramento, CA 95825

Colonial Downs
10515 Colonial Downs Parkway
New Kent, Virginia 23124

Delaware, OH Fair
236 Pennsylvania Avenue
Post Office Box 1278
Delaware, Ohio 43015

Dover Downs
1131 North DuPont Highway
Dover, Delaware 19901

Du Quoin State Fair
655 Executive Drive
Du Quoin, Illinois 62832

Freehold Raceway
Post Office Box 6669
Routes 9 and 33
Freehold, New Jersey 07728

Goshen Historic Track
44 Park Place
Post Office Box 192
Goshen, New York 10924

Harrah's Chester Casino and Racetrack
1001 Harrah's Blvd.
Chester, Pennsylvania 19013

Harrington Raceway
15 West Rider Road
Harrington, Delaware 19952

Hawthorne Racecourse
3501 South Laramie Avenue
Stickney, Illinois 60804

Hazel Park Harness
1650 East Ten Mile Road
Hazel Park, Michigan 48030

Hoosier Park
4500 Dan Patch Circle
Anderson, Indiana 46013

Indiana Downs
4200 North Michigan Road
Shelbyville, Indiana 46176

Indiana State Fair
1202 East 36th Street
Indianapolis, Indiana 46205-2869

Jackson Harness Raceway
200 West Ganson Street
Jackson, Michigan 49201

Lebanon Raceway
665 North Broadway
Post Office Box 58
Lebanon, Ohio 45036

Maywood Park
8600 West North Avenue
Melrose Park, Illinois 60160

# Modern Harness Racing Tracks

Meadowlands
50 Street Route 120
East Rutherford, New Jersey 07073

The Meadows
Race Track Road
Post Office Box 499
Meadow Lands, Pennsylvania 15347

Monticello Raceway
Routes 17 and 17B
Raceway Road
Monticello, New York 12701

Northfield Park
10705 Northfield Road
Post Office Box 374
Northfield, Ohio 44067

Northville Downs
301 South Center Street
Northville, Michigan 48167

Ocean Downs
10218 Racetrack Road
Post Office Box 11
Berlin, Maryland 21811

Plainridge Racecourse
301 Washington Street
Plainville, Massachusetts 02762

Pocono Downs
1280 Route 315
Wilkes-Barre, Pennsylvania 18702

Pompano Park
1800 South West 3rd Street
Pompano Beach, Florida 33069

Prairie Meadows
One Prairie Meadows Drive
Post Office Box 1000
Altoona, Iowa 50009-0901

Raceway Park
5700 Telegraph Road
Toledo, Ohio 43612

The Red Mile
1200 Red Mile Road
Post Office Box 420
Lexington, Kentucky 40588

Rockingham Park
(Rockingham Park Boulevard)
Post Office Box 47
Salem, New Hampshire 03079

Rosecroft Raceway
6336 Rosecroft Drive
Fort Washington, Maryland 20744-1999

Saratoga Gaming and Raceway
342 Jefferson Street
Saratoga Springs, New York 12866

Scarborough Downs
United States Route One
Post Office Box 468
Scarborough, Maine 04074

Scioto Downs
6000 South High Street
Post Office Box 07823
Columbus, Ohio 43207

Sports Creek Raceway
4290 Morrish Road
Swartz Creek, Michigan 48473

Springfield, Illinois
Horse Racing Program-Illinois Department of Agriculture
801 East Sangamon Avenue
Springfield, Illinois 62794-9281

Thunder Ridge
164 Thunder Road
Prestonsburg, Kentucky 41653

Tioga Downs
2384 West River Road
Nichols, New York 13812

Vernon Downs
Ruth Street
Post Office Box 860
Vernon, New York 13476-0860

Yonkers Raceway
810 Central Avenue
Yonkers, New York 10704

## CANADIAN
## HARNESS RACING TRACKS

Bedrock Training Centre
Site 24, Compartment 8
8127 Roper Road
Edmonton, Alberta T6E 6S4

Big Valley Raceway
Saskatchewan

Charlottetown Driving Park
14 Exhibition Drive
Charlottetown, Prince Edward Island

Clinton Raceway
Beech Street & Mill Street
Clinton, Ontario

Dresden Raceway
1244 North Street
Dresden, Ontario

Exhibition Park Raceway
Post Office Box 284
159 McAllister Drive
Saint John, New Brunswick

Flamboro Downs
967 Hwy 5
Dundas, Ontario

Fraser Downs
17755 60th Avenue
Surrey, British Columbia V3S 1V3

Fredericton Raceway
Post Office Box 235, Station A
Smythe and Saunders Streets
Fredericton, New Brunswick

Georgian Downs
7485 5th Side Road
Innisfil, Ontario

Grand River Raceway
7445 Wellington Road
21, RR2
Elora, Ontario

Grande Prairie
Box 370
Grande Prairie, Alberta

Great Western Fair Circuit
Manitoba

Hanover Raceway
269 Seventh Avenue
Hanover, Ontario

Hiawatha Horse Park
1730 London Road
Sarnia, Ontario

Hippodrome Gatineau
788 Aylmer Road
Aylmer, Quebec

Hippodrome de Montreal
7440 Decarie Blvd.
Montreal, Quebec

Inverness Raceway
Post Office Box 503
Forrest St.
Inverness, Nova Scotia

Kawartha Downs
Hwy. 28 at Hwy. 115
Fraserville, Ontario

Marquis Downs
503 Ruth Street
Box 6010
Saskatoon, Saskatchewan S7K 4E4

Mohawk Racetrack
R. R. # 1 Guelph Line
Campbellville, Ontario

Northlands Park
7600 115th Avenue
Edmonton, Alberta

Northside Downs
Post Office Box 92
105 Regent Street
North Sydney, Nova Scotia

Quinte Exhibition & Raceway
18 Yeoman Street
Belleville, Ontario

Rideau-Carleton Raceway
4837 Albion Road
Gloucester, Ontario

St. John's Racing & Entertainment Centre
Post Office Box 1090
Lakeview Drive
Goulds, Newfoundland

Sandown Park
1810 Glamorgan Road
Post Office Box 2370
Sidney, British Columbia

Stampede Park
2300 Stampede Trail SE
Calgary, Alberta T2G 2W1
Post Office Box 1060
Station M,
Calgary, Alberta T2P 2K8

Sudbury Downs
2070 Old Burwash Road
Sudbury, Ontario

Sulky Quebec
Post Office Box 2053
Parc de l'Exposition
Quebec, Quebec

Sulky Trois Rivieres
1600 Des Forges Blvd.
Trois Rivieres, Quebec

Summerside Raceway
477 Notre Dame Street
Summerside, Prince Edward Island

Truro Raceway
Post Office Box 422
73 Ryland Avenue
Truro, Nova Scotia

Western Fair Raceway
900 King Street
London, Ontario

Windsor Raceway
5555 Ojibway Blvd.
Windsor, Ontario

Woodbine Racetrack
555 Rexdale Blvd.
Rexdale, Ontario

Woodstock Raceway
Hwy. 2 & McKenzie Street
Woodstock, Ontario

Yorkton Exhibition Race Track
Box 908
Yorkton, Saskatchewan S3N 2X1

# Index

## A

Agricultural Fair Boston 129
Aintree Trotting Stakes at Liverpool 132
Aitken, Thomas D., patent 46
Akers, Dwight, author 150
Albert D, trotter 7, 8
Aldine, trotter 165, plate 12
Alexandre, J. E., Road Rider 179
Alix, trotter plate 4
Allen, Standhope I., patent 75
Alley, George B., Road Rider 179
Almont, trotter 8
Amateur Driving Clubs 179
American Driving Clubs 180
American Girl, trotter plate 7
Arab, trotter 166
Arched Axle Sulky 7
Armstrong, John Belmer, patent 58
Arrow, trotter 166
Axle Gather 28

## B

Bald, Peter H., patent 58
Ball-bearings 172 see also Hub
Barclay, J. L. & J. H., Road Riders 179
Barman, Jerry, Jerald Sulky Co. 117
Barnaby, J. B., owner plate 10
Beacon course, Hudson County, New
    Jersey 150
Berry, David, patent 46
Bibliography 189
Bicycle Sulky 7, 41
Biddle, Smart & Co., Builder 156
Bidwell-Thomas pneumatic tires 10
Bigae 1
Bigelow, Albert S., Road Rider 180
Billings, C. K. G., Road Rider 180
Billy D, trotter plate 10
Bilz, John Adolf, patent 35
Black Harry, trotter 127
Blackmore, James H., patent 38, 44
Boettcher, Theodore, patent 45
Bonner, David, Road Rider 179
Bonner, Robert, Road Rider 164, 179,
    plate 11

Boone, John L., patent 36
Booth & Bro.'s of Columbus, Ohio 12
Boston, Massachusetts 157, 158, 160
Boyd, Jesse C., patent 45
Boyd, William M., patent 45
Boyer, Michael C., patent 35
Bradley, Peter B., Road Rider 180
Brewster & Co., New York, New York
    29, 170
Bridge, Stephen 42
Britton, I. W., draftsman 170
Brockman, Clarence Eugene, patent 79
Brown, Frank E., patent 74
Brown, M. B., Road Rider 179
Brown, S. N., & Co., Dayton, Ohio 70
Brown, Thomas H., Chicago, Ill 34
Buffalo, New York plate 6
Buffalo Cycle Works, Buffalo, New
    York 10, 68
Buffalo Driving Park 135
Buffalo Tricycle Co., Buffalo, New York
    70
Bufford, J. H. 3
Bull, Willie S., patent 10, 73
Burch & Hadsell, Pontiac, Michigan 61
Burke of Hereford, tandem driver 125
Busard, Osee A., patent 91
Busbey, Hamilton, author 144
Bushor, Dennis, patent 36
Business Cart Co., Kalamazoo, MI 122
By-laws, Gentlemen's Driving Club 181

## C

Cadwell, S. W., Road Rider 179
Caffrey, Charles S., Builder 14, 36, 69,
    70, 151,
Capt. McGowan, trotter 3-4, 134
Cartoon 140
Celebrated American Trotting Horses
    plate 1
Central Trotting Circuit 124
Centreville, Long Island, track 127, plate
    2
Chamberlin, E., Builder 168
Chamberlin, Frank, Road Rider 180
Champagne, Henry, patent 38

# Index

Chandler, David, E., patent 38, 45
Chariot racing 1
Charter Oak track 124
Cheney, Frank P., patent 79
Childs, George K., Philadelphia,
    Pennsylvania 28
Cincinnati, Ohio, track 132
Circular Bar 5
Circus Maximus 1
Clark, C. F., Boston 7
Clarke, George W., patent 78
Clarke, R. A., painter plate 1
Clausen, Hermand & George G., Road
    Riders 179
Clawson, Leonard E., patent 78
Cleveland, track 123-124
Clipper Buggy 170
Coates, Joseph S., patent 105
Cohnfeld, Isidor, Road Rider 179
Colcord, Ivory G., patent 82
Columbia Pneumatic Wagon Wheel Co.,
    80
Common Sense Bicycle Mfg. Co., Phila.
    66
Confidence, trotter XII, 126, 150, plate
    2
Conner Bros., Ada, Ohio 49
Coster, J. G., Road Rider 179
Cranked Axles 6
Crawford Wheel and Gear Co.,
    Hagerstown, MD 66
Crosby, Gilzinger & Co., Rondout, New
    York 5, 27
Currier and Ives 1, plates 2-12

## D

Dan Mace, trotter 134
Davis, Nathan H., patent 47
de Cordova, Alfred, Road Rider 179
Deal, J. J., & Son, Jonesville, Michigan
    64
Deal, J. J., Jonesville, Michigan 48
Dean, Porcius F., patent 46
Decker, George W., patent 79
Deininger, axle 65
DeMott, J. H., Road Rider 179
Dentler, Frank, patent 78
Devereux, H. K., Road Rider 180
Dexter, trotter 6, plate 11

Dick Swiveller, trotter 165
Dickson, James H., patent 17, 120
Dissel, William H. C., patent 78
Doble, Budd, driver 8, 9, 36, plate 3
Doelger, Peter, Road Rider 179
Doherty, Fisher, patent 45
Donithen, Hoke W. 99
Donley, William J., patent 36
Drum, Edgar M., patent 45
Dubois, Peter, Builder 4, 16
Dutch Charley, trotter 127

## E

Early Rose, trotter 165
Eastman, T. C., Road Rider 179
Eclipse Bicycle Co., Beaver Falls, PA 67
Eclipse County, Long Island 131
Edward, trotter 165, plate 11
Ehninger, J. W., sketch artist 136
Electric Lighting for track 142
Elkland Carriage Works, Elkland, PA 73
Elliott Hickory Cycle Company, Newton,
    MA 7, 9
Elliott, Sterling, patent 7, 69, 70
Emerson, E. D., Waltham, MA 8
Empire City Park 144
Empress, trotter 134
Engles, Hugo F., patent 79
Equine Bicycles 54
Ethan Allen, trotter 134, plate 9

## F

Faber, John P., patent 188
Faber, John Peter, patent & Builder 80
Fair, W. C., Road Rider 179
Fashion Course, L. I. plate 9
Fearing, W. H., Road Rider 179
Ferguson, A. P., Ann Arbor, Michigan 50
First organized match 2
Flash, trotter 167
Flatbush Maid, trotter 164
Fleetwood Park, New York 76, 142, 143,
    179
Fleming, Will A., patent 58
Flint Wagon Works, Flint, Michigan 49
Flora Temple, trotter 3, 5-6, 129, 131,
    plate 5
Flora, trotter 129

# Index

Foote, Willis O. & Edward D., patent 78

Forbes, J. Malcolm, Road Rider 180

Foster, Frank, Houghton Sulky 103

Four-wheeled Racing Vehicles 149

Frank Verrian, trotter 134

Fraser, Edwin J., patent 36

Frazier, Edward S., patent 93

Frazier, W. S., & Co., Builder, Aurora, IL 92

Freeman, Thomas, patent 74

Frenzeny, P., sketch artist 165

Frenzeny, Paul, sketch artist 141

Fullerton, trotter 4, 137

**G**

Galbraith, William A., patent 75

Garrard, Henry H., patent 73

Gay & Son, Ottawa, IL 122

Geers, Ed 8

General Butler, trotter plate 9

Gentlemen's Driving Association of New-York 179

Gentlemen's Driving Club of Cleveland 180

George M. Patchen, trotter 131, 158

George Wilkes, trotter plate 9

Gibson, George W., sketch artist 136

Gill, driver & owner 126

Gold Leaf Maid, trotter 179

Gold Leaf, trotter 166

Goldsmith Maid, trotter 4-5, 123, 137, plate 7

Goodfellow & Babcock, Holidaysburg, PA 50

Gould, George J., Road Rider 179

Grand Circuit 8, 10

Grant, Hugh J., Road Rider 179

Gray-Parker, artist 142

Green, Charles S. 10

Greutman, George, patent 79

Grover, C. E., Road Rider 180

Gunder, J. B. 99

Gunther, W. H., Road Rider 179

**H**

Hall, Frank G., Road Rider 180

Hamill, William John, patent 36, 74

Hamlin, Harry 8

Hanaw, F. & Co., Jackson, Michigan 53

Hanna, H. M. & D. R., Road Riders 180

Harness 77, 121

Harness racing, history 124

Harper, Joseph, Road Rider 179

Harper, O. S., Sharon, Massachusetts 73

Harper, William D., patent 57

Harrell, V. R., Houghton Sulky Co. 103

Harrington, Theodore, patent 56

Hartford Horsefair 133

Haskell and Allen, print makers 124

Haslip, Joseph, Baltimore 37

Hatfield, Dan 3

Hattie R, trotter 141

Hawkey, John Rundle, patent 46

Haywood, John J., patent 56

Hazel Wilkes, trotter 8

Heath, Thomas S., patent 17

Heinemann, Henry, patent 47

Henry, trotter plate 7

Hero, trotter 127

Hessong, James, patent 58

Hetefield, Daniel G., patent 36

Hickory Wheel Co., Newton, Massachusetts 69

Higley, Eben N., patent 79

Hill, Homer C., patent 47

History of the Sulky 1

Hitchcock, Alonzo, patent 35

Hoffman, Harry A., Houghton Sulky Co. 103

Hoffman, J. P., sketch artist 135

Hollenbaugh, Sam, Houghton Sulky 103

Holliday, John W., patent 73

Hollister, Elmer P., patent 105

Hollister, W. H., Road Rider 179

Holmes, Oliver Wendell, poet 138

Honest George, trotter 8

Horses VI

Horses, history XI

Horseshoes, rubber cushion pads 148

Houghton Buggy Company 99

Houghton Sulky Co., Builder 99

Houghton, William H., Builder 98

Houghton-Merkel Co. 98

How the Old Horse Won the Bet, poem 138

Hub 83, 90, 102, 116

Hubbard, George W., patent 120

# Index

Hughson & Sullivan, Rochester, New York 48
Humphreeville, I. L., Road Rider 179
Hunt, William, Camdem, New Jersey 26
Hunting, N. L., Road Rider 179
Huntress, trotter plate 6
Hussey, Howe & Company, Pittsburg, Pennsylvania 29

**I**

Illinois Egbert 10
Ireland, L. W. 99

**J**

J. O. Nay, trotter plate 10
Jack, trotter 167
Jackey, trotter 132
Jenkins, Jesse, patent 35
Jennison, LaFayette H., patent 35
Jerald, Samuel, Builer 107
Jerald, Stanley, Builder 107, 118
Jerald Sulky Co., Builder 99, 106
Johnson, John A., patent 46
Jones, W. C. Floyd, Road Rider 179

**K**

Kalamazoo Wagon Co., Kalamazoo, Michigan 49
Kane, H. H., road rider 163
Kearney, Edward, Road Rider 179
Keeler, Harry D., patent 105
Keene, J. R., Road Rider 179
Keller, Elisha S., patent 79
Kelley, John W., patent 57
Kelling, Donnell, Jerald Sulky Co. 118
Kennedy & Lucas of Philadelphia 2
Kimberling, Philip, Houghton Sulky Co. 103
Kip, Lawrence, Road Rider 179
Kipp, Ernest, Houghton Sulky Co. 103
Knapp, Shepherd F., Road Rider 179
Knowles, Mortimer L., patent 77
Kramer & McClelland, Decataur, IL 38
Kraming, Donald, Jerald Sulky Co. 118
Kratzer, David N., patent 47

**L**

Laass, Robert, patent 105
Lady Emma, trotter plate 9
Lady Mac, trotter 165, plate 12
Lady Palmer, trotter 164
Lady Thorn, trotter 135, plate 5
Lamson, William E., patent 46
Lancet, trotter 129
Lapham, Charles C., patent 105
Lawrence, Bradley & Pardee, Builder 149
Lawrence, Williams & Co. 124
Lehner, George, Houghton 103
Limpus, William F. &Sherman E., patent 78
Lines, C. A., Builder 154
Lines, Thos. D., Syracuse, New York 62
Lingle, William H., patent 47
Little Albert 8
Locke, Daniel W., patent 74
Lohr, Frank, patent 73
Loomis, Gilbert J., patent 78
Lorillard, Louis L., Road Rider 179
Lovie, Henri, sketch artist 130, 132
Lucille's Baby 10
Lucy, trotter plates 6-8

**M**

Mac, trotter 129, 131
MacDonald, Henry R., patent 82
Mace, Dan, driver plate 9
Mail, H. W. T., Road Rider 179
Manville, B. & Co., New Haven, CT 154
Marquedant, Henry, patent 56
Maud S, trotter plate 12
Maurer, Louis plate 8
McAuliffe, J., artist plate 10
McCormick, Moses, patent 46, 74
McIntosh, Harry A. & Theodore W., patent 74
Mckerron, John A., patent 78
McLain, Walter, Houghton Sulky Co. 103
McMann, James D., driver plate 5
McMurray & Fisher, Builder 91
McMurray Sulky Company 99
McMurray, Thomas J., Builder 84

# Index

McWherter, Bert, Houghton Sulky Co. 103
Messenger, horse 2
Michigan Wheel Co., Lansing, MI 83, 172
Midnight, trotter 167
Mill Boy, trotter 166
Miller, A., patent 25
Miller Bros., Spring Valley, Illinois 50
Miller, Burt, sketch artist 141
Miller, Henry J., patent 105, 120
Miller, Jason, Road Rider 179
Milner, Edward, patent 35
Moller, Peter, Road Rider 179
Moore, T. W., inventor 54
Moore, Thomas W., patent 55
Morosini, G. P., Road Rider 179
Morris, A. Newbold, Road Rider 179
Morse, Andrew H., patent 36
Mosier, J. L. H., blacksmith 171
Mott, Jordon L., Road Rider 179
Moulton, F. C., Road Rider 179
Moutain Boy, trotter 135
Muller, Adolphus 31
Murphy, John, driver plate 10
Myndert, Starin, Road Rider 179

## N

Nancy Hanks, trotter 8, 9, plate 3
National Horse Fair, Hartford, CT XI
National Horse Fair, Long Island 131
National Wagon Company 99
Nelson, trotter plate 4
New York Driving Club 179
New York, New York 162
Newberry, Orson O., patent 46
Nickel, Samuel, patent 75
Noyes Cart Co., Kalamazoo, Michigan 48

## O

Ogden, William L., patent 105
Oliver, Elam A., patent 58
Olives, Brooklyn 12
One Wheel Sulky 59, 104

## P

Palmer, Charles H., Amesbury, MA 62
Palo Alto Sulky Co., Canton, Ohio 82
Parsons, Charles J., Builder 98
Parsons Vehicle Company 98
Parsons-Houghton Co., Marion, Ohio 96
Paterson, W. A., Co., Flint, Michigan 120
Paterson, W. A., Flint, Michigan 49
Paul, Harry B., patent 36, 57
Paulus, Ed, Houghton Sulky Co. 103
Payne, Martin, patent 44, 45, 75, 79
Peabody, A. S., Road Rider 179
Peardon, Charles, H., patent 79
Pennock, Horace A., patent 78
Penrose, W. E., Philadelphia 30
Pfifer, Dan, driver plate 5
Philadelphia, track 130
Phineas Jones & Co., Newark, New Jersey 21, 153
Pilot H, trotter 167
Pittsburgh, Pennsylvania, track 142
Pneumatic tire 7, 76, 87, 90, 102, 172
Pointer, Hal 9
Pope Manufacturing Company 7
Pratt's Perfection Road Cart 122
Pray Brothers of Boston, Massachusetts 31
Pray, Joseph, Boston, Massachusetts 6
Prince, trotter 127
Prospect Park Fair Grounds, L. I. 4, 135, 137, plate 6, 10-11
Putnam Nail Co 124

## Q

Quadrigae 1
Quadrilateral Trotting Combination 124
Quimby, T. L., Road Rider 180

## R

Radebaugh, Bert, Houghton 103
Ralph, trotter 127
Raven, trotter 10
Rease, W. H., lithograph plate 1
Reed, Milo J., patent 45
Reiff, Jacob G., patent 25
Richardson, J. B. 8

# Index

Richter, William R., patent 74
Riding (A-side), trotters plate 1
Ripton, trotter XII, 150, plate 2
Riverside Park, Cambridge, Massachusetts 134
Road Cart 113, 114, 115
Road Drivers' Association of New York City 162
Road Riders 159, 164
Road Wagon 168
Rochester 141
Rochester Driving Park 137
Rockefeller, John D., Road Rider 167
Rockefeller, William, Raod Rider 179
Roush, L. L., sketch artist 142
Rowe, Samuel, patent 74
Rudolph, Frank, patent 82
Rumsey Manufacturing Co., Detroit, Michigan 49
Russell, Charles A., patent 73
Russell, H. S., owner plate 7

## S

Safety Bicycle 9
Saffold, Ray P., patent 17
Sanford, A. Wright, Road Rider 179
Sanska, Louis, Jerald Sulky Co. 117
Schneider, Fred, Houghton Sulky Co. 103
Seabury, Thomas S., patent 35
Selligman, Henry & Simon, Road Riders 179
Sercombe-Bolte Mfg. Co., Milwaukee, WI 70
Shepard, John, Road Rider 166
Sherman Black Hawk, trotter 3, 130
Shilliam, Samuel, patent 45
Shortsleeve, William H., patent 73
Shults, John H., Road Rider 166
Siglin, Dick, Jerald Sulky Co. 117
Sinclair, James A. patent 17
Skeleton Wagon 149
Sleepy George, trotter plate 8
Sleepy John, trotter 136
Small Hopes, trotter 165, plate 12
Smith, Alphonse B., patent 59
Smith, E. W., Builder 152
Smith, H. B., Houghton Sulky Co. 103
Smith, Merton E., patent 105

Smuggler, trotter 5, 123, plate 7
Soule, Peter, patent 35
Souter, J. T., Road Rider 179
Southard, Stephen P., patent 46, 47
Speed Wagons 159, 163, 171,173, 187,
Speedway 160, 162
Spicer, George, driver 128
Splan, John, author 156
Sprague Golddust 10
Springs 2, 171
Sprout's Spring 12
St. Clair, George W., patent 56
St. Lawrence, trotter plate 2
Stair, Vernon Gordon 99
Stamped Steel Vehicle Wheel Co., Chicago, IL 83
Stanford, Leland & Charles, Road Riders 179
Steel bicycle wheels 10
Stevens, driver 125
Stillman, Charles F., patent 55, 56
Stoddard, Frederick S., patent 78
Stone, Royal Arthur, patent 47
Strauss, Nathan, Road Rider 179
Striping 81
Sulky Construction 18, 32, 59
Sulky Construction, Drawing 42
Sulky Construction, Ironing 20, 25, 30, 33, 52
Sulky Construction, Seat 24, 43
Sulky Weight 42, 51
Sweetser, trotter plate 8
Swiveller, trotter plate 11
Synoris 1

## T

Taconey, trotter 157
Tair, John Blackfan, patent 82
Tandem, trotting 125
Taylor, Alexander, Jr., Road Rider 179
Terbush, Friar, patent 38
Tethrippon 1
Thayer, John E., Road Rider 180
Timken Spring Road Cart 38
To My Horse, poem IX
Toomey, S. & Co., Canal Dover, Ohio 9, 60, 156
Toomey, S. & Sons, Canal Dover, Ohio 37

# Index

Track list for 1906  145
Tracks list for 2008  191
Tripp, George E., patent  57
Trotting Buggy  169
Trotting Park, Buffalo  136
Trotting, times  125
Trotting Wagon  170 See also Speed
    Wagons
Truss Axle  10, 60, 89, 100, 112
Turnbull, William, Road Rider  179

**U**

Union Course, Long Island, track
    127, 129
United States Agricultural Fair  3
United States Agricultural Society
    130, 132
Upington, James T., patent  36
Upington, John V., patent
    36, 44, 57, 74

**V**

Vaile, John I., patent  105
Van Ness, Frank  7
Vanderbilt, Frederick, Road Rider  179
Vanderbilt, Jacob H., Road Rider  179
Vanderbilt, William H., Road Rider  165,
    179, plate 12
Vaughn, W. A., & Son, Geenville, PA  9
Vaughn, James Wilbur, patent  47, 73
Velocipede  37
VonBlumen, Elsa, bicyclist  141

**W**

Walker, Ed, Houghton Sulky Co.  103
Walker, William, Jr. & Sr., patent  38
Wayne Sulkyette and Road Cart Co.  53
Wayne, William J., Decatuar, IL  40
Weathervanes  IV
Webb, W. W., Road Rider  179
Weigand, Charlie, patent  78
Weight of Sulkies  2, 5, 6,10, 15, 20, 59
Wells, George L., patent  79
Wesson, Isaac A., patent  45
Weston, I. A., Co., Syracuse, NY  83
Whalebone, trotter  2
Wharton, Samuel C., patent  57

Wheel Dish  39
Wheel Height  37
Wheel Strain  42
White, Horace, Road Rider  180
Whiteman, Abram V., patent  17
Wiliams, Jay C., patent  38
Wilkes Golddust  10
Wilkir, Robert D., sketch artist  134
Williams, Jay C., patent  45
Wilshire, Arthur, patent  120
Wilson, Thomas, patent  17
Wind-shield and Dirt-shield  95
Winecoff, Jesse, patent  35
Woersihoffer, C. F., Road Rider  179
Wood, Isaac, patent  58
Wood, John W., patent  36
Woodbury, Jud  8
Woodruff, Hirman, driver  128
Work, Frank, Road Rider  165,179, plate
    11

**Y**

Yale, Charles O., patent  47
Yoeman, William, patent  45
Youatt, author  VI, XII
Young, George, driver  150
Young, W. H., Road Rider  179

The **HARNESS RACING MUSEUM & HALL OF FAME** is located in the colonial village of Goshen, NY, just sixty minutes north of New York City! The museum celebrates a sport born in early America. Called "trotting," it was the nation's first national pastime, before baseball and all the other sports that attract the attention of today's public.

The institution's main building, built in 1913, was originally a stable and evidence exists today in its stall doors, hay chutes and cobblestone walk. The extensive exhibition area includes three theaters and hands-on computer displays. The museum owns the world's largest collection of Currier & Ives trotting prints and many can be found in its various galleries. Fine art abounds and includes works by Troye, Leighton and Palmer and trophies by such luminaries as Tiffany and Faberge. They all attest to the longevity of the sport. There's a unique Hall of Fame -- you won't find bronze plaques or busts; instead there are lifelike miniature statuettes of the honorees. Children find a lot to do, including rummaging through a real tack trunk to examine horse equipment, calling a race, discovering the toy exhibit or quietly spending time under the "old Oak tree" in their very own corner. The exhibit "The Evolution of the Sulky" with its high wheel sulkies, race carts and today's latest race bikes, can be found in the stable's Carriage Room; visitors will also delight in a plentiful gift shop and of course we cannot forget the star attraction - the 3D simulator that takes riders for a drive around the track in a real race!

The Peter Haughton Memorial Library contains more than 2,000 books and bound periodicals together with nearly 3,000 video and dvd recordings. They provide the serious researcher with a wealth of information on the historic sport of harness racing. The mission of the museum's Historic Collection's department is to protect the sport's great memories. The department administers more than 24,000 photographs, ephemera, objects, significant vehicles, works of art and trophies that are stored for immediate retrieval in climate-controlled storage areas.

The Harness Racing Museum is next door to the world's oldest active harness track, Goshen Historic. Founded in 1838, it is the first sporting site to be designated a National Historic Landmark. Now a year-round training facility, visitors have the opportunity to see, first hand, trotters and pacers in action!

The Harness Racing Museum & Hall of Fame
POB 590, 240 Main Street, Goshen, NY 10924
(845) 294-6330  www.harnessmuseum.com
Open daily 10-5. FREE ADMISSION.